Native Americans and the Law

A Dictionary

CONTEMPORARY LEGAL ISSUES

Native Americans and the Law

A Dictionary

Gary A. Sokolow

ABC-CLIO

Santa Barbara, California
Denver, Colorado
Oxford, England

Library of Congress Cataloging-in-Publication Data

Native americans and the law : a dictionary / Gary A. Sokolow.
p. cm. — (Contemporary legal issues)
Includes bibliographical references and index.
ISBN 0-87436-877-4 (alk. paper)
1. Indians of North America—Legal status, laws, etc.—Dictionaries.
I. Title. II. Series.
KF8203.6.S66 2000
342.73'0872'03—dc21

00-010870

05 04 03 02 01 00 99 10 9 8 7 6 5 4 3 2 1

ABC-CLIO, Inc.
130 Cremona Drive, P.O. Box 1911
Santa Barbara, California 93116-1911

This book is printed on acid-free paper ♾.

Manufactured in the United States of America

Contents

Preface

What is so important about Indian law today? The answer may lie in the simple fact that the U.S. legal system is recognizing the rights of certain distinct groups as never before. Unique among all of these assemblages stand Indian tribes. Unlike any other specific ethnic, racial, or other culturally distinct group in the United States, Indian tribes have had and continue to have a government-to-government relationship with the United States and the 50 states, and in many cases, with local governments as well. Tribes' existence as such predates the United States.

History has amply recorded the reality that U.S. society has not always dealt equitably with Indian tribes. The development of Indian law is the story of many attempts, often unsuccessful (from either or both the Native and nonnative points of view) to right some of those wrongs. The field of Indian law continues to evolve and adjust to deal with many of these wrongs.

Native Americans of all geographic areas of the country are continuing the battle for the legal recognition of and preservation of their status as quasi-independent sovereign nations. Thus, the field of Indian law is more important than ever before. As Native Americans increasingly assert their legal rights over increasingly valuable resources such as land, timber, water, and minerals, the fight becomes even more critical. Indian law affects such crucial Indian and non-Indian interests as water usage, the preservation of the environment, and the exploitation of natural energy sources, many of which are located on Indian lands. The battle has shifted from military force in the field to legal arguments in courtrooms all over the United States.

For many years, until recent times, the legal literature has referred to Native Americans (at least those of the lower 48 states) as "Indians." It was in no sense meant pejoratively. Today, although the term "Native American" is usually still understood to indicate the native peoples of the contiguous 48 states, increasingly, Native Alaskans and Native Hawaiians are also included within its meaning.

This project is the culmination of more than three years of work sandwiched in among changing a career, beginning a family, and moving halfway across the country. I would like to thank Mr. Henry Rasof and Ms. Alicia Merritt from ABC-CLIO, both for selecting me to do this work and also for their patience and understanding in the time it has taken me to complete the work. I would also like to thank Dr. Richmond Clow, of the Native American Studies Program of the University of Montana at Missoula, for all of his kind attention and advice in the writing of this book. He has answered numerous queries about various subjects in Indian law. Last but certainly not least, I would like to thank my wife, Barbara, and my young daughter, Naomi, for their untold patience while I spent many weekends and evenings hunched over the computer and piles of reference works. A number of others have also been very helpful, but it would take several pages just to list them all.

The reason for writing this book was to fill a void in the market for an easy-to-use general reference or a starting point for nonlawyers interested in the field of Indian law. Most current works dealing with Native Americans deal with particular tribes, cultures, or persons rather than with legal concepts. Oftentimes, someone trying to find out what phrases such as "trust lands" or "federally recognized Indian tribes" mean must consult the law books, which are nearly incomprehensible to the layman. It is hoped that persons interested in Indian law concepts can go to a public, high school, or college library and quickly find a definition of one of about 250 commonly used terms in this field. Readers can then look at one of about 50 bibliographic items for additional information on that particular subject. A short Internet source directory is included. As Internet addresses can change rapidly, readers are advised to also conduct a search for the particular subject in which they are interested.

A word about the criteria for the selection of topics included in this book: Because this book is concerned more with legal terminology than with the history or culture of Indian tribes, it is largely confined to a discussion of the most common terms used in the field of Indian law. No specific tribes were discussed except to illustrate a particular legal concept. Although an understanding of the history of Indian-white relations is very important to a comprehension of Indian law as a whole, that history is not the primary focus of this work. For much the same reasons, no attempt was made to write bibliographies of the many people, whether Native American or not, who have played important roles in the development and continuing evolution of Indian law. Only a few of the people who either accomplished some notable firsts as Native Americans in the non-Indian world or who have contributed key legal concepts in the field have been included.

Gary A. Sokolow

Introduction

Indian Law and History

Indian law is, simply put, the determination of the rights and obligations that Indians, their tribes, non-Indians, and all levels of governments have toward one another. It is a constantly changing field, greatly influenced by the history of Indian-white relations that began hundreds of years ago. From the earliest times, Indians lived in all parts of what is now the United States. Some Indian groups, tribes, or nations roamed over a large territory, hunting and fishing for sustenance. Others lived and farmed in a fixed location for centuries. Among the earliest recorded contacts between Indians and non-Indians (Europeans) were those with the Spanish in present-day Florida and in the American southwest. Francisco de Victoria, an early Spanish philosopher, opined that native peoples living in so-called discovered regions were entitled to live and use those lands in peace. His theory did not permit just nations to subjugate the native peoples. As history records, the Spanish rulers did not abide by this "doctrine of discovery." Instead, the Spanish enslaved the native peoples and seized their land and anything else of value. The English and the French explorers followed the Spanish; they were all looking for new lands to exploit, ultimately for the good of their respective rulers back home.

The English and French settlers initially occupied territory along the eastern seaboard of the continent and spread further inland in the late seventeenth and early eighteenth centuries. Regular contact between the new settlers and the longtime inhabitants of the so-called New World soon became inevitable. Relations between the two groups were peaceful enough initially, as long as the native peoples did not regard the newcomers as a threat to their survival or way of life. As the white population increased, so did the tension between the natives and the new settlers. At first both sides traded with one another. The Indian peoples received European-manufactured goods, and the whites received both peace and new sources of food and materials with which to build their villages. This increased contact also brought greater misunderstandings between the two sets of cultures.

The religious, cultural, and economic systems of European and native groups were profoundly different. On the one side were the European societies, which centered on the ethic of hard work to gain material goods for one's family. These European settlers stressed organized religion, held rigid concepts of right and wrong, good and evil, and worshipped a God who favored them above all others who were not like them. The Europeans saw it as their duty to acculturate, or "civilize," native peoples, an idea begun with the Spanish conquest of the Americas.

Perhaps the most significant chasm between the newcomers and the natives was that between their ideas concerning land ownership and use. These differences are still extant. The European cultures, whether Dutch, English, French, or Spanish, stressed the maximization of profits or economic use of the land and the power to exclude latecomers. Central to European theories of land ownership and use was the idea that the first to claim and successfully defend possession of the land ultimately received legal ownership of it, including the right to exclude others. These rights were backed up by their legal systems and ultimately by the use of military force. The right to own land, therefore, carried with it the right to exclude all others.

Many of the native inhabitants of America had no such concept of land ownership. Native belief essentially held that the land was a gift from the creator, to be used in common by all of the society for survival and sustenance. In many native societies, no single individual owned the land and no legal institution existed to exclude certain classes of persons from the land. Land ownership, then, was a fluid concept, especially among the nomadic tribes who moved from area to area with the seasons of the year.

Another major difference between the different cultures centered on the use, as opposed to the ownership, of the land. The new settlers' notions of land use centered on the exploitation of the land for maximum short-term economic gain. Such activities included mining, grazing, harvesting of timber and crops, and other activities intended to return the greatest economic benefits in the shortest time. The new settlers did not deem important any long-term damage that might be done to the land by the intense and short-term depletion of its resources.

Native Americans, on the other hand, lived out the philosophy of "conservation" long before the term was coined. Natural resources were extracted from the land as part of a balance with nature. The native peoples lived off the land. They did not practice wholesale extraction of resources such as timber, fish, and wildlife as did their European contemporaries. In part this was because the land could sustain their small populations and because their needs were relatively simple by European standards of their day. By contrast, the European settlers wanted the creature comforts to which they had been accustomed in Europe. These comforts included commercially manufactured food, clothing, furniture, and so on. Additionally, the new settlers needed to transfer as much wealth as possible, and as quickly as possible, from the New World to their mother countries.

Many native peoples nourished their spiritual sides by belief in one or more deities, who served them in many ways. Each Native American culture had its own system of religious beliefs. The European settlers, like all human beings, viewed the religious practices of others through the lens of their own experiences. Unfortunately, this, like the land-tenure issue, had dire consequences for the American Indians, consequences that exist to this day. As part of the acculturation process, Europeans tried to stamp out native religious practices in America.

At the time of the American colonies' formal break from England in 1776, a great deal of misunderstanding existed between the former English colonies and the Native Americans. Though many of the tribes had become economically dependent on the settlers for trade, they nonetheless were able to maintain some political independence. During the early days of the colonization of America, the new settlers could not have survived without the friendship of the Indian tribes. Ultimately the new United States, through treaties and other "agreements," forced the Indian nations to cede more and more of their lands to the new government. The balance of military power in the 1700s and into the next century was sharply shifting in favor of the new Republic. Nonetheless, in the early years after the states ratified the present U.S. Constitution, the new federal government tended to treat the Indian nations as foreign governments. This meant that, in theory at least, the new government recognized Indian nations as political sovereigns, complete with powers of self-government. Recognizing this relationship, the framers of the Constitution gave Congress, and not the states, the authority to regulate trade and Indian relations with the United States. The Northwest Ordinance of 1787, which set the pattern for the admission of new states into the Union, required that "the utmost good faith be shown in dealing with the Indians." Unfortunately, this did not always happen.

Numerous treaties were made with the Indian tribes, treaties to secure both land and peace for settlers. Recognizing the importance of stability and uniformity in the new nation's Indian policy, the First Congress passed a series of intercourse, or trade, acts (the Non-Intercourse Acts). The purpose of these laws was to regulate land transactions with Indian tribes, to put into law the relationship of Indians to the government, to regulate commercial trade between settlers and the Indian peoples, and to acculturate Indian people into U.S. society. Until the late 1700s many of the states concluded their own treaties and agreements with the Indian nations, which prevented the formation of a coherent policy toward

America's first inhabitants. The early Congresses had passed numerous laws intended to protect the Indians from further white settlement.

Despite the existence of these laws to protect Indian people, the executive branch made little effort to enforce them. Congress, which heard the increasing demands for more lands by settlers who voted, did not press the issue. In most states Indian people were denied the right to vote for U.S. representatives and senators, the very individuals who ultimately would wield the most influence over federal Indian policy.

The nation's treatment of Indians changed dramatically with the election of President Andrew Jackson in 1828. Jackson, a veteran of the early Indian wars, did not believe that Indian tribes retained the status of independent sovereigns, capable either of governing themselves or having any authority over non-Indians within their lands. Jackson publicly advocated the removal westward of the eastern Indian tribes. Under pressure from white settlers, Congress enacted the Indian Removal Act of 1830 and other measures to require Indian people, under threat of military force, to move west of the Mississippi River, a region with few non-Indian inhabitants. The governments of the eastern states were also under tremendous pressure from their citizens to "open up" Indian lands for settlement by whites. The increasing pressure of Indian-white competition for land led to violence in the southeast.

The U.S. Supreme Court was called upon to settle the land disputes in the 1830s when the Cherokee Nation fought its removal in the federal courts. Many of these cases arose when the states tried to forcibly remove Indians from their lands and to enforce state laws on those lands. Over a period of several years, Chief Justice John Marshall penned the famous "Marshall Trilogy" cases, which led to the creation of enduring principles of Indian law, many of which are still adhered to today. In one of these cases, *Worcester v. Georgia,* 31 U.S. (6 Pet.) 515 (1832), the Court ruled in favor of the Indians. President Jackson, however, refused to enforce the order of the Court and protect the Cherokee Nation from Georgia State officials. Marshall and the Court opined that the Indian tribes, no longer completely independent politically, were "domestic dependent nations." Nonetheless, Marshall reasoned that even though Indian tribes are dependent upon the goodwill of the United States for their very existence as such, they still retain all the attributes of self-government that any foreign nation would possess, unless Congress chooses to limit or abolish those powers. The aforementioned federal Non-Intercourse Acts were widely ignored by the states, which preferred to enter into their own agreements with the tribes without bothering to secure the approval of the federal government, as these acts required. The continuation of the federal removal policy into the 1880s led to much bloodshed between Indians and whites, as the former resisted the settlers' encroachments upon their lands. Among other events, the California gold rush of the late 1840s helped to fuel settlers' desire for Indian lands in the West. In an attempt both to open up Indian lands to white settlement and to ensure peace between whites and Indians, the federal government negotiated many treaties with Indian tribes, sometimes breaking them almost as fast as it made them.

The removal policy led to the creation of military posts along the western frontier. Their purpose was to ensure the safety of whites traveling throughout the West. The forts' very presence was a continuing irritation to many Indian tribes. In an attempt to "civilize" the Indian people, the Bureau of Indian Affairs (BIA, then as now the main federal agency dealing with Indian affairs) relocated Indian people to reservations with the help of the military. The government also built schools and other federal outposts such as military forts and BIA offices west of the Mississippi River to keep an eye on their Indian charges. The confinement of many Indian nations to a fixed area, often hundreds of miles away from their ancestral lands, wreaked havoc on their culture, health, and very existence. In the early 1870s, acknowledging the weakened military threat that Indians posed to non-Indians, Congress abolished the practice of making treaties with the tribes. The treaty-making process implies that each side views the other as an equal. From this time forward, the federal government would deal with Indian affairs not by treaty, which required tribal agreement, but by enacting federal laws and by executive (presidential) agreements, which did not.

By the late 1880s the government had established more than 200 day and boarding schools, with the intent of replacing Indian cultures with more "civilized" non-Indian ways of living. Both to speed up the assimilation process and to open up yet more Indian lands to white settlers on the reservations, Congress enacted the Dawes Act of 1887. This federal law forced allotments of land upon the people of many Indian tribes. This allotment process, or parceling out of land to individuals, conflicted with the long practice among many tribes of holding lands in communal ownership. By this time many Indians, once capable of living off the land, were reduced to poverty and relied on government food rations for survival. This 1887 statute provided that Indian families would each receive a parcel of land on the reservation, farm tools, and training to become a farmer in the non-Indian image. BIA agents and private charitable and religious organizations encouraged the Indians to adopt non-Indian ways of dress, to speak English, and generally to adopt non-Indian ways of life. Much of the land on the reservations allotted to Native Americans by the government was ill-suited for farming.

The 1887 act originally provided that after farming or ranching the allotments for 25 years, Indians would be considered able to handle their own affairs, and the government would then issue them a patent, or deed to the land. Once this happened, state and local governments could then levy property taxes against the land, and so over the next 47 years more reservation land was lost when many Indians could not afford to pay property taxes on it. Living on allotment and farming individual plots of land was directly counter to the communal living arrangements of many Indian nations. By the middle 1930s, when the allotment era ended, the tribal land base shrank from about 150 million acres to fewer than 50 million acres. The allotment, or assimilation, era left many Indian people landless and often destitute. Private individuals and organizations also tried to assimilate Indians into mainstream America by building churches and schools and working as missionaries in Indian communities.

By the 1930s federal policy makers had come to realize that the assimilation policy was a failure. The famous 1928 Meriam Report, commissioned by Congress, acknowledged that little had been accomplished through passage of the Dawes Act to better the lot of Native Americans. The economic depression of the 1930s had somewhat reduced non-Indians' thirst for Indian lands. The increasing public awareness of the failure of federal Indian policy inspired President Franklin D. Roosevelt to make radical changes in the way the federal government administered Indian affairs. A number of individuals in his administration worked to push Congress to enact the Indian Reorganization Act of 1934, also known as the Wheeler-Howard Act. This law stopped the further wholesale allotment of Indian lands and enabled tribes to buy back land that had passed out of Indian hands and thus to rebuild their land base. By extending federal loans for economic development of business on the reservations, the act also enticed many tribes to adopt constitutions and by-laws, patterned after the federal Constitution, and to reorganize and energize their long-dormant tribal governments. Through this law and others that followed, tribes were encouraged to reassert long-dormant powers of self-government, such as operating police forces and tribal courts of law to administer justice over their lands. The Wheeler-Howard Act also gave some preference to members of federally recognized tribes in employment with the BIA, the federal agency that wielded considerable influence over the daily lives of Indians living on reservations. Under these programs Indian tribes were able to add about 2 million acres back to their land base and to build homes, schools, roads, and other facilities to help make life better for their citizens. The onset of World War II diverted congressional attention away from Indian affairs, once—in the days when tribes were a potent military force, threatening the safety of non-Indians traveling through Indian lands—of vital concern to the federal government. In fact, during part of the war, the BIA headquarters was moved from Washington, D.C., to Chicago, Illinois.

In the early 1950s, perhaps weary of financing two major wars in fifteen years, Congress had little sympathy with the plight of Native Americans and abruptly changed course in its dealings with Native Americans. In 1953 Congress formally embarked on a policy of "getting out of the Indian business," partly to reduce federal expenses. This policy, known as "termination," attempted to end the United States' special government-to-government, or "trust," relationship with Indian tribes. Congress eventually withdrew federal recognition as quasi-sovereign nations from more than 100 Indian tribes, usually with disastrous results. Many tribes and their members, shorn of their communal and individually allotted lands, had no other resources to sustain their people once these lands were sold.

Congress further dealt a serious blow to tribal sovereignty with the passage of Public Law 280, which gave six states nearly complete criminal and considerable civil jurisdiction over any legal disputes arising on Indian lands of those tribes still recognized by Congress. Many states, with a long history of hostility to Indian interests, were all too anxious to assume legal authority over Indian affairs in their respective states. All of this was done without the consent of the affected tribes. Although Public Law 280 is still on the books, tribal consent is now required before any additional states may assume civil or criminal jurisdiction over Indian country. No tribe since has given its consent.

Federal policy toward the first inhabitants of the United States changed once again in 1970 when President Richard Nixon announced a policy of Indian self-determination. Congress formally repudiated the termination policy only in 1988. From the 1970s to the end of the twentieth century, Congress has enacted numerous laws, all designed to strengthen tribal culture and the ability of tribes to chart their own future on their own terms as much as possible. Some of these enactments include the Indian Financing Act of 1974, the Indian Education and Self-Determination Act of 1975, the Indian Child Welfare Act of 1978, the Indian Gaming Regulatory Act of 1988, and the Native American Graves Protection and Repatriation Act of 1990. The general policy of the United States in promoting tribal self-government is clear in the many laws enacted by Congress. Whether or not the United States will continue to try and respect the sovereignty of Indian nations is something only time will tell.

THE SCOPE AND MAJOR TENETS OF INDIAN LAW

Indian people and their tribes occupy a special place in the U.S. legal system. The tribes are not unlike states, or foreign countries. Yet tribes are not merely groups of people who share common ethnic, religious, spiritual, or cultural affiliations. They are distinct sovereigns with powers of self government and are often immune to state and local regulation, even though all tribal lands are located within one or more states. They may make their own laws, pass judgment on Indians who break their laws, and to some extent regulate the conduct of non-Indians living on or working in Indian country. They may even exclude from their reservations non-Indians and nontribal members whom they judge to be harmful to their societal interests—something not even the states or the federal government may do. Recognizing their semi-independent status as nations separate from the states, the Supreme Court has even ruled that the U.S. Constitution does not fully apply to Indian reservations. For instance, the Bill of Rights does not prohibit tribal governments from funding tribal spiritual or religious groups. Tribal courts do not have to provide financially poor tribal members with attorneys to represent them in criminal cases, even if the accused might be sent to jail for violating tribal criminal laws.

Indian law evolves through a constant flow of federal (and on occasion state) statutes and court cases that interpret or help define the meaning of those federal and state laws. Additionally, the president, through the appointment of officials who administer Indian programs on a daily basis, defines and shapes federal Indian policy. The role of states in the formulation of Indian policy is somewhat limited because the U.S. Constitution and federal court decisions give Congress and the president the primary responsibility in this sphere, though states may be involved in such areas as providing services to Native Americans, on or off reservations, and helping to determine Indian child custody issues in certain cases. Some states, such as Alaska, play a major role in the administration of Indian affairs in that state. Conflicts often arise between Indian tribes and the state or local governments where the tribe is situated. The federal and affected state governments may also have differing opinions as to how certain issues should be settled.

Currently, a common dispute arises over what type of gaming Indian tribes should be allowed to conduct on their lands. The Indian Gaming Regulatory Act of 1988 permits tribes to conduct gaming activities, largely independent of state regulation—a situation that does not sit well with the states. However, the extent of Indian gaming in a particular state may depend on whether that state allows non-Indian gaming activities on lands outside Indian country in that state. This law requires states and tribes to sign an agreement before certain types of Indian gaming, such as casino games, may commence. Typical areas of state/tribal dispute include which government has civil and criminal jurisdiction over these activities, how much gaming to allow, and whether the tribes must give some of the gaming proceeds to states to offset some of the expenses incurred by the state in building roads or in increased law enforcement expenses resulting from the presence of a casino. Other common disputes revolve around rights to fishing, hunting, and use of water—which states have traditionally regulated heavily to conserve wildlife—insofar as Indians' pursuit of these activities affects non-Indians.

In some cases the states and Indian tribes, like any other groups who disagree, can sit down and informally resolve their differences. If so, much emotion, time, and expense might be spared. If this is not possible, some other administrative agency, such as the Department of the Interior or a court, must resolve the issue. In rare cases, Congress may step in to attempt to solve the problem with the passage of laws. An example of this is the century-old conflict between the Navajo and Hopi Indian tribes over certain lands. After years of court cases, Congress enacted several laws, over a period of time, appointing mediators to help settle the dispute and permitting federal courts to decide the case if the two tribes could not come to an agreement.

How Native American Law Is Made

Congress, as the legislative branch of the federal government, has plenary, that is, nearly absolute, power to pass laws that shape the relationships that Indian tribes have with their citizens, federal and state governments, and non-Indians. Over the history of the United States, Congress has enacted hundreds of laws and ratified more than 300 treaties affecting Indian affairs. Unfortunately for the Indian people, until the 1960s Congress rarely consulted with Indians before enacting those laws. A major exception involved the passage of the Indian Reorganization Act of 1934. In the process of preparing this legislation to present to Congress, the BIA held hearings in Indian country across the United States to solicit the opinions of the people whom this law would most affect.

The early failure of Congress to consult with tribes primarily resulted from a lack of awareness on the part of tribes of the political process involved in the work of Congress and from the political powerlessness of Native Americans. Few tribes had any meaningful contact with their local member of Congress or senator. Since many adult Indian people could not even vote in elections until passage of the Citizenship Act of 1924, senators and representatives saw little reason to pay any attention to Indians, except when the economic or physical security of their constituents were affected.

A major source of lawmaking for more than a century was the treaty-making process between the federal government and the Indian tribes. This process is the method by which governments around the world have often worked out disagreements with one another or worked together in areas of mutual interest. Precisely this government-to-government relationship existed to a larger degree in years past between Indian tribes and the federal government. At a time when Indian nations posed a military threat to the United States, the government found it convenient to make treaties, or binding agreements, with tribes.

The president, through his agents—that is, BIA officials, army officers, or private citizens—would negotiate with the Indian tribes. If both sides could come to terms, the president would submit the proposed Indian treaty to the Senate for ratification. If two-thirds of the senators agreed to it, the treaty became part of federal law. These treaties, or agreements, often provided that tribes would give up their claims or occupancy to some lands and would cease militarily fighting the government, and in return the government promised to prevent white settlement on the remaining lands and also to provide food, health care, and farming assistance to recompense tribes for their reduced ability to sustain their people when their land base was reduced as a result of the treaties. Even though Congress stopped the treaty-making process in 1871, treaties remain a very important source of law and rights for Indian tribes. An example of this is the issue of Indian water rights. In many cases, when Congress, by treaty, or the president, through executive orders or agreements, set aside land for the use of Indian people, some of the land eventually passed out of Indian hands.

Executive orders are official commands or decisions by the president to do something. Congress in many cases has delegated to the president the authority, for example, to set aside lands owned by the people of the United States for the use of Indian tribes and their people. Indian tribes rarely used all of the water to which they were entitled when their reservations were created. Nonetheless, if tribes now want to use water to further the purposes for which the reservation was created, they can do so. The tribes have a right to use the water that flows on or under reservation lands, even to the detriment of their non-Indian neighbors or the states. The right to receive services from the federal government may often be grounded in treaties as well as in federal laws such as the Snyder Act of 1921. Although Congress may unilaterally abrogate, or cancel, treaties, even without the consent of Indian tribes, it has rarely done so.

A third major source of law in Indian affairs are court decisions. The federal and state courts are called upon to make decisions to settle disagreements among the tribes, Indian people, and state, local, and federal governments. The highest court in the United States, the Supreme Court, has issued many opinions touching the lives of Native Americans. These court decisions, once the appeals process is complete, have the force of law and must be obeyed. Over the centuries, the courts have made decisions affecting all areas of Indian life, such as religious practices, civil rights, the ownership and use of lands, and the quantity and quality of services delivered to Indian tribes and their citizens. Frequently the courts must interpret federal Indian laws to determine just what they mean to all interested people. For example, in the northwestern United

States the courts have been called upon to determine just how much fish Indian tribes are entitled to take from streams and rivers. Over time, the Supreme Court has developed a set of rules, known in Indian law as the "Canons of Construction," to guide themselves and the lower courts when they need to interpret or determine the legal effect of a certain statute, treaty, or executive order. These canons arose out of the trust relationship and treaties between the United States and the various Indian tribes. Such special rules are necessary when a statute or provisions of a treaty can be defined in more than one way and the parties to a legal dispute cannot agree on which interpretation to use.

These rules of interpretation assume that Congress's intent toward the Indians is benevolent and that when treaties, statutes, and other federal rules and actions could be interpreted in more than one fashion, they should be read as protecting Indian rights and in a manner favorable to Indians. The United States had the upper hand in the bargaining that went on in the treaty-making process. Government agents had superior knowledge of the English language and of the precise legal meaning to be afforded to specific legal terms. U.S. and English legal concepts and terminology, especially those dealing with land ownership and use, were foreign to the Indian tribes.

The legal precepts, or canons, that have been developed by the federal courts are these:

1. Treaties are to be construed (interpreted) liberally in favor of the Indians.
2. Ambiguous terms of treaties and other federal actions be resolved in favor of the Indians. In other words, when a treaty or law can have two or more meanings or interpretations, the meaning that would be most favorable to the Indian or tribe should be adopted.
3. Treaties or other federal decisions should be interpreted as the Indians would have understood them at the time they were made. Treaties are still an extremely important source of the legal rights of Indians and of obligations to Indians by the federal government.
4. Before a treaty or law will be interpreted as extinguishing or eliminating the rights of the Indians, it must be shown that Congress had a "clear and plain" intent to eliminate Indian treaty rights. In this situation, the courts use a narrow interpretation of the federal action to be reviewed. In other words, the courts want to see some strong evidence that Congress, in enacting laws, clearly meant to reduce or eliminate Indian rights when they study federal actions.

The courts use the canons in analyzing many facets of Indian law issues that come before them. For example, Public Law 280 provided that state law and the jurisdiction of state courts was to be extended to Indian country in many cases. No specific mention was made in that law of the states' right to tax nontrust lands, that is, private property located in Indian country, or commercial activities arising in Indian country. In the case of *Bryan v. Itasca County,* 426 U.S. 373 (1976), the Supreme Court applied the canons when it decided that the state may not tax private activities or property on Indian lands. That decision has been modified over the years.

A final major source of Indian law are the decisions of administrative agencies. Congress allows many federal agencies, such as the BIA, to make decisions in areas of the law where it does not have the time or expertise to do so. Examples might involve the issuance of grazing permits on Indian lands or the probate of the estates of Native Americans who live on a reservation or hold a legal interest in trust lands or other tribal property. Special judges, called administrative law judges or hearing officers, make thousands of decisions settling cases. The vast majority of these are never appealed to any courts. To guide them, these judges or hearing officers apply federal statutes and administrative regulations to make their decisions. Congress, when enacting new laws, often give these governmental agencies the power to make rules to guide the hearing officers. One example of this is the process by which the federal government officially recognizes a group of people as an Indian tribe. Instead of deciding these cases one by one, Congress delegated to the BIA the right to make detailed rules that established criteria or standards by which applications to be acknowledged or recognized as an Indian tribe are judged. Most of these rules affecting Indians are found in Title 25 of the *Code of Federal Regulations,* a multivolume publication containing all of the administrative rules for all federal agencies.

WHO IS INVOLVED IN THE SYSTEM?

There are thousands of individuals involved in the making of Indian policy. At the top of the executive branch of the federal government is the president of the United States. Through the appointment of the top federal officials in the Department of the Interior and other agencies, the president has a great deal of power to shape policy. These officials are directly responsible to the president in carrying out the administration's programs. If, for reasons of conscience or otherwise, they can no longer do so, they either resign or are fired from their positions. Although Congress may ultimately have the last word as to policy, it usually follows the lead of the president and these top officials. Examples of presidential influence include Roosevelt's stopping the assimilation and allotment era in the 1930s and Nixon's issuance of a presidential proclamation declaring an end to the termination era of Indian policy and promoting Indian self-determination beginning in 1970.

Congress, as the lawmaking branch, plays a key role in the formulation of Indian policy. The House and Senate possess not only the authority to enact laws but the ability to fund any programs they create. Congress may also withhold funding for presidential programs with which it disagrees. Although Congress has a moral obligation to legislate in the best interests of Indians, it has not always done so. Indeed, Congress alone possesses authority to unilaterally terminate federal recognition of a tribe, thus ending the tribe's unique political relationship to the United States. Congress exercised this authority a number of times during the termination era of the 1950s and 1960s, though it has subsequently restored some terminated tribes to their former status as federally recognized tribes.

The third branch of the federal government, the federal court system, also has a hand in the formulation of policy. Through the power of judicial review of the constitutionality of statutes and by their interpretation of those statutes, the courts wield tremendous influence. An example of their influence, even at the federal district court level, over Indian affairs is the famous Boldt Decision of 1974 (*United States v. Washington*, 384 F.Supp. 312 [W.D. Wash. 1974]), in which the federal district court in the state of Washington determined the rights of Indians and non-Indians over fishing and water in the northwest. This decision is still widely followed today by other courts in addressing similar issues. Indeed, the U.S. Supreme Court, as the court of last resort in the federal system, has the last word as to the legality of federal laws affecting Indian people.

Probably no agency of government has more to say about the daily life of Indian people, especially those living on a reservation, than the Bureau of Indian Affairs. The BIA is one of the oldest of all federal agencies. It was founded in the 1820s under the auspices of the former War Department, and its mission was to help open up Indian lands for white settlement and to pacify Indian tribes wherever possible. Today the BIA supervises the delivery of a myriad of federal services to Indian tribes and manages the trust property of the tribes and individual tribal members. The BIA also deals with such issues as the approval of changes to many tribal constitutions, the funding of educational programs on the reservation, environmental and land use issues in Indian country, economic assistance to Indian tribes and their members, and tribal housing. On many reservations, this agency may also provide law enforcement services as well.

The overwhelming number of Indian reservations, unfortunately, are highly dependent upon federal funding for their very survival. Although some reservations may boast of natural resources such as timber, water, wildlife, coal, oil, gas, and other minerals, these are often not enough to sustain the tribes. Even Indian gaming may not necessarily be the tool to enable tribes to achieve economic independence on many reservations. In fact, federal agencies are often the largest employers on the reservations. Many commentators believe that such monies represent a payment for lands and ultimately for a way of life taken away by treaty or other "agreements" made between the Indian tribes and the federal government long ago.

The BIA, an agency of the Department of the Interior, is headed by an assistant secretary for Indian affairs. Its headquarters are currently located in Washington, D.C. The BIA also maintains some area offices, each of which is headed by a director. Further down the BIA chain of command are the agency offices, usually serving specific reservations. Each agency office is supervised by a superintendent. Except for the top BIA officials, most employees are protected by the federal civil service. Many of the BIA's officials and employees are enrolled members of Indian tribes.

The BIA is not the only federal agency involved in Native American life. The Indian Health Service (IHS), an agency of the federal Department of Health and Human Services, provides health care services to many reservation Indians. The IHS operates numerous hospitals and clinics on the reservations. Many of these institutions are staffed by a full complement of doctors, nurses, counselors, other health care professionals, and supporting staff.

The U.S. Department of Housing and Urban Development also provides technical assistance and funding to many tribal housing authorities. These tribally controlled housing authorities manage and maintain housing for tribal members. Other federal agencies, such as the Departments of Agriculture, Commerce, Education, Justice, and Veterans' Affairs, also play a role in providing a myriad of other programs designed to better the lot of Indian people.

The practice, as opposed to the formulation, of law as it affects both Indians and non-Indians also involves a wide array of players. At the local level, many Indian tribes operate their own tribal courts that have both civil jurisdiction over all who reside or work in Indian country and criminal jurisdiction over Indian people. Most tribes have considerable authority over people and activities in their territory. Many of the tribal courts are staffed by law-trained judges and lawyers. This was not always the case. Many early tribal courts were staffed by members who had no formal legal training. Even today, not all tribal courts require such training. Some tribes allow their members who have little or no legal training to act as advocates for anyone appearing in tribal court proceedings. As recently as 30 years ago, many of the lawyers and judges working in the tribal courts were non-Indian. Tribal courts must attempt to blend the Anglo-Saxon tradition of an adversarial relationship between the parties with the different Native American cultural traditions of many tribes. The U.S. system of law often takes on a "winner take all" attitude in which the parties battle it out in court while the judge ensures the fairness of the process by which this is done. However, in the tradition of many Indian tribes, disputes are mediated by elders or other respected members of a tribe, with the primary goal not that one side or the other takes all but that fairness reigns and that the peace and harmony of tribal relations is preserved. Tribal court judges, then, must often balance the two ways of looking at things. More and more tribal court judges and the attorneys who appear before these courts are members of the tribes where they work as well as members of state bar associations. The cases that tribal courts hear are the same as any state or federal court might hear: minor criminal cases, landlord/tenant conflicts, and contract, tort, employment, and even tax cases.

Tribal governing bodies are also heavily involved in the practice of Indian law. It is an unfortunate fact of life for many tribes that they are often forced to go to court to defend their legal rights. As many tribes become increasingly aggressive about exercising and testing the limits of their inherent sovereignty, the non-Indian world just as vigorously opposes them. Especially since the 1970s and President Nixon's Indian Self-Determination policy, for example, tribes have attempted to regulate the use of non-Indian-owned land within the borders of their reservations. Extensive court litigation was necessary to help settle this issue, not entirely in favor of tribes. Tribes that operate casinos find it necessary to employ consultants and legal counsel to help them understand the maze of federal regulations that apply to gaming and to negotiate gaming compacts with state governments. Environmental issues also require a great deal of legal attention on the part of the tribes. Some of the larger Indian tribes may employ one or more in-house attorneys, who work full time advising the tribes and in some cases representing them in the state and federal courts as well.

State courts may be involved in Indian law issues as well. State courts whose territory lies near Indian country may be called upon to decided whether they or the tribal courts have the authority to try Indians accused of crimes. That question depends, among other things, on whether the criminal act took place in Indian country. Civil litigation is another area of Indian law in which state courts may be called upon to decide their own authority to hear a particular type of case. Indian law is of increasing importance to state courts under the provisions of the Indian Child Welfare Act of 1978, for example. Many courts in states distant from any Indian reservations are called upon to decide whether child custody cases involving Indian children must be returned to the courts of the child's tribe for a decision. State courts, however, may be asked to retain authority over the case if a state official or other interested party so requests. The state courts must then apply Indian law to help them decide these and other issues.

More and more tribal courts are meeting traditional U.S. legal due process requirements of notice of cases, of opportunity to defend or answer charges or civil lawsuits brought in tribal courts, and about the conduct of hearings or trials and the keeping of records of these proceedings. Because of this, state courts are increasingly asked to treat tribal court judgments rendered in those cases as their own. Under the principles of comity, states may choose to treat tribal court decisions as their own and thus enforce tribal court orders as if the state courts themselves had rendered them. Because tribes are not exactly the same as states, the Full Faith and Credit Clause of the U.S. Constitution does not require state courts, as a matter of law, to recognize tribal court decisions in most cases. An unusual exception to this are tribal court Indian child custody decisions, under the terms of the aforementioned Indian Child Welfare Act.

State executive officials, from governors and attorneys general on down, must often deal with Indian tribes on a number of issues such as the negotiation and approval of Indian gaming compacts and whether Indian tribes should be able to take lands back into trust status and thus off state and local tax rolls. Increasingly, state or local museums that receive federal funding are required under federal law to return many Indian artifacts to Indian tribes. The authority of state social service agencies to deal with child custody, abuse, and neglect and related matters are also a matter of concern to state authorities. Law enforcement issues in Indian country are also of some concern to state officials. The resolution of disputes requires a working relationship between state law enforcement officials and the local U.S. attorney, who is generally responsible for prosecuting all serious crime that occurs in Indian country regardless of the race of the victims or accused.

CURRENT ISSUES

There are a number of issues of current concern to state officials. The resolution of these issues depends on the extent to which states and Indian tribes within their boundaries share or contest goals and interests. Unfortunately, the long history of state-tribal interaction does not augur well for a harmonious relationship between the two sovereigns. From the earliest days of our Republic, states have rarely acted with any real concern for the welfare of Indian people within their domain. The pressure on elected and appointed state officials was always to seize Indian lands for settlement by whites, most of whom were eligible to vote. For many years, Indian people were not eligible to vote in state elections. Some states, such as Utah, only lifted the ban against the Indian vote in the middle 1950s. Unless a tribe had a significant ability to use military force, the states prevailed upon Congress to take lands away from Indians and open them up for white settlement. Moreover, states resented the freedom from state regulation that many Indian tribes possessed. Perhaps this indignation is due to widespread ignorance on the part of the general public of the fact that Indian nations are self-governing entities, predating the United States.

The allocation of civil and criminal jurisdiction in Indian country among state and tribal authorities is of continuing concern to them both. Sometimes the two sides are able to settle their differences. In other cases the courts must decide. For example, the authority of states to regulate activities on state highways crossing reservations is always a concern. On many occasions, the U.S. Supreme Court has had to settle disputes arising from the ability of states and local governments to tax activities arising in Indian country, especially those of non-Indians. The profits from Indian casinos are also eyed by states as potential revenue and are usually one of the subjects of negotiations of tribal gaming compacts. Indian people are citizens of the state where they reside as well as of their tribes. Therefore, states often provide services to residents of reservations or off-reservation Indian country, so naturally, states attempt to reduce some of those expenses by taxing as many activities as possible.

Numerous private organizations exist to lobby Congress and the states on behalf of Indian interests, to help smaller tribes with litigation to safeguard their interests, and to help tribes manage their resources by providing technical assistance. With the increased public demand for minerals, oil, gas, and geothermal resources located on certain tribal lands, natural resource law is becoming increasingly important to the tribes. The Council of Energy Resource Tribes is a group composed of tribes who possess such reserves. This organization provides member tribes with technical expertise to help them develop and manage their resources wisely. The Indian programs of the federally funded Legal Services Corporation (LSC) assist Native Americans who are unable to afford their own attorneys to represent them in tribal, state, or federal courts. In its early days, the LSC brought many civil rights lawsuits to end discrimination by states against Indians and tribes. The National Congress of American Indians lobbies Congress to help voice Indian concerns about any legislation that might either help or harm Native Americans. This group and others helped to shape such legislation as the Alaska Native Claims Settlement Act of 1971, the Indian Gaming Regulatory Act of 1988, and a host of other legislation. Still other organizations, such as the Native American Rights Fund (NARF), help tribes to protect and advance their own interests through litigation in federal and state courts. The NARF takes on cases of national significance to Indians. It also maintains an Indian law library for the use of those working in the field of Indian law. These groups and others serve as training grounds for the future leaders of Indian nations.

THE FUTURE

Given the history of Indian-white relations, Indian tribes will have to be ever vigilant about protecting their legal rights and maintaining the ability to plan their own futures as semi-independent nations with a minimum of interference from other governments. The battleground has shifted from the military campaigns of a century or more ago to the courtrooms and the halls of Congress and the state legislatures. Even though many Indian tribes have full-time legal counsel, they are realizing that litigation is both time-consuming and very expensive. The smallest tribes, as just as the vindication of their legal rights may be, often cannot afford the expense of lawsuits. Even the larger tribes want to put their resources to better use. With the information explosion and the ready accessibility of the public to both the state and federal legislative processes, it is becoming easier for Indian tribes to maintain a political presence in state capitals and in Washington, D.C., to monitor any legislation affecting their interests. The real test of Indian self-determination will come when tribes are able to survive as such without financial assistance from any other government.

A

Aboriginal Possession or Title

Aboriginal Possession or Title The principle of aboriginal possession or title, which is a principle of real estate law, holds that the indigenous people who occupied the soil before European settlement still retain certain rights in the land. A most recent example can be found in the United States, where Indian nations had lived on or occupied the land for centuries prior to European contact. This aboriginal concept traces ownership of land from the earliest recorded occupants to those who "discover" the land. However, it has long been held that rights to land springing from discovery still are subject to the right of the original possessors to continue to occupy the land. The theory of aboriginal title holds that the consent of the aboriginal, or original, occupier is necessary before dominion may be exercised by the "discoverer." However, the Trilogy Cases (a set of three early Supreme Court cases that established how the young United States would treat American Indians from a legal perspective) gave Congress the legal ownership in Indian lands and left the Indians themselves with only the continued right of possession or occupancy. The federal government must give its consent before such lands are sold or otherwise transferred to anyone.

See also **Indian Title; Victoria, Francisco de**

Administration for Native Americans

Administration for Native Americans The stated goals of the Administration for Native Americans (ANA), an agency within the U.S. Department of Health and Human Services (HHS), are to further tribal self-governance and economic independence. It provides a variety of services to all native peoples, whether federally recognized or not. The ANA provides technical assistance to tribal government in the administration of their programs as well as monetary grants for various economic, educational, governmental, health, and other programs to benefit native peoples. The ANA is but one of many organizations seeking to implement the current official governmental policy of promoting Indian self-determination, a policy that originated in the 1970s.

This HHS agency is unusual among the many federal agencies and programs that deal with Native American peoples in that it extends its services to indigenous groups in all geographic regions of the United States, including Hawaii, and in territories of the United States such as American Samoa and the Marshall Islands. Additionally, official federal recognition of a tribal group as such is not a requirement to participate in many ANA programs.

Most federal agencies, notably the Bureau of Indian Affairs (BIA), require official federal recognition of an Indian tribe before it extends services to them. Individuals must also be enrolled as members of a recognized tribe as a prerequisite to eligibility for most governmental services targeted toward American Indians. The BIA, which is the primary U.S. government service provider to American Indians, generally does not provide services to Native Hawaiian groups, to Native Alaskan groups, or to those indigenous peoples located outside the fifty states.

ADMINISTRATIVE LAW The branch of the law that deals with rules issued by administrative agencies under the executive branch of government (such as the Bureau of Indian Affairs), as opposed to statutes passed by legislative bodies like the U.S. Congress, is called administrative law. Administrative law rules are of necessity more detailed and specific than are statutes. When a legislative body enacts a law, it cannot be aware of every possible situation that might arise under the statute. Administrative law rules can be issued and changed much more easily and more quickly to respond to changing situations. Generally, proposed rules or regulations are published in the *Federal Register,* and the agency proposing the rules seeks public comment on them, which may take the form either of letters or testimony taken at a hearing. After the agency considers the public input, it may modify, cancel, or go ahead with the proposed rules. To make the proposed regulations legally effective, the agency must then publish the final version of them in the *Federal Register.* States follow similar procedures for their own administrative rules.

Disputes under the rules can be settled more quickly before an informal tribunal presided over by an administrative law judge or hearing officer, a quasi-judicial official, than before a court. All parties to the dispute present evidence in the form of live testimony, documents, or other items at the hearing. Formal evidentiary rules are often relaxed, the hearing is more informal than courtroom proceedings, and the judge or hearing officer, not a jury, decides the dispute. Any party to the administrative hearing has the right to appeal its decision to a court of law, but only after going through all administrative channels.

Once the judge, hearing officer, or other official has decided the case, the losing party may then appeal to the secretary, commissioner, or other head of the agency where the case was heard. Only after that official has made a decision may the dissatisfied party then appeal to a court of law. This doctrine is called the "exhaustion of administrative remedies."

ADMINISTRATIVE PROCEDURES ACT OF 1946

The federal Administrative Procedures Act (APA) of 1946 governs the adoption, interpretation, and revision of the rules and regulations of all federal administrative agencies. The rules and regulations do not become official until their publication in the *Code of Federal Regulations.* The APA also establishes the duties of hearing officers or administrative law judges and the manner in which they decide cases, what evidence they may consider, and the degree of formality of the hearings. The Act also grants appeal rights to the parties, establishing specifically what matters may be appealed to the federal courts, who may appeal, and how long after a decision or ruling is made an appeal may be made. Many states have similar acts in place to govern their administrative proceedings.

See also **Code of Federal Regulations**

ADVERSE POSSESSION

The theory of adverse possession sets out the legal conditions under which a person who does not have formal ownership of land may nevertheless legally acquire it, as against the wishes of the owner of record. There are several requirements for this to occur. First, the person who is trying to get title (or formal ownership) of a parcel of land must have physically occupied it for a continuous period. In many states, that period is about 20 years. Second, the adverse possessor must occupy the land in a manner inconsistent with or "hostile" to the uses of the true owner. For example, an owner of record grows crops on her land. An adverse possessor moves his cattle to graze on part of the land where the crops are growing. Use of the land for grazing is inconsistent with that of growing crops. Third, the current legal owner (that is, the owner of record) must have some notice, such as through fencing or signs, that the adverse occupier has an interest in the land and is claiming it.

The main points are that the person claiming title, or ownership, must have the intent to claim the title and must have physical possession of the land—for anywhere from 5 to 20 years, depending on which state the land is situated in—and that the true, or legal, owner of record must be aware of this possession. If all of these requirements are met, the adverse possessor may then bring a lawsuit in a court where the land sits and ask that court to declare him or her the new legal owner of that real estate.

AGENCY SUPERINTENDENT The head of a local office of the Bureau of Indian Affairs (BIA) is called an agency superintendent. The BIA is a part of the federal government. It is contained within the U.S. Department of the Interior, a cabinet-level organization of the executive branch of the U.S. government. The agency superintendent's immediate supervisor is an area director. There is a local agency office located on all major Indian reservations. The agency handles such matters as maintaining trust land records, handling the financial affairs of the local BIA office, managing local welfare programs, forestry management, and the like. The superintendent is covered under the federal Civil Service Act and is often a member of a federally recognized Indian tribe. An effective superintendent will usually maintain a close working relationship with the Indian tribe or tribes that he or she serves.

See also **Area Director; Bureau of Indian Affairs; Indian Preference**

AHUPUA'A The ahupua'a was a unit of land used in Hawaii in preterritorial days (before 1893). The parcels ranged in size from 100 to 100,000 acres. Ideally, it was an economically self-sufficient, triangular unit that started at a point on a mountaintop and extended downward to a base along the seashore. Thus, this parcel included farmland, water, and access to the sea. The ahupua'a provided everything the people living on it needed for subsistence. Unlike under traditional Western ideas of land ownership, the chief did not own the ahupua'a. Instead, he managed it for the benefit of or in the best interests of the people. This notion is similar to the Native American conception of land ownership, which held that the land was not really "owned" by any one person but, rather, was used communally for the benefit of all tribal members. If the Native Hawaiians living on an ahupua'a were dissatisfied with the way it was managed, they could move to another area.

ALASKA ALLOTMENT POLICY The federal Alaska Allotment Act of 1906 initiated the federal policy of enabling Native Alaskans to acquire legal title to land in Alaska. Under the Act, Native Alaskans could apply for land allotments of up to 160 acres (a quarter section). The restrictions on the transfer, state control, and taxation of such lands were very similar to those imposed on Indian allotments elsewhere under the General Allotment Act of 1887. In the 1950s, Congress removed many of these restrictions so that Alaska natives could sell their allotments. Unlike the 1887 law, which promoted Native American "mainstreaming" into American society, the Alaska policy was designed primarily to allow Native Alaskans to gain legal title to the lands upon which they lived and worked.

With the passage of the Alaska Native Claims Settlement Act of 1971 and the Alaska National Interest Lands Conservation Act of 1980, the government no longer accepted new applications for allotment of public lands. Under these laws, however, pending applications are in the process of getting approval. Currently, about 800,000 acres of land are still held in allotments by individual Native Alaskans.

See also **Allotments**

ALASKA FEDERATION OF NATIVES

The Alaska Federation of Natives (AFN) is a major statewide Alaskan political action group that advocates for the rights of Native Alaskans there. It was founded in the late 1960s as an organized attempt to persuade Congress to settle native land claims. In part because of the activities of the AFN, Congress passed the Alaska Native Claims Settlement Act of 1971 (ANCSA). The AFN also operates programs to deliver services to Native Alaskans. Although the federal and state governments contract with the AFN to deliver various services, the AFN is not considered a "tribe" or a tribal governing body. Besides attempting to secure and maintain political rights for Native Alaskans, the AFN also conducts various activities to preserve their customs, history, and traditions. The federation membership is composed of ANCSA regional corporations, other organizations, and both Native Alaskan and non–Native Alaskan individuals. The AFN is still currently involved in many issues concerning ANCSA and subsistence rights of Native Alaskans.

ALASKA INDIAN REORGANIZATION ACT OF 1936

The federal Alaska Indian Reorganization Act of 1936, 25 U.S.C. § 473a, extended many of the benefits of the Indian Reorganization Act (IRA) of 1934 to Native Alaskans. The IRA was originally designed to stop the massive erosion of the tribal land base that began when Congress passed the General Allotment Act of 1887. The 1887 law discouraged tribal organization and attempted to eradicate Indian culture by breaking up Indian reservations. As a result of this policy, millions of acres of tribal lands passed forever into non-Indian hands.

The IRA as originally enacted intended that tribal governments would exercise self-governance over a well-defined geographic area—that is, a reservation. Except in a very few cases, Native Alaskan groups did not have well-defined geographic areas. Tribal "governments," if they existed at all in Alaska, were very informal. Their powers of self-government were largely undefined.

Congress amended the IRA in 1936 to extend its benefits to Alaska Natives. These amendments used a more flexible definition of a tribe. Rather than applying the IRA only to reservations, Congress included those Native Alaskan groups that were based on a "common bond of occupation, or association, or residence within a well-defined neighborhood, community, or rural district." As the original Act did for other Native Americans, the 1936 amendments granted Native Alaskan groups access to federal loans for economic development, required tribal approval for disposition of its own property, and allowed the tribes to hire their own attorneys, with limited federal supervision. Before the Native Alaskan organizations could receive these benefits, however, they had to reorganize their governmental structures under IRA constitutions, many of which contained standard, or boilerplate, language. Notwithstanding the federal encouragement of tribal self-government through the IRA, these constitutions often required federal approval of many of the tribal governments' decisions, such as enacting tribal ordinances, calling tribal elections, and so on. Approximately 70 IRA tribal governments were organized in Alaska, many of which still exist today.

See also **Indian Reorganization Act of 1934**

ALASKA NATIONAL INTEREST LANDS CONSERVATION ACT OF 1980 The federal Alaska National Interest Lands Conservation Act (ANILCA) of 1980, 16 U.S.C. § 3111 *et seq.*, addresses the subsistence rights of Alaskans on public lands in that state. The Act was intended to settle the issue of the hunting and fishing rights of Native Alaskans, which had allegedly been extinguished by Congress in 1971 with the passage of the massive Alaska Native Claims Settlement Act (ANCSA). When Congress enacted ANCSA, it did not provide directly for subsistence rights of Native Alaskans. Nonetheless, the intent of Congress was that the State of Alaska and the U.S. Department of the Interior would protect native hunting and fishing rights on federal lands. Because they did not, Congress stepped in with ANILCA to address subsistence issues, that is, hunting and fishing for survival. These activities are important not merely for physical survival; they also have great cultural and spiritual significance for Native Alaskans.

The ANILCA, as originally enacted, allowed the state to establish and maintain a scheme to regulate hunting and fishing on federal public lands. The state was required, however, to give subsistence hunting and fishing by rural Alaskans priority over commercial and recreational uses. However, since nonnatives wielded considerable political clout, Congress required that this hunting and fishing (subsistence) preference apply not only to Native Alaskans but also to nonnatives who relied on hunting and fishing for survival. In order to claim the subsistence rights under ANILCA, persons must show that they hunt and fish for survival and that their ability to obtain food from other sources is limited. For instance, a person who lives in a remote village, 50 miles from the nearest grocery store, probably has no real alternative to hunting and fishing. The issues of hunting and fishing rights are still being resolved, but as of 2000, after much wrangling between the state regulatory agencies and Native Alaskans in the courts over a number of years, it appears that an Alaskan citizen seeking a subsistence permit need not actually live in the area where the food is to be taken.

ANILCA also requires that those federal agencies with land management responsibilities give significant priority to subsistence uses when making decisions to lease, reserve, or otherwise dispose of federal public lands. For example, before the Interior Department could lease land to an oil company for drilling, it must provide notice and a hearing to subsistence users and it must take steps to minimize the impact such activities would have on subsistence hunting and fishing activities, if possible. There may be situations in which commercial or recreational uses of particular public lands would so interfere with subsistence uses of the land that the federal agency could not allow the other activities.

See also **Alaska Native Claims Settlement Act of 1971; Subsistence**

ALASKA NATIVE BROTHERHOOD AND SISTERHOOD The Alaska Native Brotherhood and Sisterhood (ANB/S), a major statewide Alaskan political action organization that advocates for the rights of Native Alaskans, is composed of descendants of the aboriginal peoples of Alaska and of those persons married to those descendants. The ANB/S, founded in 1912, is the oldest statewide native political action group in Alaska. Unlike an allied organization, the Alaska Federation of Natives (AFN), the ANB/S's early goals were to encourage the assimilation of Native Alaskans into the nonnative, that is, white, culture. Nonetheless, the latter group has worked over the years to advance the social, political, and legal interests of Native Alaskans. Like the AFN, the ANB/S has also been heavily involved in land claims issues and activities to end racial, social, and political discrimination in the state. The federal and state governments do not consider the ANB/S a tribe or tribal governing body.

ALASKA NATIVE CLAIMS SETTLEMENT ACT OF 1971

ALASKA NATIVE CLAIMS SETTLEMENT ACT OF 1971 The Alaska Native Claims Settlement Act (ANCSA) of 1971, 43 U.S.C. §§ 1601–1628, settled once and for all the claims of Native Alaskans to aboriginal title in Alaska. It provided land and cash to natives of Alaska, including Aleutian Islanders and Eskimos, in exchange for their extinguishing any claims to aboriginal title to any land in the State of Alaska.

NATIVE-WHITE RELATIONS IN ALASKA PRIOR TO 1971

The region that is now Alaska has been inhabited for thousands of years by three ethnically diverse peoples: The Aleuts live on the Alaska Peninsula and the Aleutian Islands in the southwestern part of the state. Eskimo people live in the western and northern regions of Alaska. Several groups of Indian people also inhabit the state. Federal Indian policy made no distinction among any of the first people to live in Alaska. The term "Native Alaskan," then, deals with all groups of aboriginal people in Alaska—Aleuts, Eskimos, and Indians.

Before Russian contact with Alaska in the mid-1700s, there was little, if any, contact between whites and the native peoples of the region. Native Alaskans had exclusive possession to their lands. From the mid-1700s to 1867, Russia exercised domination over Alaska. Some of the native peoples of Alaska were enslaved to work for Russian-dominated business enterprises. In 1867, by treaty, the United States purchased the territory of Alaska from Russia for more than $7 million. This purchase gave the federal government exclusive control over Alaska.

In reference to native people, this treaty of purchase only said that the "uncivilized tribes" would be subject to all laws and regulations enacted by the United States. For a number of years, through such agencies as the Navy, Treasury, and War Departments, the federal government exercised only minimal supervision over the region. In 1884, Congress enacted the Organic Act for Alaska. This law, which established a civil government for the territory of Alaska, never settled any native land claims. The Organic Act simply provided that "Indians or other persons . . . shall not be disturbed in the possession of any lands actually in their use or occupation." Under the terms of the Organic Act, Congress reserved for itself the right to determine the nature of the title that people may hold in such lands. This law did not explicitly differentiate between natives and whites. There has always been some confusion over whether any Indian country ever existed in Alaska, even though the federal government did provide a modicum of services such as education and health care to the native peoples of Alaska. The question of the existence of Indian country in Alaska was (and is) important to any analysis of the nature and extent of inherent tribal sovereignty in Alaska.

In the early 1900s, the native-white relationship began to change through administrative rules, court decisions, and congressional enactment of legislation such as the Alaska Indian Reorganization Act (IRA) of 1936, which extended the benefits of the Indian Reorganization Act of 1934 to the native groups in Alaska. In the early 1930s, responsibility for native affairs in Alaska was transferred to the Bureau of Indian Affairs, the agency that managed federal Indian policy issues for the lower 48 states. At that time, the U.S. Department of the Interior established few reservations like those it had created in other states. Instead, most Native Alaskans lived in numerous small villages all over the territory. Whether or not these "reservations" constituted trust property or even Indian country was always questionable. Unlike in the rest of the United States, in Alaska, prior to passage of ANCSA, there was only a fragmented trust responsibility toward the native peoples of Alaska.

PASSAGE OF THE ALASKA NATIVE CLAIMS SETTLEMENT ACT

There was a great deal of uncertainty regarding the legal status of millions of acres of land that Native Alaskans used and occupied. Traditional and legal notions of Indian title, that is, of aboriginal title, did not apply with any uniformity to land in Alaska. Even the few Indian reservations in that state were subject to much litigation over their very status as reservations. No treaties were ever made between the United States and Alaska Natives.

Even judicial and legislative opinion was divided on whether the federal-Indian trust relationship applied to Alaska's natives. The Alaska IRA amendments of 1936 did little, in the long run, to settle the legal status of lands used or occupied by Alaska Natives. In fact, a 1955 decision of the U.S. Supreme Court, *Tee-Hit-Ton Indians v. United States,* 348 U.S. 272 (1955), held that Alaska Natives were not entitled to any monetary compensation if Congress took their lands for some public purpose such as a national forest or park. In response to a federal district court decision that held that the Tyonek tribe had the exclusive right to try one of its members for a crime, Congress, in 1958, extended Public Law 280 to Alaska, implying that Native Alaskan villages and tribes then had inherent powers of self-government. Public Law 280 extended state civil and criminal authority to Indian lands. This law did not extinguish a tribe's power to regulate the conduct of persons on its lands. It only opened up the courts of the territory (later the state) to hear civil and criminal matters arising within Indian lands. In many situations, then, the state and native groups had concurrent jurisdiction over cases arising on Indian lands.

Until the early 1960s, there was little pressure to settle the question of title to Alaskan lands. The state was remote and the climate is harsh. Non-Indians had little economic motive to exploit land, whether Indian owned or not. Except in areas where fish and wildlife were plentiful, there was little need to deal with these issues. Therefore, there was no great hurry to settle the question of the extent of native title to Alaska.

All of this changed when great reserves of oil were discovered in Alaska. When the State of Alaska was admitted to the Union under the Alaska Statehood Act, 72 Stat. 339, it was able to select 100 million acres of federal land for itself. At the same time, the statehood act required Alaska to give up any rights or jurisdiction in land to which the "right or title" may be held by any Native Alaskans. This meant that the new state could not choose for its own use any lands to which natives could claim aboriginal title. The state wanted the lands richest in the newly discovered oil, but much of that land was claimed by native peoples. Much litigation ensued over the new state's land selections. Secretary of the Interior Stewart Udall temporarily froze state selections in 1968. No large-scale extraction of natural resources from the land could take place until the question of land title was settled among all of the citizens of the new state. Energy companies were unwilling to make extensive economic commitments to do business in Alaska until this issue was settled. Native peoples, oil companies, and state officials all realized that the title question needed to be settled. Thus, ANCSA became the vehicle by which aboriginal land claims were settled. Whether this Act was truly satisfactory in the long run to all groups is for the reader to decide.

THE ALASKA NATIVE CLAIMS SETTLEMENT ACT OF 1971: MAJOR PROVISIONS

Overview

This Act is but one of the many native-white land settlements made in the history of the United States. Many such settlements were enacted by treaty: Land was exchanged for money or the provision of services to native peoples. What makes the ANCSA so unusual is its sheer size in terms of land and money. Since passage of the Act, most federal legislation providing for services or special protection to other Native Americans has also been applied to Alaska Natives. In summary, the Act provides Native Alaskans with fee title (that is, ownership) of approximately 44 million acres of land and nearly $1 billion in exchange for their relinquishing any aboriginal or other land claims—including hunting, fishing, mineral, or other rights—to non-ANCSA lands. In other words, after passage of the Act, Native Alaskans made no claim to the rest of the state. The State of Alaska could then proceed with its selection of 100 million acres of federal land guaranteed to it under the Alaska Statehood Act.

Land Transfer

As part of the Act, Congress allowed Alaska Natives to choose about 44 million acres of land from their claimed aboriginal territory. This territory is an area that Native Alaskans have used or lived upon. The surface (above-ground) estate of approximately half of this amount went to about 200 native villages, which were organized as corporations under state law. The subsurface estate of this same 22 million acres was given to 12 regional corporations, also organized along ethnic and racial lines, and incorporated according to state law. (A subsurface estate means legal rights to valuable minerals, water, or anything else of value found underneath the ground.) All of the village corporations are situated in one of the regional corporations.

Of the 12 regional corporations, 6 were entitled to select another 16 million acres of land, to which they had both the surface and subsurface rights. The remainder of the lands were to be allotted to Native Alaskans individually, pursuant to pending applications for individual allotments, and to parks, historic sites, or other uses by Native Alaskans. That portion of these "remainder" lands not set aside for such purposes was to be transferred to the regional corporations based on their individual populations.

Cash Settlement

Under the terms of the Act, Congress established the Alaska Native Fund as a mechanism to manage and distribute the monies allocated by Congress as part of the land settlement. Over an 11-year period, Congress appropriated about $462 million for the fund, and another $500 million dollars were generated from annual revenues collected by both the federal and state governments from mineral leases on Alaskan lands. The fund then contained just less than $1 billion. The monies were to be distributed to the regional corporations, which in turn were required to give about 50 percent to their own stockholders and to the village corporations within each region. A thirteenth regional corporation was composed of Native Alaskans living outside the state. This corporation received a share of the ANCSA cash settlement but no land.

Alaska Native: Definition

The Act specifically defined an Alaska Native as a person who is a citizen of the United States and who has a blood quantum of one-fourth or more of Alaska Indian, Aleut, or Eskimo blood. A person who cannot prove the blood quantum but who is regarded as an Alaska Native by a village or other native group, whose father or mother was also regarded as a native by a village or group, and who was alive on December 18, 1971, is also considered an Alaska Native under the Act The definition is important because it takes into account a more flexible concept of native culture by accepting proof that the native community regards the person as one of its members rather than merely relying on a blood-quantum measurement. In the lower 48 states, the boundaries of reservations and Indian communities have been fairly well defined after two centuries of clarification through presidential orders, congressional enactments, and litigation in the state and federal courts. None of this has occurred to any great degree in Alaska. The government has always taken a piecemeal approach to defining the Indian-white relationship in Alaska.

The definition of "Alaska Native" is also crucially important for another reason: Many federal enactments extending legal protection or offering other benefits to Native American people and groups because of their status have adopted the legal definition of an Alaska Native first established under ANCSA.

Participation in ANCSA by Alaska Natives

The Act originally provided that each Alaska Native alive on December 18, 1971—the date President Richard Nixon signed ANCSA into law—would receive 100 shares of stock in a regional corporation and would also receive shares of stock in the village corporation to which he or she belonged. Under the original act, until Congress amended the ANCSA in 1988, this stock could not be sold or transferred until after 1991 (there were a few exceptions, such as transfer as a result of a divorce settlement). The 1988 ANCSA amendments extended these restrictions on the sale of such stock until such time as the village or regional corporations themselves, by amending their articles of incorporation, authorized the transfer of shares of stock to others, including non–Native Alaskans. Under current law, the corporations could simply choose to maintain these restrictions on the sale or other transfer of their stock.

The 1988 amendments to ANCSA were intended to prevent the control of the corporations from passing out of native hands. These restrictions on alienation, that is, selling or otherwise transferring ownership, are similar to those established by the General Allotment (Dawes) Act of 1887, which held that Indian lands in the lower 48 states could not be sold or otherwise transferred without federal approval.

The 1988 amendments to ANCSA also allowed the corporations to sell shares of stock to Native Alaskans who were born after December 18, 1971, or to persons otherwise eligible for enrollment as Native Alaskans.

Status of Reservations at the Time of Passage of ANCSA

Several reserves, analogous to Indian reservations elsewhere in the United States, existed in Alaska prior to passage of the Act. ANCSA abolished all except the Annette Island Reserve of the Metlakatla Indian Community. Several village corporations elected to take full fee title to their former reservation lands and forfeit further benefits under ANCSA. These former reserves are contained within one or more of the regional or village corporations, and as such they enjoy protected status as ANCSA lands.

Taxation and Transfer of ANCSA Lands

The lands selected by the regional and village corporations were deeded to them in fee simple—the same form of ownership, for example, that a non-Indian might receive when buying land to build a house. This meant that after 1991, the corporations could, with few restrictions, sell their interests in the lands to anyone. This raised the potential for large tracts of Indian lands to pass out of Indian hands, as had happened to other Indian peoples after passage of the General Allotment (Dawes) Act of 1887, which allotted parcels of land to individual Indians and after a fixed period of time ended congressionally imposed restrictions on the sale or transfer (trust status) of such lands. During the allotment era, from 1887 to 1934, the Indian people of the lower 48 states lost more than 80 percent of their land base.

The Act originally provided that ANCSA lands were exempt from state and local property taxes for a period of 20 years as long as the corporation that owned the land did not develop it or lease it to third parties. The 1988 ANCSA amendments extended that period indefinitely. Perhaps Congress feared that the land would pass to nonnatives if Native Alaskans were unable to pay property taxes. (The inability to pay state or local taxes was a major factor in the erosion of the Native American land base during the allotment era.) The ANCSA amendments also protect undeveloped ANCSA lands from being seized by creditors to whom individual natives or corporations owe money or from being lost through bankruptcy or other legal proceedings.

Hunting and Fishing Rights

On its face, the Act extinguished Native Alaskan hunting and fishing rights that might have existed on native lands under the theory of Indian title (aboriginal title). In Indian country elsewhere in the United States, tribes or tribal members may retain certain rights to hunt or fish on privately owned lands even though the land may no longer have the status of Indian country or be within an Indian reservation. The courts have held that unless Congress expressly terminated those rights, they remain. ANCSA is an example of a case in which Congress, as part of the land settlement giving Native Alaskans title to 44 million acres of land, did expressly extinguish aboriginal hunting and fishing rights to all lands of Alaska. That is, if a private landowner were to be taken to court for developing land in a way that would interfere with native fishing rights, because of ANCSA the courts would not judge that those rights still exist, other federal and state laws notwithstanding.

However, even though such rights were extinguished, Congress still intends for the ANCSA lands to be used in a way that will respect Native Alaskan subsistence rights, and it intends state and federal laws and policies to be applied in the same way. This is especially important in

Alaska, which is one of the last parts of the United States where a significant portion of the native people still earn a living off their lands by hunting and fishing. The treaty-making process and the extensive encroachment of non-Indians into Indian country has all but eliminated native hunting and fishing as a means of subsistence for Indians in most other parts of the country. The subsistence rights of nonnatives and Alaska Natives alike were recognized and further clarified by Congress in 1980, when it enacted the Alaska National Interest Lands Conservation Act.

Alaska Native Government under ANCSA

ANCSA was unclear as to whether it intended Native Alaskan governments to continue to exist. In fact, Congress dodged the issue of inherent sovereignty altogether by failing to address it in the Act, which stated that Congress did not want to "establish any permanent, racially-based institutions" or a "lengthy wardship or trusteeship." Nonetheless, by 2000 the courts had not yet reached the conclusion that the Act disestablishes preexisting (that is, pre-ANCSA) Native Alaskan governments. Prior to the Act, the federal government recognized two types of native governments: traditional and IRA (Indian Reorganization Act).

It appears that these governments may continue to operate or may begin operations as sovereigns, with inherent powers of self-rule, notwithstanding the existence of ANCSA and Public Law 280. In fact, federal Indian policy in 2000 seems to encourage the strengthening of Alaska Native self-rule. Since 1971, Congress has passed a number of significant laws that explicitly recognized the existence of native governments. Among them are the Indian Self-Determination and Education Assistance Act of 1975 and the Indian Child Welfare Act of 1978. Both of these laws give Alaska Native governments and other Native American tribal governments significant roles to play in the specific issues that they address, namely, the education of children, strengthening of native governments, and the temporary or permanent placement of children within their native communities, if possible. The regional and village corporations under ANCSA are profit-making entities; their function is to manage the land and funds that they have been entrusted with rather than to regulate the civil activities of their members or to punish criminals. The geographic area that traditional or IRA governments serve may be coterminous with the boundaries of a village corporation, that is, they may cover the same ground.

CONCLUSION

Although the settlement between Native Alaskans and the U.S. government is by far the largest such settlement in the history of the United

States in terms of land and money. ANCSA has a long way to go, according to some critics. Some people have asked whether the non-Indian business concept of corporations can be meshed with Native Alaskan culture. Just as Congress tried to turn Indians into farmers with the General Allotment (Dawes) Act of 1887, it tried to turn Native Alaskans into corporate executives and shareholders with the passage of ANCSA nearly a century later. These corporate forms of business are responsible for the management of large tracts of land and other assets. Corporations are designed to exploit the earth for the maximization of profits. Although native cultures also exploit the earth for survival, they stress respect for the land and recognize that resources must be conserved to last. Additionally, whereas corporations run on a fixed calendar year, most indigenous cultures revolve around the earth's seasons and migratory patterns of wildlife. Native Alaskan assimilation into the dominant non-Indian culture seems to have been far slower than that of Native Americans in the rest of the United States. It remains to be seen whether these interests can be reconciled with one another in the long run. Other critics have questioned whether ANCSA is really just a resurgence of the 1950s termination policy of the U.S. government. These critics suggest that the native corporations, which are organized under state law, might eventually replace the Native Alaskan traditional and IRA governments in governing the lives of their people.

See also **Alaska National Interest Lands Conservation Act of 1980;** ***Alaska v. Native Village of Venetie Tribal Government;*** **Public Law 280: Indian Self-Sovereignty; Regional Corporation; Subsistence; Trust Responsibilities; Village Corporation**

ALASKA V. NATIVE VILLAGE OF VENETIE TRIBAL GOVERNMENT (1998)

The U.S. Supreme Court decision in *Alaska v. Native Village of Venetie Tribal Government*, 522 U.S. 520 (1998) discussed for the first time the question of whether Indian country still existed in Alaska after passage of the landmark Alaska Native Claims Settlement Act of 1971 (ANCSA). The case interpreted 18 U.S.C. § 1151(b), which includes "dependent Indian communities" within the definition of Indian country. For particular lands to be considered "dependent Indian communities," there must be some intent by the government to set aside the lands for the use of Indians and to supervise activities on those lands such as education, health care, land use, and so on. This determination is important because if a particular region is considered to be Indian country, a tribe might be allowed to exercise its civil and criminal jurisdiction over activities occurring there.

In this case, the federal government, under the terms of ANCSA, transferred former reservation lands to two village corporations, which in turn retransferred those lands to the Venetie tribal government. The court reasoned that because Congress had enacted ANCSA to further native self-determination by abolishing all Alaskan reservations (except one, the Annette Island Reserve of the Metlakatla Indian Community), there was no intent to set aside the land in question for Indian use or to continue federal supervision. Therefore, the Court ruled that these lands were not Indian country. This case signals the Court's unwillingness to expand tribal autonomy in the wake of ANCSA. Self-determination would seem to include a tribe's increased ability to exercise its governmental powers. Unfortunately for Alaska Natives, however, Congress has never squarely addressed the status of Alaska IRA or traditional tribal governments in ANCSA.

See also **Alaska Native Claims Settlement Act of 1971; Indian Country; Inherent Sovereignty**

ALLOTMENTS Beginning in 1887 with the passage of the General Allotment Act (also known as the Dawes Act), the U.S. government, on a comprehensive and nationwide basis, distributed allotments, or parcels of land, to individual Indians in an attempt to create a system of land ownership that would make the American Indians into farmers or ranchers. The United States was, at that time, primarily a nation of farmers and ranchers. The Act allotted, or parceled out, up to 160 acres (a quarter section) to the head of each Indian household on a reservation.

For the first 25 years after an individual Indian or Indian family received an allotment, the United States held the land in trust for the benefit of the family or individual. During this time, the land could not be taxed, mortgaged, sold, or otherwise burdened with a lien without the express approval of the government. After that time, the allottee could apply for a land patent. If the patent was granted, the owner could sell or mortgage the land without restriction and it could be taxed, just like real estate anywhere else.

With the aid of federal personnel trained in such areas as farming, ranching, cooking, and so on, the Bureau of Indian Affairs tried to teach the Indian people how to farm the European way. In the process, the allottee was also to learn the European system of land ownership. This allotment policy was carried out regardless of the cultural characteristics of the Indian tribe or nation concerned. For example, the Sioux of the northern plains were a nomadic people, moving from place to place depending on the season of the year. Most of their food was derived from the buffalo and other animals, not grains, as is the case with farming.

The policy of allotment eventually failed because the Act failed to account for these cultural differences. One could not turn a person into a farmer simply by government decree. Because of the rapid erosion of the tribal land base under the allotment practices and other factors, the government ceased wholesale land allotments in 1934 with the passage of the Indian Reorganization Act.

See also **Fee Patent; Indian Reorganization Act of 1934; Trust Lands**

AMERICAN INDIAN MOVEMENT The American Indian Movement (AIM) was organized in the 1960s and worked to change the policy of the federal government toward American Indians. The group, mostly composed of members of federally recognized Indian tribes, organized in response to the termination and assimilationist policies of the government. Other important goals included Indian self-determination and international recognition of the plight of indigenous (native) peoples worldwide by such groups as the United Nations.

AIM was involved in such confrontations as the 1972 takeover of the Bureau of Indian Affairs headquarters building in Washington, D.C., and the 1973 "occupation" of the Pine Ridge Indian Reservation village at Wounded Knee, South Dakota. These activities brought the group worldwide publicity, not all of it positive. Whether or not the group advanced its worthy cause of world respect for Indian people is open to question. AIM did not, and does not today, necessarily have the support of all Indian people in the Midwest or elsewhere. Indian people, like all other groups, have differing opinions on the merit of such groups as AIM.

AMERICAN INDIAN POLICY REVIEW COMMISSION In 1975 Congress established a study panel, the American Indian Policy Review Commission (AIPRC), for the purpose of making a comprehensive survey of the living conditions and legal status of today's American Indians. This commission conducted the first comprehensive survey of American Indian affairs since the 1928 Meriam Report. The AIPRC was composed of three U.S. senators, three members of the U.S. House of Representatives, and five American Indians, three from federally recognized tribes, one from a non–federally recognized tribe, and one urban Indian.

The commission conducted a number of hearings all over the United States. AIPRC task forces, staffed in part by Indian people, investigated tribal governments, health and education among Indians, reservation economic development, and other issues in Indian life. In 1977, the AIPRC released its final report, which contained more than 200 specific recommendations that focused largely on enabling Indian people to determine their own future without paternalistic supervision by the federal government. Some of the recommendations favored expanding the federal trust responsibility and tribal sovereignty. In response to these suggestions, the AIPRC vice chairman, Representative Lloyd Meeds of the State of Washington, wrote a strong dissent. Among other things, he questioned the objectivity of the commission's work and the very existence of tribal inherent sovereignty. Although Congress acted on almost none of the AIPRC's recommendations, the AIPRC's work was nonetheless valuable as a chronicle of contemporary Indian life and the relationship of Native Americans to non-Indian society. Unlike in the 1928 study, Indian people themselves were heavily involved in all phases of the AIPRC's work.

AMERICAN INDIAN RELIGIOUS FREEDOM ACT OF 1978 The American Indian Religious Freedom Act of 1978, 42 U.S.C. § 1996, was designed to ensure that state and federal agencies take Native American religious beliefs into account when making decisions that affect the practice of Indian religions. The statute makes it official federal government policy to respect and protect Native American spirituality wherever possible. Additionally, the Act directs the president to survey all federal agencies to examine their enforcement of any federal laws that may hinder the practice of Native American religions. In response to the Act's mandate, the president convened a task force that identified numerous instances in which the government had disregarded Indian religious practices when making decisions. Such actions dealt mainly with land use policies in national forest or park areas containing lands sacred to Native Americans. Despite its title, however, this law offers only minimal protection to American Indians concerned with the practice of their spirituality. As the U.S. Supreme Court pointed out in its decision in *Lyng v. Northwest Cemetery Protective Association,* 485 U.S. 439 (1988), this law is only a resolution of Congress. Such a resolution merely expresses Congress's feelings about a certain issue, and there is no penalty for violating the resolution. Additionally, the Act creates no right to sue in the federal courts. Later decisions of the Court, such as *Employment Division, Department of Human Resources of Oregon v. Smith,* 494 U.S. 872 (1990), followed *Lyng* in giving short shrift to this Act and to Indian religious interests. *Smith* involved several people who were fired from their jobs because they used peyote as members of the Native American Church. One employee was Indian, and the other was white. Peyote, whose use is illegal under most state and federal drug laws, is a sacrament (religious object) in the Native American Church. Because they were fired, both workers were denied unemployment benefits by the State of Oregon. They sued the state, and the Oregon Supreme Court ultimately found that the state had violated their First Amendment rights by denying them benefits because they used peyote, which was part of the practice of their religion.

In 1994, Congress responded to the *Smith* decision by amending the American Indian Religious Freedom Act to legalize the use of peyote for legitimate religious purposes. The amendment prohibits both criminal punishment and denial of public welfare or other benefits because of the use or transportation of peyote by an Indian in connection with the practice of his or her religion. Although the law only explicitly exempts Native Americans from legal consequences for the religious use of peyote, the prosecution of non-Indians for such use may also be problematic. Non-Indian members of the Native American church also have First Amendment freedoms to practice their religion.

See also ***Lyng v. Northwest Cemetery Protective Association***

AREA DIRECTOR

A Bureau of Indian Affairs (BIA) area director oversees the activities of a group of local BIA offices. The BIA delivers services to Indian tribes and their members through its headquarters in Washington, D.C., and 12 area offices throughout the United States. Each of these area (regional) offices is headed by a director, who is a federal civil service employee.

See also **Bureau of Indian Affairs**

ARIZONA V. CALIFORNIA (1963)

Arizona v. California, 373 U.S. 546 (1963), is an important U.S. Supreme Court case dealing with Indian water rights. When two states sue each other, the Supreme Court has original jurisdiction; that is, it hears the case as a trial court rather than as an appeals court. Since such cases are lengthy, the Court appoints a "special master," or referee, to take written evidence and testimony from witnesses. This case dealt with the use of water from the Colorado River, a major water source for many western states, including California. Ultimately, these states were unable to agree on just how much water each state could draw from the river. Five Indian reservations, in Arizona, California, and Nevada, were involved in the lawsuit.

The Court continued to rely on the *Winters* Doctrine, which was formulated in the early 1900s and held that the Indian reservations were entitled to a significant share of water. Under the principle of prior appropriation, the normal rule governing water usage in the West, if the tribes had not used their share of water for an extended period of time, they would have lost the right to that water for good. *Arizona* is important because the Court held that the tribes could count on the use of some of the Colorado River water for future needs as well as for the needs of the reservations at the time the case was heard. Large users of water had to continue to take into account Indian reservations' needs when seeking additional water supplies. Additionally, Indian reservations created by executive order are given the same rights to water as are those reservations created by treaties.

See also **Indian Water Rights; *Winters* Doctrine**

ASSIMILATION Until recently, the federal government followed a policy of assimilation with respect to Native Americans—that is, a policy of absorbing Native Americans into the mainstream of American life and culture. National political leaders of the nineteenth century thought that Indians needed to be "civilized," for their own benefit as well as for the benefit of white culture. The government established reservations, allotted land to individual tribal members, established day and boarding schools to teach American culture to Indian children and to discourage the children in the use of their own languages and customs, and hired farmers, skilled tradesmen, and others to teach Indians white skills—all in an effort to turn Indians into white Americans.

ASSIMILATIVE CRIMES ACT OF 1825 The Assimilative Crimes Act (ACA) of 1825 and the Indian Country Crimes Act of 1948 extend the reach of federal authority over criminal cases arising in Indian country. Essentially, the Assimilative Crimes Act, 18 U.S.C. § 13, applies a state's criminal law to crimes committed in Indian country in that state. The ACA and the Indian Country Crimes Act are intended to fill some gaps in federal law. For instance, a crime may be committed on an Indian reservation, an act that would be a crime in the state in which the reservation is located, but the tribe may not have jurisdiction over the case. If there is no federal criminal statute that applies to the offense, then the federal government invokes the ACA to "borrow" the appropriate state criminal law. If there is a federal criminal law that applies to the wrongdoing in Indian country, then the ACA is not needed.

Until relatively recent times, Congress, unlike the states, had not enacted a comprehensive criminal code. Therefore, there were many types of criminal activity occurring in Indian country that were not addressed by federal law. The ACA was written in the early 1800s to cover crimes committed on federal lands such as post offices, national parks, and military installations. Congress never meant to utilize it in Indian country. However, in *Williams v. United States,* 327 U.S. 711 (1946), the Supreme Court applied the ACA to Indian country. This law does not confer any additional jurisdiction upon the states to prosecute crimes occurring in Indian country. It only allows the federal government, in the absence of a controlling federal criminal law, to utilize the state criminal law to see justice done in a particular case.

See also **Indian Country Crimes Act of 1948**

ASSOCIATION ON AMERICAN INDIAN AFFAIRS

The Association on American Indian Affairs (AAIA) is a national organization that provides some legal and technical assistance to American Indian tribes. The AAIA, founded in the 1920s, is one of the older organizations dealing with Indian issues. It provides assistance to tribes in such issues as economic development, health, education, and the administration of justice in Indian country. The organization publishes a newsletter, *Indian Affairs,* with a circulation of about 40,000.

B

Bill of Rights The first ten amendments to the U.S. Constitution, the Bill of Rights, were all proposed by the Founding Fathers in 1789, the first year of the Republic. They were adopted by all 13 original states by 1791. Scholars generally agree that the Constitution that established our present republican form of government (that is, government in which power is shared among the people and the federal and state governments) could not have been approved if these ten amendments had not also been proposed. The new states were wary of a too-strong or too-centralized federal government. These amendments, therefore, are designed to limit the national and state governments' authority and power over the people. They address the relationship of all levels of government to the people as individuals.

The First Amendment deals with religion. No government except Indian tribes may establish an official religion. However, not even Indian governments may limit the practice of other religions. All governments must allow the press freedom to report facts. The Founders believed that a free press is important so that voters may be fully informed about the doings of their government. The free speech provisions allow people to speak and write whatever they choose, subject to restrictions on obscene, libelous, and slanderous matters. The rights of assembly allow people to form groups and organizations for all lawful reasons. Finally, the people also have the right to lobby governmental agencies to make their wishes known. With the exclusions noted above, the First Amendment applies everywhere in the United States.

The Second Amendment allows the people to bear arms, in the context of allowing states to maintain militias or national guard organizations. This amendment has no binding force in Indian country.

The Third Amendment forbids governments to station troops in private homes in peacetime; nor may governments do so in wartime unless regulations are established by statute. This amendment, too, is ineffective in Indian country.

The Fourth Amendment prevents governments from arresting people or searching private property unless they first get a warrant to do so from a judge. (However, there are exceptions to the warrant requirements that are beyond the scope of this book.) This amendment is fully applicable in Indian country. In fact, the impetus for passage of the Indian Civil Rights Act of 1968 stemmed largely from the concern that some tribal governments were routinely disregarding any personal rights individuals should have on the Indian reservations.

The Fifth Amendment is not completely applicable to tribal governments. Unlike all other governmental units in the United States, tribes need not use grand juries to help prosecute serious crimes (felonies). The Double Jeopardy Clause forbids a government, tribal or otherwise, to try a person twice for the same crime. Also, no government may force a person to testify against himself or herself in court proceedings, when that might tend to expose his or her guilt for a crime (self-incrimination). All governments must provide the basics of a fair hearing (due process) in civil and criminal court proceedings. These include the right to advance notice of the specific nature of the charges or civil claim; the right to have an impartial judge hear the case, and the right, in criminal cases, to an attorney to help prepare the case. Unlike other levels of government, however, tribes need not bear the expense of court-appointed attorneys in criminal cases. The accused in tribal courts must pay for their own lawyers. Finally, no government may take private property for public use without paying the owner a fair price for it (Just Compensation Clause, or eminent domain rights).

The Sixth Amendment pertains to the rights of individuals charged with criminal offenses. Indian tribes and all other governments must give the accused speedy and public trials. In addition, persons who are accused of crimes and who might therefore be subjected to jail time are generally entitled to trial by jury. The length of the possible jail sentence that triggers the requirement of a jury trial depends upon which government is bringing the charges. The U.S. Supreme Court has interpreted the Sixth Amendment as generally requiring a jury trial in any criminal case, whether federal, tribal, or state, in which a convicted defendant could be sentenced to more than six months in jail. Any state or tribe can enact a stricter requirement that mandates a jury trial when a defendant is subject to even one day in jail. Imprisonment is not an issue in civil cases, except that persons may be held in contempt of court for such things as refusing to obey a lawful court order or showing great disrespect to a judge while court is in session. At all levels of government, defendants are entitled to receive advance notice of the specific charges so that they may properly prepare their cases, to subpoena witnesses in their favor, to have the government's witnesses testify in person (confrontation rights), and to have lawyers help prepare the cases. However, unlike other governments, Indian tribes need not pay for the attorneys. Defendants must hire their own lawyers at their own expense.

The Seventh Amendment requires a government to provide a jury trial in certain civil cases. It does not apply on Indian reservations.

The Eighth Amendment prevents governments from setting excessively high bail amounts for criminal defendants. The bail has to be appropriate to the seriousness of the crime, to the risk that the defendant might flee, and to a number of other factors, and all governments must establish specific guidelines for setting bail. Additionally, the severity of punishment for a crime must be somewhat in proportion to the seriousness of the offense (Cruel and Unusual Punishments Clause). This amendment applies to all governments. However, unlike other levels of government, no Indian tribe may impose a punishment greater than one year in jail, a fine greater than $5,000, or both for a single criminal offense.

The Ninth Amendment provides that the people may have additional rights besides those stated in the Constitution. It states that the rights contained in the federal Constitution are not a complete and full listing. The Ninth Amendment does not apply in Indian country.

The Tenth Amendment states the people retain all powers not explicitly given to either the states or to the federal governments. The Tenth Amendment also does not apply to Indian country.

See also **Civil Rights; Eminent Domain; Indian Civil Rights Act of 1968**

BLOOD QUANTUM

The term "blood quantum" is used to refer to the fraction of Indian blood present in an individual applying for membership in a federally recognized Indian tribe. To count toward membership in a federally recognized Indian tribe, Indian blood must be that of a recognized tribe. A person can have blood from more than one Indian tribe, but most tribal constitutions and existing federal law allows a person to claim membership in only one Indian tribe.

The quantum of Indian blood (from none to entirely Indian blood) necessary to be considered for membership varies from tribe to tribe. Some tribes will allow as little as one-sixty-fourth of Indian blood for membership, whereas others require a minimum of one-fourth or higher. Blood quantum figures may also be used in determining what governmental or tribal services a person is eligible to receive. Not all tribes and federal agencies define an "Indian" in the same way.

See also **Federally Recognized Tribe**

BRENDALE V. CONFEDERATED TRIBES AND BANDS OF YAKIMA (1989) In *Brendale v. Confederated Tribes and Bands of Yakima*, 492 U.S. 408 (1989), the U.S. Supreme Court limited the authority of a tribe to zone fee land owned by non-Indians located on an Indian reservation. Fee land is land that the owner can sell or otherwise transfer without asking the federal government's permission. The case concerned two sections of a reservation. One section was closed to the general public, contained very few privately owned parcels of land, and had little, if any, commercial development. The second section of the reservation was open to the general public, and a substantial part of that section comprised privately owned parcels, some of which were already developed. Both the tribe and county governments had enacted zoning ordinances purporting to regulate the use of privately owned fee land on the reservation. These ordinances conflicted with one another.

The *Brendale* Court, following the case of *Montana v. United States*, 450 U.S. 544 (1981), a fishing and hunting rights case, found that a tribe ordinarily has no authority to zone non-Indian-owned fee lands on a reservation. The *Montana* case severely limited tribal self-rule by finding that Congress had not delegated such authority to the tribes. As a result of the *Montana* and *Brendale* decisions, unless a tribe can prove that it has some business relationship with private landowners or that the regulation of private lands is necessary to protect the political integrity of the tribe or the health, welfare, or safety of its members, it has no power to zone non-Indian-owned fee lands on reservations.

In this case, the Court did find that the tribe had the authority to zone non-Indian-owned lands in the closed area of the reservation. Because that area had not been developed commercially and contained little non-Indian-owned land, the Court was persuaded that the tribe had a great interest in regulating land use there. Conversely, the portion of the reservation that was open to the general public had received significant commercial development and contained many non-Indian-owned parcels. The Court reasoned that the tribe had a minimal interest in regulating land use there. The proportion of non-Indian-owned land and the extent of existing private land development on a reservation are important factors that a court must consider when evaluating a tribe's authority to regulate the use of these lands.

BRYAN V. ITASCA COUNTY (1976) In *Bryan v. Itasca County*, 426 U.S. 373 (1976), the U.S. Supreme Court decided that states do not have the authority to tax the personal property of Indians located on reservation trust lands. The decision limited the reach of Public Law 280 (PL 280) on Indian lands. At first glance, PL 280 seems to enable states to take complete civil and criminal jurisdiction over Indian reservations.

Russell Bryan was a member of the Minnesota Chippewa Tribe located at the Leech Lake Indian Reservation in Minnesota, which is a Public Law 280 state. (Public Law 280 states have specific civil and criminal jurisdiction over Indian country. Alaska, California, Minnesota, Nebraska, Oregon, and Wisconsin are the states that Congress, in enacting PL 280, has allowed to assume criminal and civil jurisdiction over people and activities arising on some or all of the Indian reservations within those states.) He lived in a mobile home located on trust land on his reservation. The State of Minnesota assessed a personal property tax against his home, which Bryan refused to pay. Not surprisingly, the Minnesota state courts interpreted PL 280 as conferring authority on the state to tax personal property located on an Indian reservation.

The *Bryan* Court, in reviewing PL 280, which applies to all or parts of five states, ruled in essence that state civil jurisdiction over the tribe is limited to opening state courts to private lawsuits arising on the reservation. For instance, under PL 280, if two tribal members are involved in an automobile accident on the Leech Lake Reservation, the victim would have to sue the other person in state court, not tribal court.

This case is important because it was the first time the Supreme Court had applied the Canons of Construction in Indian law to a tax issue in a PL 280 state. Using those rules of legal interpretation, the Court resolved the ambiguity in PL 280 in favor of the tribe. On its face, it appears that that law is a broad grant of power to a state to extend its civil authority, including the power to tax, over Indian country. However, in interpreting PL 280, the Court upheld the general principle that a state's power to tax tribal members or property located in Indian country will be upheld only if Congress has clearly granted that power to the states. It is also significant that despite the broad grant of authority to states over civil matters in Indian country, in invalidating the state tax, the *Bryan* Court to a large degree sustained the existing relationship between federal and tribal governments.

See also **Canons of Construction; Public Law 280: Indian Self-Sovereignty**

BUREAU OF INDIAN AFFAIRS

HISTORY AND EARLY MISSION

The Bureau of Indian Affairs (BIA) is a part of the federal government contained within the U.S. Department of the Interior, a cabinet-level organization of the executive branch of the U.S. government. The BIA was one of the first administrative agencies to be set up by the U.S. government. Its early mission was to administer Indian treaties entered into by the various tribes and the U.S. government, to carry out the policies of the government, and to regularize the conduct of Indian affairs on the part of the government. The BIA, by establishing the reservation system, became the government's key tool in its efforts to "civilize" the American Indians.

The agency established a system of local Indian agents to supervise the Indian people on the reservations. The local agent was responsible for distributing items required under the terms of the treaty, such as food, clothing, blankets, medical care, seed, and expert assistance to help the Indian people learn how to farm their allotments. Depending on the size of the reservation and of the agency, the agent, later called the superintendent, might come to oversee a large number of employees.

THE BUREAU IN 2000

The BIA has grown into a large federal agency, with an annual budget, as of 2000, of nearly $1 billion. The United States is divided into 12 geographical regions, each supervised by an area office. There are area offices in Oklahoma City, Oklahoma; Albuquerque, New Mexico; and Aberdeen, South Dakota, among others. Each area office oversees a number of agencies, which are located on most reservations where members of one or more federally recognized tribes live. The area office is headed by an area director, who, like the local agency superintendent, is a covered employee under the federal Civil Service Act and, more likely than not, a member of a federally recognized tribe. (An employee covered under the federal Civil Service Act cannot be disciplined or fired except for a good reason, for example, committing serious crimes such as stealing property from the government.)

The BIA today performs many functions to carry out its trust responsibilities. Each agency office has a number of divisions charged with specific responsibilities. Among the more important branches are these: (1) Finance, which handles the bookkeeping matters for the individual Indian money accounts, lease payments, and other fiscal chores; (2) Realty, which supervises the issuance of leases for tribal and individual trust lands; This branch also keeps track of tribal allotments and investigates whether or not land, pursuant to specific criteria, should be either taken out of or placed into trust status; (3) Natural Resources, which is responsible for managing the natural resources, such as water, oil, minerals, timber, and so on, on Indian lands; (4) Social Services, which administers various welfare and educational programs on the reservations; and (5) The Office of Superintendent, which oversees and coordinates all of the activities of the local office. Most employees of the BIA are Native Americans. The agency is headed by an assistant secretary for Indian affairs, of the Department of the Interior.

See also **Allotments; Indian Preference; Trust Responsibilities**

BUREAU OF LAND MANAGEMENT The Bureau of Land Management (BLM), created by Congress in 1946 as an agency of the Department of the Interior, is responsible for the proper administration of federally owned or controlled public lands throughout the United States. The bureau's duties include preserving the wildlife and natural habitat of public lands and developing and maintaining recreational opportunities. Other responsibilities include developing and conserving forest and natural resources. The bureau also provides technical support to other federal and state agencies in the use and management of public lands.

Among the agencies assisted by the BLM is the Bureau of Indian Affairs (BIA). The BIA administers hundreds of thousands of acres of tribally owned or controlled lands for the benefit of the tribes and their members. The BLM assists the BIA in developing land use plans and provides other technical assistance to the BIA and the tribes in the administration of these lands. Such plans balance recreation, mining, grazing, and other activities to develop the land to its maximum potential while also attempting to preserve the land.

The BLM traces its origins to 1812, when Congress created the General Land Office (GLO) to administer the public domain (that is, public lands). Its main function until the close of the frontier in the late 1800s was to oversee the survey, sale, and settlement of public lands by both individuals and business enterprises. During this time, the GLO helped administer the General Allotment Act of 1887 (also known as the General Severalty Act or the Dawes Act), under which Indian lands were distributed to tribal members. The GLO also administered other congressional acts that "opened up" Indian lands to white settlement. After the close of the American frontier in about 1890, the GLO's mission shifted to one of conservation, land management, and allocation of natural resources, such as timber, mining, or grazing lands. These missions are still carried out, largely by the BLM. The BLM, just as the GLO did earlier, maintains some field offices across the United States. Other federal agencies, however, such as the U.S. Fish and Wildlife Service, the U.S. Forest Service, and the Office of Surface Mining, Reclamation, and Enforcement, also have a hand in land use and management activities.

BURKE ACT OF 1906 The federal Burke Act of 1906 allowed the secretary of the interior to shorten the period of Indian land trust status. The General Allotment Act of 1887 (the Dawes Act) had provided that lands allotted to Indians would remain in trust status for 25 years. The Burke Act allowed the secretary of the interior to terminate that trust status early. The 1906 Act was passed to speed the assimilation of Indian people into mainstream American culture. Federal officials had long believed that Native Americans could become better citizens by owning private property. The Act also accelerated the transfer of individual allottees' trust land to deeded status, which meant the owner could sell or mortgage the land and that the land could eventually be taxed by state and local governments.

Another significant feature of the 1906 Act was that issuance of deeds was no longer automatic after a 25-year trust period. Instead, an allottee had to be declared competent (that is, able to manage his or her business affairs in the European mold) before a deed was granted. The secretary had the discretion to issue the deed earlier upon proof of competency. The task of determining competency was often delegated to local agents and to the Bureau of Indian Affairs bureaucracy.

Finally, under the Burke Act, Indian allottees could become citizens only after the secretary had issued the deed. (Under the original Dawes enactment an Indian became a citizen when the allotment was first granted.) However, the Citizenship Act of 1924 granted U.S. citizenship to virtually all remaining noncitizen American Indians.

See also **Allotments; General Allotment Act of 1887; Trust Lands**

BUY INDIAN ACT OF 1908 The federal Buy Indian Act of 1908, 25 U.S.C. § 47, encourages the Department of the Interior and other federal agencies serving Native Americans to purchase goods and services from Indian-owned individuals and businesses. Until the 1960s, the Bureau of Indian Affairs (BIA) was not required to publicly advertise when asking for proposals to provide the BIA or other federal agencies with various products and labor. Since then, federal agencies must generally let the public know when they need to buy such items. However, the Buy Indian Act still allows agencies dealing with Indians to give them preference over non-Indians when such goods and services would benefit Indian tribes, their programs, and individual tribal members. For instance, the Indian Health Service may give preference to Indian contractors for the construction and supply of a health clinic that would primarily benefit Native Americans.

See also **Indian Preference**

C

California v. Cabazon Band of Mission Indians (1987) In *California v. Cabazon Band of Mission Indians*, 480 U.S. 202 (1987), the Supreme Court ruled that a Public Law 280 (PL 280) state (Alaska, California, Minnesota, Nebraska, Oregon, and Wisconsin are the states that Congress, in enacting PL 280, has allowed to assume criminal and civil jurisdiction over people and activities arising on some or all of the Indian reservations within those states.) had no authority to regulate bingo games conducted on the reservations of two Indian tribes. In this case, two Indian tribes were conducting bingo games, poker, and other card games on their reservations to raise money for economic development. The games were played predominantly by non-Indians. The profits from these enterprises were the main source of tribal income. The Court decided that since California permitted bingo and other forms of gambling within the state, the laws governing these activities were of a civil or regulatory nature. If the state had prohibited bingo or other forms of gambling, the Court might have come to the conclusion that such laws were criminal or prohibitory and that the state could have prevented the tribe from operating such games. Congress, partly in response to this decision, passed the Indian Gaming Regulatory Act of 1988, which in effect nullifies the Court's decision. Nonetheless, *Cabazon* still serves as a modern guide to evaluate the reach of PL 280 state authority on Indian reservations.

Canons of Construction When federal or state courts need to interpret a question involving Indian law, they look to certain court-made rules, called statutory constructions, to help them determine what is meant by a certain statute, treaty, or executive order. Statutory construction is that branch of the law that interprets laws passed by a state legislature or Congress. The Canons of Construction are a special set of statutory construction rules that apply only to Indian law issues. They arose out of the trust relationship and treaties between the United States and the various Indian tribes. Such special rules are necessary when a statute or provisions of a treaty can be defined in more than one way and the parties to a legal dispute cannot agree on which interpretation to use.

These canons, or rules of interpretation, assume that Congress's intent toward the Indians is benevolent and hold that treaties, statutes, and other federal rules and actions should therefore be read as protecting Indian rights and in a manner favorable to Indians. These canons originated in the interpretation of treaties. The United States had the upper hand in the bargaining in the treaty-making process. Given that in the treaty era, American concepts of the law and legal terms were foreign to the Indian tribes, the government had, in all probability, superior negotiating skills and knowledge of the English language, especially of the precise legal meaning given to legal terminology.

The federal courts have developed the following precepts: (1) Treaties should be construed (interpreted) liberally in favor of the Indians. (2) Ambiguities in treaties and other federal actions should be resolved in favor of the Indians. In other words, when a treaty or law can have two or more meanings or interpretations, the meaning that would be most favorable to the Indian or tribe should be adopted. (3) Treaties should be interpreted as the Indians of their day would have understood them. Treaties are still an extremely important source of the legal rights of, and obligations to, Indians by the federal (and sometimes state) governments. (4) Before a treaty or law will be interpreted as extinguishing or eliminating the rights of the Indians, it must be shown that Congress had a "clear and plain" intent to eliminate Indian treaty rights.

These are the basic rules. When Indian rights are to be reserved or established, these canons give a broad interpretation to the federal action to be taken. Conversely, when Indian rights are to be limited or extinguished, the courts use a narrow interpretation of the federal action to be reviewed. The courts use the canons in analyzing many facets of Indian law issues that come before them. For example, Public Law 280 provided that state law and jurisdiction was to be extended to Indian country in many cases. No specific mention was made in that law of the states' right to tax in Indian territories. However, the U.S. Supreme Court, in *Bryan v. Itasca County,* 426 U.S. 373 (1976), applied the canons in its decision that the state may not tax activities on Indian lands. That decision has been modified over the years.

See also **Trust Responsibilities**

CEDED LANDS TRUST When the U.S. government formally annexed Hawaii in 1898, the Republic of Hawaii ceded, that is, turned over, nearly 2 million acres to the United States. The United States took title to these "ceded lands," with the condition that they be used for their historical purpose of supporting and sustaining the Hawaiian people. The Hawaiian monarchs formerly owned these lands and managed them for the benefit of their people. Land use practices in Hawaii prior to Western contact in the 1700s stressed not land ownership in the American tradition but land stewardship, that is, the management and use of the land for the benefit of all of the inhabitants of the Hawaiian nation.

The federal government turned over management of this property to the Territory of Hawaii when it was organized in 1900. The United States, however, retained legal title to the lands. Upon statehood for Hawaii in 1959, the new state received the legal title to most of these ceded lands, subject to the requirement that it use and manage them for the benefit of the Hawaiian people. The federal law admitting Hawaii to statehood established five specific trust responsibilities that the new state had concerning these lands: (1) to support schools at all levels; (2) to better the living conditions of Native Hawaiians; (3) to develop farm and home ownership among the people; (4) to develop public improvements upon the lands; and (5) to make the best public use of this ceded lands trust. Currently, the Office of Hawaiian Affairs (OHA), established in 1979, is the primary state agency charged with the management of these lands. Any use to which the OHA puts these lands must fall within one or more of the five categories just mentioned. Some of these trust obligations are fulfilled through income the OHA earns by leasing the ceded lands to private parties. Unlike the general trust responsibility the federal government owes Indians in the mainland United States, these trust obligations are administered by the State of Hawaii, not the federal government. In theory at least, Native Hawaiians have more direct input into the management of these lands than do Native Americans elsewhere in the country. In the rest of the United States, the Bureau of Indian Affairs, an executive agency, administers most federal Indian programs and trust lands. Its top officials are appointed by the president and the secretary of the interior until the Supreme Court decision in *Rice v. Cayetano* (2000). The OHA board of directors is elected by Native Hawaiians. Many Native Hawaiians today continue to be skeptical of the OHA's ability to carry out the trust responsibilities imposed upon it by the federal government and the Hawaiian state constitution.

See also **Hawaii Homes Commission; Office of Hawaiian Affairs; *Rice v. Cayetano;* Trust Responsibilities**

Checkerboard Lands The term "checkerboard" describes land within a specific area, such as an Indian reservation, as containing both land owned by Indians and land owned by non-Indians. It is distinguished from the term "fractionalized interest," which refers to joint ownership of a parcel of land by a number of people, regardless of race, at any specific point in time. Under the General Allotment Act of 1887 (also known as the General Severalty Act or the Dawes Act), the U.S. government, on a national basis, began allotting Indian lands to individual tribal members. After a specified number of years, they received a deed to the parcels they had been allotted. On many reservations, the tribal members eventually lost that allotted land. Some, for example, could not afford to pay state or local property taxes, and the state or local government would then auction the land to the highest bidder. Others mortgaged part or all of their allotment to finance the building of a house or other buildings or improvements to their parcels. As a result, some or all of a member's allotment passed into non-Indian hands.

Over the decades, much of the land on a given reservation became non-Indian. As is discussed elsewhere in this encyclopedia, state and local governments acquire criminal and civil jurisdiction over activities occurring on land that has passed into non-Indian ownership.

Checkerboarded reservations today often present considerable problems. For example, local law enforcement officials may have to determine whether a given parcel of land is in trust status or is privately owned land before arresting a person found there for a crime. The ownership status of the land where criminal activity has occurred may determine whether the state, federal, or tribal government may prosecute a person for a given crime. Checkerboarding also presents problems in zoning and land use issues. The ownership status of a given parcel will help determine whether the state or the tribe has the right to regulate the use of the land in question.

See also **Civil Jurisdiction; Criminal Jurisdiction; Fractionalized Interests; Jurisdiction; Zoning**

***Cherokee Nation v. Georgia* (1831)** *Cherokee Nation v. Georgia,* 30 U.S. (5 Pet.) 1 (1831) is the second of the so-called Trilogy Cases, in which the U.S. Supreme Court, for the first time, discussed whether or not Indian tribes were states or foreign nations within the meaning of the U.S. Constitution. The Cherokee Nation was at that time located on its ancestral lands, in what had by that time become the State of Georgia. The Cherokees brought a suit under the original jurisdiction powers of the Supreme Court, asking it to prevent Georgia from applying its laws to the Cherokee Nation.

Chief Justice John Marshall, along with his fellow justices, concluded that the Court had no jurisdiction, or authority, to decide the case. The Court then dismissed it. In Marshall's view, the tribes were neither states nor foreign nations as those terms are used in Article III of the Constitution when dealing with the Courts. Under the Constitution, when a state or foreign nation is a party to a lawsuit, with certain conditions, the case can be heard directly in the Supreme Court. Even though the Court refused to hear the case, it is still very important in Indian law because Marshall, for the first time, opined on the status of Indian tribes and their relationship to the United States.

Marshall referred to the tribes as "domestic dependent nations" with very limited aspects of sovereignty. The Indian nations have the right to occupy their territory, subject to the government's right to eliminate their ownership of the land. The tribes were not considered foreign nations because the worldview appeared to be that the United States would see any attempt by another country to seize Indian lands as an act of hostility toward the United States. And yet Marshall did not consider the tribes to be states because they look to the national government for protection and petition it to address their needs and wants. In the language of *Cherokee Nation,* the tribes' relationship to the government is that of ward to guardian. Though Marshall's opinion was not that of the majority (the Court was split with three different opinions, all for dismissal of the case, but for different reasons), nonetheless, later decisions of most other courts, both federal and state, continue to adopt Marshall's reasoning and categorization of Indian tribes.

See also **Trilogy Cases**

CHOICE OF LAW

The legal principle of choice of law allows one court, on the grounds of justice, courtesy, and convenience to the parties, to apply or enforce the laws of another jurisdiction in the forum court (that is, the place where the controversy is being decided). Typically, under principles of comity, or judicial courtesy, a state court may, under certain circumstances, apply the law of an Indian tribe to a case pending in that state court.

A choice of law question may occur when the parties to a transaction have contact with more than one jurisdiction. For example, two parties may begin to make a contract on an Indian reservation, intending to enforce it under tribal law. Before the contract is completed, both parties move off the reservation and seek to enforce it under state law. If justice demands it, and due process is followed, a state court may apply tribal law to interpret or enforce the agreement. Some states with Indian reservations within their borders may have special laws that deal with such situations. The Full Faith and Credit Clause of the U.S. Constitution does not apply to the relationship between state and tribal governments.

See also **Comity; Full-Faith and Credit Clause**

CITIZENSHIP ACT OF 1924 Under the federal Citizenship Act of 1924, 8 U.S.C. § 1401(b) *et seq.*, U.S. citizenship was granted to all American Indians who were not already citizens under other provisions of federal law or treaties. It must be remembered that Indian people are members of tribes that are somewhat sovereign (that is, independent of the United States or the fifty states). As such, prior to passage of this Act, Indian people were not automatically U.S. citizens by reason of birth or residence in the United States.

Before this Act, there were two ways for Indians to gain citizenship. The first was by treaty: Treaties often provided that a person must either accept U.S. citizenship or retain tribal membership and move wherever the tribe went. A second method was by specific federal statute: Some such laws granted citizenship to all members of a tribe who served in the military during a particular time of war and who were honorably discharged. Another type of federal statute granted blanket citizenship to all Indians coming under its terms.

The 1924 Act was a catchall act that conferred citizenship on all Indians born within the territorial United States and those Native Americans not granted citizenship under other federal treaties or laws such as the General Allotment (Dawes) Act of 1887. The Citizenship Act today means that virtually all Indians are citizens of their tribes and of the United States. This Act does not impair the trust relationship that Indians have with the U.S. government.

CIVIL JURISDICTION A government's civil jurisdiction in Indian country is its power to regulate the noncriminal activities of people or property there. This authority also includes the right of a particular government's courts to decide civil disputes that arise in Indian country. If a tribe or other governmental entity could not exercise these powers, self-rule would be meaningless. There are three factors to be considered when deciding which government—the tribe, the state, or the federal government—may exercise authority over a given situation: (1) the identity of the parties, that is, whether they are Indian or non-Indian; (2) the land or actual location that gives rise to the dispute in question, that is, whether the dispute arose on tribal trust land or on fee-owned (deeded) land; and (3) the particular subject involved.

Under the Plenary Powers Doctrine, Congress may at any time allocate the power to regulate a given situation in Indian country among the three sets of governments. Therefore, to decide this question, federal statues, treaties, and federal court decisions must be reviewed. As a general rule, Indian tribes, as political entities that predate the founding of the United States, retain all powers of self-government not taken away by Congress through legislation.

FEDERAL JURISDICTION

The federal government does not have civil jurisdiction over matters arising in Indian country unless Congress has given its express consent. Usually, all laws passed by Congress apply to all states in the country. However, since Indian tribes are considered semi-independent nations, Congress must signify its intention for federal laws to apply in Indian country. Congress has extended federal civil authority to the reservation in several instances. For example, Congress has assumed authority over Indian trust lands and the sale of reservation resources such as timber, oil, and gas. Generally, however, Congress has left the Indian tribes to manage most of their own affairs. Even where Congress has given the federal government some authority to act in Indian country, tribes may regulate activities that Congress has placed under federal jurisdiction as long as the tribe's laws do not conflict with the federal laws. This is known as concurrent jurisdiction.

STATE JURISDICTION

Congress and the federal courts, recognizing the long history of hostile state-tribal relations, have generally refused to permit the states to assume much authority over civil matters arising in Indian country. At any time, however, under the Plenary Powers Doctrine, Congress could choose to allow the states additional authority over activities occurring in Indian country. Again, Congress must expressly intend to grant the states regulatory authority in Indian country. It has occasionally done so. For instance, in 1953, Congress enacted Public Law 280 (PL 280), which gave certain states the authority to open up their courts to hear civil disputes (and also criminal cases) arising in Indian country. Even though this appears to be a broad grant of authority to the states, Congress specifically limited state power over such matters as taxation, the sale or lease of Indian trust lands, and hunting, fishing, and water rights issues arising in Indian country. Under this law, states have concurrent jurisdiction in Indian country with the tribe. PL 280's major feature is that it opens up state courts to hear civil disputes in Indian country. A litigant may still choose, in many cases, to have the tribal court resolve the dispute instead.

Early U.S. Supreme Court cases, such as *Worcester v. Georgia,* 31 U.S. (6 Pet.) 515 (1832) and the other two of the Trilogy Cases heard under John

Marshall's Court, recognized the sovereign status of Indian nations. These early cases, interpreting treaties and federal laws, found that states generally could not assume power over Indian country without the consent of Congress. Nonetheless, the states have often tried to assume some measure of authority in Indian country in such areas as taxation and the regulation of land use (and they sometimes succeeded).

Since the *Worcester* case, the federal courts have applied two tests to determine whether or not state authority over activities in Indian country would be acceptable. The first test, that of infringement, asks whether or not the proposed state action "infringe[s] on the right of reservation Indians to make their own laws and to be governed by them." The second test, preemption, asks whether or not the federal or tribal governance of a particular activity is so extensive so as to preclude any state regulation of that activity. For instance, federal regulation of the sale, leasing or other transfer of Indian trust lands is so extensive as to prevent any state from applying its real estate laws over such territory. States, of course, can always claim a legitimate interest in regulating health, safety, and other matters within all land in their borders. However, each of these tests constitutes a challenge to a state's asserting civil authority in Indian country, notwithstanding the state's interest in such matters. The burden of making and meeting such a challenge rests on the state. Until recently, there have been few situations where a state's interests prevailed over a tribe's when the tests were applied. Ordinarily, only where the activities involve non-Indians conducting activities on non-Indian-owned lands within a reservation have the state's interests in regulation been found sufficiently strong to overcome tribal autonomy when applying these two tests. For example, despite the fact that the power to tax is important to true self-rule, states have been given the power to tax non-Indian-owned land, to regulate hunting and fishing activities, and to zone private property located in Indian country. The power to tax also includes the right to collect levies from the sale of goods by non-Indians to non-Indians from businesses located on such privately owned land within an Indian reservation.

Far less clear, and generating the most litigation, are those cases involving activities on Indian-owned or tribally owned land or in which one or more of the parties concerned is Indian. In these situations, the infringement and preemption tests are crucial. Since the 1980s, the Supreme Court has been increasingly skeptical of Indian rights and has reduced the importance of the infringement test, relying more heavily on a determination of whether or not Congress intended, by federal legislation, to exclude state civil authority in Indian country. In other words, inherent tribal sovereignty, the fundamental interest of a tribal government in self-rule, has been given a lesser role by the Supreme Court in adjudicating tribal-state disputes over civil authority within Indian country. Since the 1980s the Court has generally required that before state authority over activities in Indian country is ruled out, some specific tribal interest must be involved. In other words, either the territory in which the activity is concerned must be in Indian hands or one or more of the parties concerned to the dispute must be Indian, either a tribal member or a nonmember Indian. Currently, when a tribe's assertion of authority over any non-Indian activity or person is challenged, the burden seems to shift to the tribe to show why state regulation should be forbidden.

Unless the tribe can show that its regulation of non-Indian activities arising on non-Indian lands has a direct impact on the political integrity or welfare of a tribe, or that the non-Indians entered into a voluntary agreement (that is, a business license) with the tribe, tribal authority will be denied over such matters. Furthermore, U.S. Supreme Court decisions require that tribes show that Congress positively granted them the authority to regulate non-Indian activities on Indian lands. This, of course, reverses the legal principles in Indian law, developed over many years, that held that tribes, as sovereign nations, have all powers of self-rule except those Congress expressly removed from them.

For example, the 1997 case *Strate v. A-1 Contractors,* 520 U.S. 438 (1997), found that tribal courts did not have authority over a motor vehicle accident involving two non-Indians on a state highway crossing a reservation. That case decided that even though the regulation of highway safety might have some impact on the health, welfare, and safety of tribal members, the tribe's interests in such regulatory authority was not strong enough to overcome state regulatory authority in such areas. Other cases have held that tribes lack the jurisdiction to regulate the use of non-Indian lands on a reservation, especially if the land is located in an area of Indian country where many parcels of deeded land are intermingled with trust lands. Still other cases have found that tribes lack the right to regulate hunting and fishing activities of non-Indians on lands located on a reservation but owned by non-Indians.

However, whenever Indians or Indian property is involved in reservation activities, the tribe usually possesses the jurisdiction to control those activities. For example, a non-Indian who runs a grocery store on the reservation and trades with Indians and non-Indians is subject to tribal business license and health and safety laws. If a person, regardless of race, is injured on the premises, he or she must bring any lawsuit against the store in tribal courts, if the tribe has one. Unless a law such as PL 280 covers the situation, the state courts have no power to hear the case. Occasionally, there may be situations in which a tribal legislature has not authorized its courts to hear a certain type of case, and a person wishing to bring such a case may have no tribunal in which to bring it.

TRIBAL JURISDICTION

Unless Congress, the federal courts, or the tribe itself has forbidden it, tribal courts usually hear the same variety of civil cases as their state counterparts do. These cases include child custody cases, divorces, personal injury cases, debts, contract disputes, and many others. As stated previously, in order for a tribal court to hear a particular case, some interest of the tribe must be involved: At least one of the parties must be Indian or the property involved must have some connection with the reservation, that is, must be owned by Indians or located in Indian country. With tribes becoming increasingly adept at the regulation of commerce, land use, recreation, activities affecting the environment, and other activities arising in Indian country, non-Indians will continue to challenge the tribes' authority over these matters.

See also **Infringement Test; Jurisdiction; *Montana v. United States;* Preemption; Public Law 280: Indian Self-Sovereignty; *Strate v. A-1 Contractors***

CIVIL RIGHTS

CIVIL RIGHTS Civil rights are those legal rights or liberties that are personal, natural rights guaranteed by the U.S. Constitution and many tribal constitutions. Under political theories advanced hundreds of years ago by such noted philosophers as Voltaire and Thomas Locke, men and women have certain natural rights that no government may take away. The term "civil rights" also deals with that body of law—constitutional, statutory, and decisional (court decisions)—that deals with the liberty of mankind. Such liberty is considered to be a restraint on all levels of government from interfering with certain personal freedoms of individuals.

Among the personal rights or liberties guaranteed to all are the rights to freedom of speech, peaceable assembly, and freedom of religion. Many of these rights are found in the first ten Amendments to the U.S. Constitution, known popularly as the Bill of Rights. Depending on the personal liberty involved, some or all of these rights may apply to Indians on Indian reservations. The U.S. Constitution does not fully cover people in Indian country. The Indian Civil Rights Act of 1968 addressed some of these issues.

Although government cannot legally restrict certain civil rights, it sometimes does so, either intentionally or negligently. For example, a governmental agency may, because its policy makers or top officials find some type of speech offensive, try to regulate or prevent a person from using certain so-called obscene words in public. Or, for example, some types of parades or public demonstrations may be offensive to a particular group—such as a neo-Nazi rally in a Jewish suburb—and a governmental agency, whether it be city, state, or federal, may try and prevent such a parade.

Civil rights are actually enforced or protected by the judicial branch of government. To encourage governments to refrain from invading a person's civil liberties, a court may issue an injunction preventing the governmental agency from acting in such a manner. Alternatively, the court may award the person whose rights were violated a sum of money, called damages, that the government must then pay. Although civil rights usually deal with the relationship between a citizen and a government, in some cases a private individual or legal entity (such as a corporation) may also be legally liable for violating another person's civil liberties.

See also **Bill of Rights; Indian Civil Rights Act of 1968; Injunction**

CODE OF FEDERAL REGULATIONS

The *Code of Federal Regulations (CFR)* is an official publication of the U.S. government in which all federal rules and regulations of an administrative nature are published for the use of the public and government officials. When a rule or regulation is published in this set of more than 100 volumes, the regulation is then effective and in force. This multivolume set is updated annually. Rules and regulations that deal with Indian affairs are found in Title 25 of the *Code*. Depending on the topic, some other federal regulations and rules affecting Native Americans may be found elsewhere in the *CFR*.

See also **Administrative Law; Administrative Procedures Act of 1946**

CODE OF FEDERAL REGULATIONS COURT

Code of Federal Regulations (CFR) courts are tribal courts named after Title 25 of the *Code of Federal Regulations*. They exist only in Indian country. Only those tribes that retain their own sovereignty and do not come under the Indian Reorganization Act of 1934 (Wheeler-Howard Act) or other federal acts have these courts. They conduct their own affairs and deal with certain crimes as defined in the *Code*, which is a compilation of all administrative regulations of the United States that carry out, in detail, a multitude of federal laws and programs. Title 25 of the *Code* also deals with the rules of procedure of the courts themselves. These tribal courts are also known as Courts of Indian Offenses.

The Bureau of Indian Affairs (BIA) established these courts in 1883, after a steady decline, beginning in the eighteenth century, of tribal institutions that had provided for law and order on the reservations. The CFR courts, as the name implies, dealt mostly with law-and-order matters, but some came to deal with various civil matters such as divorce and landlord-tenant relations as well. They were and are highly regulated by the BIA, which often selects and pays the judges and police officers. In the 1930s, the BIA issued a *Code of Tribal Indian Offenses,* which, with some changes, is still in effect for those tribes that still choose to utilize these tribunals. As part of the current trend toward Indian and tribal self-reliance, most tribes today operate their own court systems, complete with their own tribal code and regulations. The tribes choose their own judges, other court personnel, and police departments.

See also ***Code of Federal Regulations;*** **Indian Reorganization Act of 1934**

COLLIER, JOHN (1884–1968) A long time critic, ideologue, and social reformer of U.S. society, John Collier left a legacy in the field of federal Indian policy. As a social reformer, he first became interested in American Indians and their social problems during a visit to the Taos Pueblo of New Mexico in the early 1920s. Appointed commissioner of Indian affairs during the New Deal era of President Franklin D. Roosevelt, Collier served in that office from 1933 to 1945, helping to redefine the U.S. Government's relationship with the Native American people. His major accomplishment while in office was to secure passage of the Indian Reorganization Act of 1934. This Act stopped the wholesale allotment of Indian lands and helped to check the erosion of the Indian land base that had resulted from enactment of the General Allotment Act of 1887 (the Dawes Act).

During the 1920s and until his appointment as commissioner, Collier frequently criticized the Bureau of Indian Affairs (BIA) for its mismanagement of trust assets and for its treatment of its charges—the Indian people. During his tenure as commissioner of Indian affairs, Collier was often forced to respond to many of the same charges that he had leveled at previous BIA officials and other public figures. Collier's refusal to accept compromise over certain parts of the 1934 Act led to feuds with Congress, which ultimately has the final say over Indian affairs. However, he did sincerely want to thoroughly reform the bureau and make it into an agency that would provide economic and technical assistance to the tribes that were attempting to exercise powers of self-governance. It is probable that until his tenure, no high-ranking BIA official had consulted with Indian tribes with any regularity. Before Collier's administration, the BIA was largely concerned with governing and overseeing the tribes rather than with working with them as equal partners in the management of their lands and tribal institutions.

After leaving office in 1945, Collier, as a college professor and commentator, continued to write and speak out on matters of importance to

Native Americans. He died in 1968, while living in retirement at Taos, New Mexico.

See also **Indian Reorganization Act of 1934**

COMITY The term "comity" refers to the legal principle by which one government may, at its option, recognize and treat as its own the court orders, decrees, judgments, and other legal pronouncements of another government. For example, an Indian tribe may, as a courtesy to a state, choose to recognize a state court's divorce decree when the tribal court hears a child support dispute. Whether or not comity applies depends on whether the tribal legal code allows it. Comity is recognition based on courtesy or respect of one government for another. The Full Faith and Credit Clause of the U.S. Constitution does not apply to Indian tribes. Therefore, only the principles of comity determine whether tribes and states recognize each other's laws and court orders.

See also **Full Faith and Credit Clause**

COMMISSIONER OF INDIAN AFFAIRS "Commissioner of Indian affairs" was formerly the title of the highest federal official directly responsible for Indian affairs, the head of the Bureau of Indian Affairs (BIA). The post was first created in 1832, when responsibility for such matters was under the authority of the War (now Defense) Department. The head of the BIA is now known as the assistant secretary of the interior for Indian affairs. The president, with Senate confirmation, has appointed the chief of the BIA throughout its history.

CONCURRENT JURISDICTION When the courts of two or more governments have the authority to decide a legal dispute, whether civil or criminal, they are said to have concurrent jurisdiction. For example, under the federal Major Crimes Act of 1885, both the federal and tribal courts, in many circumstances, would have the authority to try a person accused of certain serious crimes occurring on an Indian reservation. Furthermore, Congress has given certain states the responsibility to enforce their criminal laws on an Indian reservation. In those states, both the state and the tribe could probably try a tribal member for a single offense. In practice, at least where the federal and tribal governments are concerned, the two governments might come to some type of agreement as to which court would take control over certain types of cases. For instance, in the case of certain serious offenses, even though a tribe could try an Indian, both governments would probably agree that the federal courts would take the cases. Federal prosecution would be more appropriate for some crimes because Congress has limited the punishments that tribal courts may mete out to persons convicted of crimes to one year in jail and a $5,000 fine.

Often, both tribal and state courts may have the authority to decide certain types of civil cases. To illustrate, the Indian Child Welfare Act of 1978 allows both the tribal and state courts to deal with the placement of Indian children in foster homes or with adoptive parents. The state courts may notify the tribe and transfer the case to the court of the tribe where the child is enrolled. If the tribal court declines to take the case, however, it remains in the state court.

COOPERATIVE ASSOCIATION Any association or corporation organized for the benefit of its members is a cooperative association. Like a corporation, a cooperative is a separate legal entity, capable of holding and disposing of property, entering into contracts, and doing many of those things that a natural person may do. The cooperative has a board of directors to act for the benefit of the members. Unlike a corporation, however, a cooperative renders services to its members for their direct benefit rather than for economic gain for the cooperative. In other words, the cooperative itself receives no direct economic benefit from its activities, as does a corporation.

Cooperatives are traditionally organized for such purposes as selling members' crops for them, selling various products to members, holding savings for members, and making loans to members. Permitted activities vary according to state law. The formation and operation of cooperatives in Indian country is governed by tribal law, unless there is a special federal law that grants jurisdiction over such activities to the state or the federal governments.

See also **Public Law 280**

CORPORATION A corporation is a legal entity created according to state or federal law. Typically, these organizations are created for some business purpose, whether for profit or not. They are sometimes called "artificial persons" because they have many of the same powers a real person has: to enter into contracts, to sue and be sued in the law courts, to hire and fire employees, and to carry on business activities. Each state and the federal government has specific procedures that people or organizations must follow to form a corporation. One of the major advantages of forming a corporation is that it provides protection against personal liability for any injuries the corporation may cause.

If, for example, an employee of a corporation causes an accident and hurts someone, the directors or managers normally cannot be personally sued for damages arising out of the accident. The injured person must sue the corporation itself, not its directors.

In Indian country, corporations are formed for the same reasons as elsewhere. Many tribal legal codes have provisions governing the formation and operation of these organizations. Some corporations are formed for the purpose of obtaining so-called 638 contracts from the federal government in order to provide services such as housing to tribal members. (These contracts are named after Public Law 93-638, which regulates them. Congress enacted this law to encourage tribes to manage their own affairs with their own employees and forms of business such as corporations, rather than having the federal government directly manage these activities.)

COUNCIL OF ENERGY RESOURCE TRIBES The Council of Energy Resource Tribes (CERT), a consortium of more than 50 American Indian tribes with lands containing energy resources, was formed in the 1970s to help reverse the long history of non-Indian exploitation of such Indian-owned natural resources as coal, oil, natural gas, and uranium. Over the years, tribes and their members saw their natural resources being exploited when the federal government permitted private business interests to lease Indian lands at rates often far below their market value. CERT provides a number of services to its members, including technical expertise in the management of tribal natural resources, environmental protection advice and assistance, and the monitoring of federal energy legislation. This organization, based in Denver, Colorado, has an annual budget of approximately $1 million and employs a staff of about 20 people, including attorneys, economists, and engineers. CERT is managed by a board of directors composed of officials from member tribes.

CRIMINAL JURISDICTION The power of a particular sovereign—state, federal, or tribal—to punish violators of that sovereign's criminal laws is called criminal jurisdiction. In Indian law, determining which one of the three governments has such authority requires an analysis of several factors. First, where was the crime committed? Second, what is the race of the parties involved, both the assailant and the victim? Third, does a special federal jurisdictional statute, such as Public Law 280 (PL 280), apply to the situation?

This analysis is necessary because, over the years, the U.S. Supreme

Court has decided that although Indian tribes have some powers of self-government as quasi-independent sovereigns, their authority is limited, especially where non-Indians are concerned. Congress has enacted various measures defining criminal sovereignty, and the Supreme Court has somewhat limited the reach of tribes in criminal cases. As a general rule, a state cannot exercise criminal jurisdiction in Indian country unless Congress has expressly permitted it to do so. Congress has nearly complete (that is, plenary) authority to limit tribal self-rule in all areas of law, including the authority to limit the tribes' rights to try people for crimes committed in Indian country.

LOCATION OF THE CRIME

State and federal courts have jurisdiction over crimes that are not committed in Indian country, regardless of the race of the victim or aggressor. Tribal courts have no authority over such cases. Indian people are fully subject to the authority of the state or federal courts in such a situation. If a crime takes place in Indian country, and no special federal criminal jurisdictional law, such as PL 280 or the Kansas Act of 1940, applies, then the race of the parties will determine which courts have the power to try and punish the offender.

RACE OF THE PARTIES: CRIMES COMMITTED IN INDIAN COUNTRY

Crimes by an Indian against an Indian

If a crime is committed by an Indian against an Indian, then state courts have no jurisdiction. If the crime is listed in the Major Crimes Act of 1885, 18 U.S.C. § 1153 (for example, murder or rape), then the federal courts have authority over the case. The Indian Country Crimes Act of 1948 does not apply to these situations because cases of Indians versus Indians are specifically exempted under that law. If the crime is not a "major crime" under the Major Crimes Act, then the federal courts also have no jurisdiction. Only tribal courts have the power to try and punish offenders in this category. For the purposes of criminal jurisdiction, the tribal affiliation of either the victim or perpetrator is irrelevant. Tribal courts normally have jurisdiction over such parties, regardless of where they are enrolled. The U.S. Supreme Court ruled in the case of *Duro v. Reina,* 495 U.S. 676 (1990) that the tribal courts lacked the power to punish nonmember Indians. Congress later overruled this decision by amending the Indian Civil Rights Act, at 25 U.S.C. § 1301(4) to restore tribal courts' criminal jurisdiction over nonmember Indians.

However, even where the tribal court has the power to punish an offender, the Indian Civil Rights Act, 25 U.S.C. § 1302(7), limits the maximum punishment that a tribal court may impose for a single offense to one year in prison and a $5,000 fine, regardless of the seriousness of the offense. Many tribal codes may also punish such "nonmajor crimes" as repeat drunk driving or unlawful sexual contact, but one year in prison and a $5,000 fine is still the maximum punishment federal law allows tribes to mete out to offenders.

Crimes by an Indian against a Non-Indian

State courts also have no authority over crimes by an Indian against a non-Indian. If the crime is covered under the Major Crimes Act of 1885, then federal courts may try the case. Under the Indian Country Crimes Act of 1948, also known as the General Crimes Act of 1948, if an Indian commits a crime against a non-Indian, and if the crime violates a federal "enclave law," then the federal courts can try the offender.

A federal enclave is land under federal supervision, such as an Indian reservation, national park, military base, or post office. Congress enacted laws such as the Indian Country Crimes Act of 1948 (General Crimes Act) and the Assimilative Crimes Act of 1825 (18 U.S.C. § 13) to govern activities at these places. The latter statute makes it a federal crime to engage in activities in a federal enclave (including an Indian reservation) if those activities violate the criminal law of the state where the enclave is located. In other words, the federal Assimilative Crimes Act "borrows" state criminal statutes and converts them to federal crimes. The combined effect of these two federal laws greatly expands the reach of federal courts on Indian reservations.

Generally, the tribal courts have concurrent jurisdiction with the federal government to try such cases. If a crime comes under the Indian Country Crimes Act of 1948 (General Crimes Act), and the tribal court has already tried the offense, the General Crimes Act specifically prevents the federal government from also taking jurisdiction in that particular case. Otherwise, however, the Double Jeopardy Clause of the U.S. Constitution does not prevent both the tribe and the federal government from trying a particular case. However, as noted earlier, the power of tribal courts to punish Indians is very limited. As a practical matter, the tribe would probably want the federal courts to handle serious felony cases so that the punishment may extend to many years' imprisonment, a large fine, or both, if necessary.

Crimes by a Non-Indian against an Indian

State courts do not have any authority over crimes by a non-Indian against an Indian. Under the Indian Country Crimes Act of 1948, the federal government would have the power to prosecute the non-Indian if a federal enclave statute was violated. The Assimilative Crimes Act would also give the federal government authority over cases where a state law was violated in Indian country. The Major Crimes Act of 1885 does not give the federal government jurisdiction because that law only applies to crimes committed by Indians. The Supreme Court, in the case of *Oliphant v. Suquamish Indian Tribe,* 435 U.S. 191 (1978), forbade tribes to prosecute non-Indians for any criminal offenses committed in Indian country. Therefore, only the federal government would have the authority to try crimes committed by a non-Indian against an Indian in Indian country.

Crimes by a Non-Indian against a Non-Indian

The state alone has jurisdiction over crimes by a non-Indian against a non-Indian, even for those occurring in Indian country. Despite the great respect originally accorded tribal sovereignty by the Supreme Court in the 1832 case *Worcester v. Georgia,* 31 U.S. (6 Pet.) 515, in 1881 the Court changed all that in its decision in *United States v. McBratney,* 104 U.S. 621. After the McBratney case, the Supreme Court was never willing to accord tribes as sovereigns much authority over people, especially non-Indians, who commit crimes in Indian country. The *McBratney* rule excludes both tribal and federal jurisdiction over such cases. Despite inherent tribal sovereignty, the *Oliphant* decision, as mentioned earlier, prevents any tribal criminal jurisdiction over non-Indians. If a state refuses to prosecute a crime on a reservation in which two non-Indians are involved, no other government may prosecute them. Because of limited resources or for other reasons, state officials give law enforcement work on Indian reservations a low priority.

Victimless or Consensual Crimes Committed by an Indian

So-called victimless crimes or consensual crimes are those in which there is no readily identifiable victim, such as gambling, tobacco, or drug offenses. Examples of these two types of crimes include illegal drug usage, where there is no specific human victim, or adultery, where both parties commit the crime. As part of their inherent sovereignty, tribes would normally have exclusive (that is, sole) jurisdiction over such offenses. Some courts have held, however, that the federal government can try cases under the Assimilative Crimes Act. Neither the Major Crimes Act nor the General Crimes Act appears to apply to such victimless crimes. Despite these Acts, the federal government retains the jurisdiction to try general federal offenses such as tax evasion and mail fraud, even if committed in Indian country.

SPECIAL JURISDICTIONAL LAWS

Public Law 280

Public Law 280, 18 U.S.C. § 1162 (criminal jurisdiction), is perhaps the most wide-ranging special jurisdictional statute. Although it also deals with civil jurisdiction, only its effect on the criminal jurisdiction of the federal, state, and tribal governments will be briefly discussed here. For a fuller discussion of this law, please see the article in this encyclopedia. The statute, passed in 1953, originally imposed upon five states the responsibility of enforcing state criminal laws in Indian country within those states' borders. In 1958 the law was expanded to include Alaska. With some exceptions, PL 280 gives Alaska, California, Minnesota, Nebraska, Oregon, and Wisconsin the authority to apply their criminal laws in all Indian country within those states. Until the law was amended by the passage of the Indian Civil Rights Act of 1968, 25 U.S.C. § 1301 *et seq.*, the tribes had no right to prevent state assumption of such authority. Since 1968, when tribal consent became needed for states to assume criminal or civil jurisdiction in Indian country, no state has done so.

PL 280 grants states concurrent jurisdiction with the tribes to try criminal offenses in all but two areas of the law: First, the state cannot tax or regulate the use or transfer of Indian trust lands in a manner inconsistent with federal law. Second, the state cannot restrict a tribe's rights under federal treaties or statutes to regulate Indian hunting, fishing, or trapping. The states cannot impose criminal penalties in Indian country based on laws that deal with these two fields. For instance, a state law that punishes hunting out of season would not apply to federally protected hunting in Indian country. Tribes have never lost their authority to try Indian defendants for crimes committed in Indian country located in so-called PL 280 states. However, as a practical matter, because tribes' power to punish violators of the tribal criminal law is so limited, they sometimes prefer to have the state deal with the matter.

PL 280 does not directly affect the federal government's criminal jurisdiction in Indian country. Nonetheless, since states may punish serious crimes committed within those states, the federal government, with limited resources, may choose to let the states handle criminal cases arising in Indian country, unless the federal government is a "victim" of such a crime. Examples of offenses the U.S. government might choose to prosecute include assault on federal employees or the theft of funds from federal programs operated on an Indian reservation.

Other Jurisdictional Acts

From time to time, Congress has passed special jurisdictional acts granting selected states criminal jurisdiction over all or some of the Indian lands within those states. In the 1940s, Congress granted Iowa, Kansas, New York, and North Dakota criminal jurisdiction over crimes committed on all or some Indian reservations within those states. As a general rule, these special laws, like PL 280, do not foreclose tribal or federal concurrent jurisdiction over the same offenses committed in Indian country.

See also **Indian Country; Indian Country Crimes Act of 1948; Major Crimes Act of 1885; Public Law 280: Indian Self-Sovereignty**

D

DECLARATORY JUDGMENT

A declaratory judgment is a decision in which a court determines what particular rights parties have in a particular dispute. For instance, an insurance company may decide not to honor a claim for injuries on the grounds that the policy it issued did not cover the particular type of accident that caused the injuries. The insured person may disagree and bring an action or lawsuit asking a court to declare that the insurance company must cover him or her for the injuries in that accident. The court, after hearing the evidence from both parties, would make a declaratory judgment as to who is right.

Other examples of declaratory judgments are those deciding whether an Indian tribe, for instance, may own a particular piece of land or whether a tribal court has the authority to decide a particular type of case involving a non-Indian. As with other types of judgments, most declaratory judgments may be appealed to a higher court.

See also **Judgment; Judicial Review**

DECOTEAU V. DISTRICT COUNTY COURT (1975)

DeCoteau v. District County Court, 420 U.S. 425 (1975), an important case, involved a dispute over state criminal and civil jurisdiction on the Sisseton-Wahpeton Sioux Tribe Reservation in northeastern South Dakota. The lands in dispute were the fee lands within the original 1867 boundaries of the reservation. The state claimed that it had jurisdiction over those nonallotted lands, but Cheryl DeCoteau claimed that such lands were still a part of Indian country and so were not subject to state jurisdiction. In 1889, the tribe signed an agreement (not a treaty) "to cede, sell, relinquish all right title, and interest . . . to the United States." Congress ratified the agreement in 1891. The Supreme Court decided that the quoted passage in the 1889 agreement, along with the history of the negotiations leading up to the pact, showed that the tribe meant to give up all of its interests in the unallotted lands. Among other things, non-Indian settlers eventually bought those lands to live and work on.

The *DeCoteau* case supports the proposition that if the tribes and Congress make clear, by agreement or otherwise, that they intend to "disestablish" a reservation, the courts must honor that intention. This decision reaffirms a long line of earlier cases in which the courts ruled that former Indian lands give up their reservation status only if Congress clearly and unambiguously indicates its intention to change the status of those lands. As a result of the *DeCoteau* decision, the courts ruled that reservation lands not otherwise reserved for the tribe or for individual Indians were no longer part of a reservation and thus are subject to state jurisdiction, for they are no longer considered to be "Indian country" under federal law.

See also **Allotments; Fee Patent**

DEEDED LANDS

DEEDED LANDS The term "deeded lands" is used in real estate law to describe land in which an individual (or legal entity such as a corporation) has written evidence, called a deed, that shows ownership of the land. The land may be subject to government regulations, such as zoning and environmental regulations. The owner may generally sell the land to anyone and may mortgage it to raise money. Deeded land is subject to taxation. The vast majority of land in the United States is deeded land.

This may be contrasted with much of the land in Indian country, which is in trust status. Trust land may not normally be sold by the person who occupies it, for strictly speaking, it is owned by the U.S. government, and it is not subject to taxation by states, counties, public schools, or cities.

See also **Trust Lands**

DELEGATED POWERS

DELEGATED POWERS The U.S. Constitution has delegated certain powers to each of the three branches of government. The Indian Commerce Clause—Article I, Section 8, Clause 3—gives Congress the authority to regulate Indian affairs. This includes, among other things, the authority to recognize "new" tribes, to define the boundaries of reservations, and to deny tribes the jurisdiction to regulate their own affairs.

Neither the judicial nor the executive branch of government has the power to regulate Indian affairs. Although Congress can call upon the executive branch to investigate matters for it, under the Delegated Powers Doctrine, Congress must still make the final decision on all specific matters entrusted to it under the Constitution. For example, if a tribe wants to expand its jurisdiction to act on its own reservation, the Department of the

Interior may conduct an investigation, but Congress must still make the final decision on whether to grant such additional jurisdiction to the tribe.

DEPARTMENT OF HAWAIIAN HOME LANDS The Department of Hawaiian Home Lands, an agency of the State of Hawaii, is charged with the administration of the federal Hawaii Homes Commission Act (HHCA) of 1921. This office is directed by the state Hawaii Homes Commission, a board of nine members (eight members plus a chair), all appointed by the governor of Hawaii with the consent of the state Senate.

Each of the eight members of the commission must come from a specific geographic area of the state of Hawaii so as to achieve some geographic balance. At least four of the eight members must be Native Hawaiian, which is generally defined as a person with at least one-quarter blood quantum from a descendant of those who lived in Hawaii before 1778, which is thought to be when first contact occurred between Caucasians and natives of the Hawaiian Islands. The chair is the full-time member of the board and as such is a member of the governor's executive cabinet. All other members of the commission serve on a part-time basis. The commission chair is also the director of the Department of Hawaiian Home Lands. Under the terms of the HHCA, the governor, when appointing board members, need not consult with those who benefit from the Act (that is, with Native Hawaiians).

The department performs the day-to-day functions required of it under the Act, such as managing the lands entrusted to it, administering the lease program, and attempting to arrange for homesteads for Native Hawaiians. The department has a staff of about 100 people and has headquarters in Honolulu, the state capital. It also maintains some district offices, with limited staffs on each island where homestead lands (those under the HHCA) exist.

See also **Blood Quantum**

DEPARTMENT OF HOUSING AND URBAN DEVELOPMENT The department of Housing and Urban Development (HUD) is a cabinet-level agency of the U.S. government. It is headed by a secretary who is appointed by the president, with the approval of the U.S. Senate. Its major functions are to administer the many housing programs for communities and to promote access to safe and affordable housing for all in the United States. Under certain conditions, the department provides mortgages and other funding for the construction and renovation of housing. Like the Department of the Interior, the Department of Housing and Urban Development maintains a significant presence on Indian reservations.

An assistant secretary for public and Indian housing oversees all programs relating to housing on Indian reservations. This office works with Indian housing authorities, which are local tribal entities that supervise the construction, leasing, and management of tribal housing on the reservations. Among the programs that help those on Indian reservations are those dealing with the construction and renovation of Indian housing and the removal of lead-based paint and other hazardous materials from existing housing. The assistant secretary also provides technical assistance to the Indian housing authorities in carrying out their programs.

DEPARTMENT OF THE INTERIOR The Department of the Interior is a cabinet-level agency of the U.S. government. It is headed by a secretary appointed by the president, with the approval of the U.S. Senate. The department is responsible for the management, care, and protection of the nation's natural resources on public (federal) lands and also for Indian affairs. Among the bureaus and agencies contained in this department are the Office of the Special Trustee for American Indians, which oversees Indian trust assets (both of tribes and of individual tribal members) and individual Indian money accounts and seeks to cure the problem of fractionalized interests in Indian lands. The Office of the Special Trustee is a relatively new office, having been established only in 1994. (By contrast, the Bureau of Indian Affairs originated in 1824 as an agency of the old War Department.)

Other bureaus within the Department of the Interior are the Fish and Wildlife Service; the National Park Service; the National Biological Service; the U.S. Geological Survey; the Office of Surface Mining, Reclamation, and Enforcement; the Bureau of Land Management; the Bureau of Reclamation; and of course the Bureau of Indian Affairs. It is interesting to note that except for the Office of the Special Trustee and the Bureau of Indian Affairs, all the offices in the department are concerned with wildlife, fish, land, and the environment, not people.

See also **Allotments; Bureau of Indian Affairs; Checkerboard Lands**

DEPENDENT INDIAN COMMUNITY The term "dependent Indian community" as used in the Indian Country Crimes Act of 1948, 18 U.S.C. §§ 1151–1152, legally defines certain non-reservation lands as "Indian country." Examples of such off-reservation Indian lands might include tribal housing projects or other communities that are populated primarily by Indians and that have a distinct Native

American character. When such areas acquire the status of a dependent Indian community, they are considered to be Indian country. As a result, the state in which they are located may not have civil or criminal jurisdiction over them. The tribe and the federal government exercise authority over these areas.

The courts ask several questions in order to determine whether a particular area is a dependent Indian community: (1) Has the federal government retained title to the land and continued to exercise some supervision over the area? (2) What is the land used for, and how have state and local governments treated the area in the past? For example, have the county and the Indian tribe treated that particular area as an Indian community? (3) Are there economic and cultural interests held in common in the area? For instance, are there tribally operated schools and Indian-owned businesses in the area that may give the region a distinct Indian flavor? Finally, has the federal government set aside the area for the occupancy, use, and protection of the Indian residents? No one factor alone settles the question. The fact that non-Indians also live in the area does not determine the question.

The legal status of the area in question may be of great concern to local governments, for they may seek to prosecute crimes committed there or to regulate or tax the parcels of land in the region. Generally, if an area is legally considered to be a dependent Indian community, state and local governments can do neither.

See also **Indian Country; Indian Country Crimes Act of 1948**

DIMINISHED RESERVATION

An Indian reservation that has been reduced in size as a result of surplus land acts passed by Congress is called a diminished reservation. In many cases, so-called surplus lands sold by order of Congress no longer have the status of Indian country, although Indians may retain water rights and hunting, fishing, or trapping rights there. If a court finds that a given area is no longer part of Indian country, tribes may no longer have any power to regulate activities occurring on those lands. That task then falls to the federal or, more commonly, state governments.

During the latter part of the nineteenth century and the early part of the twentieth century, under pressure from non-Indians, Congress enacted laws opening up parts of Indian reservations to white settlers. Reservation lands that were not allotted to individual tribal members or otherwise used (according to European or non-Indian concepts) by a tribe were declared "surplus" by Congress and sold to the general public.

The Supreme Court, in nearly a dozen cases, has considered the question of whether a particular piece of land that was once considered Indian country remained so even though it had passed out of Indian hands years earlier. Because no clear-cut rules have emerged from these decisions, the Court answers this question on a case-by-case basis. Among the factors often used to determine the answer are these: (1) the history of the land, that is, whether it, albeit informally, continues to have an "Indian" character, primarily occupied by Native Americans; (2) the language of the laws allowing the sale of such lands; (3) whether the tribes received a fixed sum for the land cession or whether it instead received the proceeds from land sales; and (4) whether or not the tribe agreed to the reduction in its land base (as may have occurred by treaty years ago). Interestingly enough, the Supreme Court and lower federal courts appear to give short shrift to the Canons of Construction in Indian law. Instead of resolving uncertainties in the language of statutes and regulations in favor of Indian sovereignty, as the Canons of Construction direct, the courts analyze the matter by considering some of the issues just discussed.

The question of what makes a piece of land Indian country is relevant today, for the answer determines, among other things, whether or not the state may prosecute an Indian for crimes committed in a disputed territory or whether the tribe, to the exclusion of a state, may impose environmental regulations over the lands at issue. For instance, in one case, *South Dakota v. Yankton Sioux Tribe,* 522 U.S. 329 (1998), the Court found that former reservation lands no longer had Indian country status; therefore, the state was able to regulate the placement of a landfill there. Environmental regulation, which is but one aspect of tribal self-rule, is an increasingly important issue for Indian tribes as the new century begins.

See also **Indian Hunting and Fishing Rights; Indian Water Rights**

DOCTRINE OF DISCOVERY

The doctrine of discovery encompasses several European theories that justify a political or economic entity's taking the lands of indigenous peoples. This doctrine dates back to the medieval Roman Catholic church, which was the prevailing political, religious, and social institution of its time. These theories essentially held that non-Christian nations and peoples, as "infidels," had no real rights and that it was the responsibility of Christian sovereigns and of the church itself as a civil or political entity to Christianize heathen peoples.

Additionally, European nations regarded as savage and in need of "civilization" those people who did not possess such trappings of life as clothing, money, metal goods, and other belongings. Furthermore, the Europeans viewed land as free and uninhabited if it was not regularly used for agricultural, industrial, or residential purposes. Indian lands in America were not occupied in the European sense. Many tribes in what is now the United States were nomadic, moving from place to place during the four seasons. As a result, much of the land had no apparent occupants. To the Europeans, this meant the grounds were unoccupied, and the first to locate them, then, was the "discoverer." This doctrine of discovery gave the discoverers legal title or ownership of these lands.

This desire to Christianize the natives as well as to make better use of the land led to rationales intended to provide some moral justifications for taking the land by force, purchase, or treaty. Early decisions of the U.S. Supreme Court adopted these rationales. *Johnson and Graham's Lessee v William McIntosh,* 21 U.S. (8 Wheat.) 543 (1823), and other decisions of the U.S. Supreme Court at least found that the Indian people retained some right of possession in the lands that were "discovered" by Europeans. Nonetheless, largely for political reasons, until the late 1700s American colonists, representatives of the great trading companies, and the oversees sovereigns often found it necessary to purchase, instead of taking by force, so-called unoccupied lands from the various Indian tribes. Until the early to mid-1800s in the United States, the Indian people were much more powerful militarily than the colonists, and the latter had to take this into account when they dealt with the tribes.

DOMESTIC DEPENDENT NATION The legal theory of a domestic dependent nation was first enunciated in *Cherokee Nation v. Georgia,* 30 U.S. (5 Pet.) 1 (1831), the second of the Trilogy Cases of Indian law decided by the U.S. Supreme Court. This principle holds that although Indian tribes retain some measure of political independence like that which states possess, they are nonetheless subordinate to the federal government and dependent on it for physical sustenance and for protection from state intrusion into their internal affairs.

The Court reasoned that Indian dependency upon the United States resembles the relationship between a ward and his or her guardian. According to the *Cherokee* case, the Court declared that the Indians rely on the federal government for its "kindness and power. . . . They [Indians] are considered by foreign nations, as well as by ourselves, as being so completely under the sovereignty and dominion of the United States . . . that any attempt to . . . acquire their lands [by a foreign nation] would be considered by all to be . . . an act of hostility."

See also ***Cherokee Nation v. Georgia;*** **Guardianship**

DUE PROCESS The term "due process" refers to certain legal rights guaranteed to all in the United States, including Native Americans. Some constitutional due process rights are guaranteed to Native Americans under the Indian Civil Rights Act (ICRA) of 1968. Under procedural due process, all levels of government must treat individuals fairly when attempting to take or limit their use of their own property or when attempting to limit their rights to liberty by imprisoning them.

For example, before Indian tribes may jail tribal members for violating tribal laws, they must first take several steps to ensure fairness to the defendants. Defendants must be given specific written notice of the charges against them. They need to know exactly what the tribe is accusing them of. Alleged wrongdoers must also be given time to prepare a defense to the charges so as to deny them if they so choose. A hearing or trial of some type is guaranteed as well. Some neutral party, such as a judge or jury, must decide guilt or innocence. Whoever decides a case can have no financial or personal interest in the case.

Similar rights are also guaranteed to persons in civil cases whenever the government seeks to limit the use of or take private property for public use. If a tribal ranch, for example, wants to expand its acreage and take land owed by private individuals, it must pay the owners a fair price. The tribal government cannot just take property and decide on its own what to pay the owners. Just as criminal defendants have the right to notice of the charges, the right to defend themselves, and the right to impartial hearings, property owners have the right to advance notice of the government's intention to take or limit the use of property, the right to the opportunity to oppose the request, and the right to an impartial hearing before a judge or jury to rule on the government's request.

The legal source for these due process rights is found in the Fifth and Fourteenth Amendments to the U.S. Constitution. These amendments were originally adopted by the states as a limit on the arbitrary or capricious exercise of governmental authority against the people. Until the passage of the ICRA, tribal governments were not required to extend these rights to reservation residents. The ICRA extends due process rights to both Indians and non-Indians living on a reservation.

See also **Indian Civil Rights Act of 1968**

E

EASEMENT An easement is a license or permission given by a landowner for another to enter a parcel of land for a specific purpose. Easements are typically granted for the right to lay water, sewer, electric, or telephone lines or to provide other utility services. A landowner may also grant an easement allowing an adjoining property owner to reach his or her own parcel by crossing the first owner's land. Another example of an important easement is that granted to a governmental agency, such as a state or county, to build a road across private property.

A person or government grants another an easement in exchange for money or something else of value. These special rights in real estate are often recorded in the same land office where deeds of ownership in the land itself are recorded.

ECONOMIC DEVELOPMENT ADMINISTRATION The Economic Development Administration (EDA), an agency of the U.S. Department of Commerce, was established in 1965 to generate jobs and stimulate business and industrial activities in economically depressed areas of the United States. The eligibility criteria for EDA assistance include high unemployment, low per capita income, or other severe economic distress, such as that caused by natural disasters (for example, earthquakes or floods) or the closure of a military base. Unfortunately, many Indian reservations, for a variety of reasons, are among the most economically depressed areas in the United States. In some cases, unemployment approaches 90 percent.

Although the Indian Financing Act of 1974 shifted the responsibility for many Indian economic development programs to the Bureau of Indian Affairs, the EDA still maintains an Indian program. According to its own data, in 1996 the EDA spent just less than $3 million dollars on Indian programs directed to about 65 tribes.

EMINENT DOMAIN The power of a government entity—such as the United States, an Indian tribe, a state, a county, a city, a school, or certain private persons or corporations authorized to exercise certain public functions—to take private property for public use is called eminent domain. This power is derived from the Fifth Amendment to the U.S. Constitution.

It is sometimes necessary for a public entity to take private land for public purposes. For instance, a state may plan to build a new highway, and the most direct route may take the highway across private property. This property would undoubtedly be taken for a public purpose—to build a road for all to use—but the Fifth Amendment to the U.S. Constitution requires that the landowner be given just compensation, that is, that he or she be paid for his or her land and home. If the government and the property owner cannot agree on the sum to be paid for the land, then a judge or jury will have to decide how much the parcel is worth. In order to help the court decide the property's value, expert witnesses, such as land appraisers, testify as to their professional opinion on this point.

Since most Indian land is subject to some control by the federal government, the tribal government's condemnation, or eminent domain, rights are not at issue. Various federal statutes authorize the federal government to take tribal trust lands for public purposes. However, the Supreme Court's rulings in *Menominee Tribe v. United States,* 391 U.S. 404 (1968), and *United States ex. rel. Hualapai Indians v. Santa Fe Pacific Railroad,* 314 U.S. 339 (1941), provide, consistent with the Canons of Construction of Indian law, that the federal government may not condemn Indian trust property unless Congress has clearly and plainly authorized such an action. To hold otherwise might mean that the government could feel free to take Indian lands for any purposes it thinks best, thus further eroding the Indian land base. At the end of the twentieth century, eminent domain is invoked in Indian lands largely in the area of water rights. For example, the federal government may wish to build a dam that will control flooding at the cost of flooding Indian lands, or it may wish to work on other water projects. In years past, Indian lands taken for railroads and other public purposes was the issue.

Under limited circumstances, state governments or private entities such as public utility companies may condemn tribal lands for public purposes, including, for example, rights-of-way for electric or telephone lines. However, this too requires explicit authorization by the U.S. Congress.

See also **Canons of Construction; Just Compensation Clause**

ENROLLMENT PROCESS An individual purporting to be a member of a federally recognized Indian tribe may apply for membership through an enrollment process. Each tribe, with the approval of the Bureau of Indian Affairs, establishes the criteria a person must meet to be considered for tribal membership. A tribe's right to establish such criteria is an inherent part of its sovereignty, as the Supreme Court confirmed in *Santa Clara Pueblo v. Martinez*, 436 U.S. 49 (1978). That case placed the primary responsibility for the determination of membership upon the tribe.

There are a number of reasons why people apply for tribal membership. Some applicants are looking for a sense of identity or "community": A person who never lived on an Indian reservation or close to his or her people may feel a sense of loss, a sense that "something is missing" with regard to his or her cultural or ethnic identity. Others apply for membership in order to be eligible for federal or tribal benefits accompanying membership, such as free or reduced-cost health care, housing, scholarships, and federal and tribal employment preference. Finally, still others, who are close to an Indian community, want another tie to that community (although, of course, the mere fact of enrollment would not necessarily make a person more accepted in a community).

As discussed earlier, each tribe sets it own enrollment criteria and processes. Some tribes merely require that one of an applicant's parents or grandparents be a member. Others, either in addition to or instead of a parental requirement, may demand that an applicant have a certain blood percentage of tribal or Indian lineage. A person who wishes to apply for membership must present some evidence of an ethnic tie or blood percentage to the tribal office in charge of such matters, which is often called the tribal enrollment officer. The tribal enrollment officer will then investigate the accuracy of the applicant's evidence. If the applicant appears to meet the tribe's membership requirements, a membership committee of the tribal council (which is often considered the legislative branch of the tribal government) will meet and recommend to the full council that the applicant be either accepted or rejected.

It is important to keep in mind, however, that although the tribe may define who is or is not an Indian, that definition might not be accepted by the federal government. In other words, the U.S. government may consider a person Indian for some purposes even though he or she is considered non-Indian by a tribal government. In many cases, however, the federal and tribal definition of Indian is the same, so that for all practical purposes, once a tribe accepts a person as a member, he or she is considered Indian for all federal purposes and is eligible for the federal housing, educational, and health programs set aside for members of Indian tribes.

Once a tribe has properly determined that an applicant is a member of a federally recognized tribe, however, that member has a property interest in his or her tribal membership that may not be arbitrarily taken away by the tribe. According to the Supreme Court, the tribe must follow certain due process rights before revoking a person's membership. This means that there has to be specific reasons to revoke the membership (a fraudulent application, for example), the person is entitled to advance notice of the reason for revocation, and the applicant must be given some kind of hearing before an impartial hearing officer or a judge before membership may be taken away by the tribe.

See also **Blood Quantum; Indian Preference**

EQUAL PROTECTION CLAUSE The Equal Protection Clause of the Fourteenth Amendment to the U.S. Constitution prohibits states from denying any person within their jurisdiction the equal protection of the laws. Under this amendment, no state or local governmental agency may deny any protection or benefit of any laws to any person or class of persons based on such criteria as gender, race, or national origin. For instance, a person who applies for a state-guaranteed housing loan may not be refused solely on account of his or her race or gender. If a person or group of persons meets all the criteria for the application or protection of a law, they must receive the benefits of that law.

Indians who do not live or work on a reservation enjoy the same rights under the Equal Protection Clause as do all other persons. Under the Indian Civil Rights Act of 1968, tribal governments must also grant the equal protection of their laws to all residents, Indian and non-Indian alike, except in one situation: Tribes are permitted to practice racial discrimination in their voting practices because tribal membership is determined on the basis of race. Tribal governments, as sovereign entities, would cease to exist as such if non-Indians or nonmember Indians were permitted to vote in elections.

ESTABLISHMENT CLAUSE The Establishment Clause of the First Amendment to the U.S. Constitution forbids the state or federal governments from establishing an "official" church or religion. This clause also forbids the government from passing laws that aid or grant preferences to any religion or that force a person to believe or disbelieve in any religion. This provision forms the basis for the principle of the separation of church and state.

The Establishment Clause, however, does not apply on Indian reservations. Because some tribal governments are theocratic (that is, based in religion), Congress chose to exempt tribal governments from the Establishment Clause when the Indian Civil Rights Act of 1968 extended most of the Bill of Rights to Indian country. Native religions are a crucial part of tribal cultures, and modern federal Indian policy has attempted to preserve Indian tribes as such.

EX PARTE CROW DOG (1883) *Ex Parte Crow Dog*, 109 U.S. 556 (1883), an early U.S. Supreme Court case, examined the jurisdiction of Indian tribes to punish criminal wrongdoers. This case concerned two members of the Sioux Nation, one of whom, Crow Dog, murdered the other in Indian country. Notwithstanding treaty language by which the Sioux people submitted to the jurisdiction of the United States, the *Crow Dog* Court recognized that the Sioux had exclusive criminal jurisdiction over tribal members for crimes committed on their reservation.

At the time of the murder, tribal law required that the offender make restitution to the victim. The killer was compelled to support the dependent relatives of the victim. Imprisonment was not a form of punishment used by traditional Sioux society. The federal criminal justice system in what was then the Dakota Territory intervened and tried Crow Dog, convicted him, and condemned him to death. He then appealed his conviction and sentence. The Supreme Court narrowly construed (that is, interpreted) treaty provisions so as to avoid infringing on the power of the tribe to punish its own members. The Court upheld the principles of inherent tribal sovereignty and set Crow Dog free. According to the Court, unless Congress clearly says otherwise, tribes are to handle reservation criminal matters concerning tribal members themselves because criminal jurisdiction over their own members is one of their powers of self-government. This is still one of the rules of Indian law today, but both Congress and later court decisions have greatly narrowed the authority of tribal governments to punish criminal offenders.

Many historians suggest that the decision in this case motivated Congress to pass the Major Crimes Act of 1885, which gave the federal government the authority to try crimes committed in Indian country in federal court. At least one commentator, however, has suggested that the *Crow Dog* case was simply part of a long campaign by the Bureau of Indian Affairs to get Congress to pass the Major Crimes Act.

See also **Criminal Jurisdiction; Major Crimes Act of 1885**

EXCLUSION FROM RESERVATION As part of its attributes as a sovereign power or state, every recognized tribe has the right to exclude "undesirable" nonmember persons from its reservation. Typically, this is defined in a tribal law-and-order code. For instance, one tribe in the midwestern United States, the Rosebud Sioux

Tribe of South Dakota, has a detailed and specific procedure for the removal of nonmembers (which means Native Americans who are members of a different tribe as well as non-Indians). The procedure lists about 20 detailed reasons to exclude a nonmember, ranging from the use and possession of illegal drugs, to excavating in areas of archaeological interest without tribal permission, to violating tribal customs.

A tribal right to exclude is analogous to a country's right to expel citizens of another country for activities the host country deems harmful to itself. The United States, from its founding to the present, has always recognized that this right is not granted by the federal government but, rather, is an inherent part of sovereignty. Such exclusion is closely tied to a tribe's ability to protect its own law and order, its integrity, and the welfare of its members. This right of exclusion is embodied in some of the earliest federal court decisions and treaties and, later, in federal statutes.

EXCLUSIVE JURISDICTION When the courts of only one government or when only a specific type of tribunal has the authority to decide a legal dispute, whether civil or criminal, that government or tribunal is said to have exclusive jurisdiction. For instance, if a non-Indian commits a crime against another non-Indian on a reservation, generally only the courts of the state where the crime occurred may try the case. Neither the tribe nor the federal government may deal with the case. In states or tribes with specialized courts, the legislative branch of the government may decide to allow only those specialized courts to try cases that fall within their area of concern. For example, a state or tribe with a special tax court may require anyone with a dispute over taxes to bring the case to that court and no other.

EXECUTIVE ORDER The president of the United States may issue executive orders, that is, official commands or directives, instructing a federal agency under his or her control to take a specific action. Before such an order becomes effective with the force of law, it must be published in the *Federal Register,* the official publication of the U.S. government that deals with administrative issues. Under certain circumstances, Congress can overrule an executive order by passing a law. A president often, either orally or by letter, directs a federal agency to do something. An executive order, however, is a much more formal proclamation, often implementing a public policy as established by Congress or the Constitution. Generally speaking, it is up to Congress to set overall federal policy and up to the executive branch of the government, through the president, to implement it.

Many Indian reservations were created by executive order rather than by treaty (which were no longer used to create reservations after 1871). The federal courts have consistently upheld the president's right to make such reservations, essentially because Congress did not protest such a practice. However, Congress ended this practice in 1919.

See also **Administrative Law**

EXECUTIVE ORDER RESERVATION A parcel of land set aside by the president of the United States for the use and occupation of a specific Indian tribe and its members is called an executive order reservation. Executive order reservations were created, without specific approval from the U.S. Congress, from 1855 to 1919. During this period, more than 20 million acres of land were set aside for this purpose, and Congress agreed with the practice by its silence. In 1919, Congress passed a law, found at 43 U.S.C. § 150, which specifically stopped the practice of establishing Indian reservations in this manner. However, in 1934 Congress gave the secretary of the interior, who is appointed by the president, the authority to acquire land for Indian reservations, to proclaim the establishment of new ones, or to enlarge existing ones. As of 2000, the courts had not yet determined whether the 1934 Act would allow the president, acting through the secretary of the interior, to create additional executive order reservations.

Many executive order reservations still exist. As a practical matter, reservations that were created by this method, as opposed to treaty or statute, ordinarily have the same legal status as far as criminal and civil jurisdiction is concerned. Many federal statutes dealing with Indian lands draw no distinction among them based on their origin.

Depending on the executive order reservation concerned, however, it is questionable whether the president or the secretary of the interior can remove the land from reservation status and restore it to the public domain without express authorization from Congress. Reservations created by treaty or by statute require specific congressional approval for any change in their boundaries. The general rule is that if the boundaries of an executive order reservation are changed, even with the approval of Congress, the government is not required to compensate the Indian tribe for its loss. Nonetheless, Congress has on occasion compensated a tribe for such a reduction in its land base.

See also **Executive Order**

EXHAUSTION OF REMEDIES DOCTRINE Under the Exhaustion of Remedies Doctrine, the judicial branch of government will not interfere in a dispute until all possibilities of resolving the problem through an appropriate administrative agency have been exhausted. This is an administrative law doctrine, often established by statute. Administrative agencies were given the authority to try to resolve many disputes of a somewhat technical nature, such as worker's compensation, labor disputes, Indian probate, or tax issues. Parties to a dispute cognizable (that is, subject to resolution) by an administrative agency must take the dispute to the agency first. The agency employs hearing officers or administrative law judges who are experts in the agency's field of law. Judges in courts of law are generalists and are not usually experts in a specific field of the law. In most systems of administrative law, the judicial branch is required to give great deference, or weight, to the decisions of the hearing officers or administrative law judges.

The Exhaustion of Remedies Doctrine is meant to allow agencies with expertise in particular types of problems to try and solve them. Without the doctrine, such agencies would be rendered useless, for many people would go directly to courts of law instead of to the agencies. A person with a dispute over grazing rights on Indian lands, for example, may have to go through the tribe or the Bureau of Indian Affairs (BIA). If dissatisfied with the decision of the BIA agency superintendent or area director, the person may have to take the dispute all the way up to the secretary of the interior. If not satisfied there, he or she then would have the right to file a lawsuit, or appeal of that last decision, with the nearest U.S. district court. Settling disputes through an administrative agency may be less expensive than going to court.

Many tribal governments also follow this practice, requiring that disputes of a technical nature first be resolved, if possible, by a tribe's administrative agency. Other tribes simply require that all disputes go directly before the tribal courts. Not all Indian tribes are able to maintain administrative agencies with the ability to resolve disputes.

See also **Administrative Law**

EXTRADITION

Extradition is a procedure whereby a person who is charged with a crime in one jurisdiction and who flees to another may be returned to the first jurisdiction for prosecution. The U.S. Constitution provides that one state must surrender a fugitive to a requesting state upon demand and after a brief legal inquiry. Generally, however, Indian tribes, as sovereigns, are not answerable to the states in these matters, and they are not required to surrender a fugitive to a state. Although there has been no direct decision on this point by the U.S. Supreme Court, conventional wisdom has it that the constitutional state-to-state extradition provisions do not apply to the tribes. States may, however, voluntarily enter into extradition agreements with the tribes.

This discussion applies to Indians who may flee to their home reservation. Less clear is the status of non-Indians who flee to a reservation. Because tribal courts have criminal jurisdiction only over member Indians and for misdemeanor offenses, a state is rarely interested in extraditing an Indian for minor offenses. Extradition typically involves an Indian person who is charged with a serious crime off the reservation and who then flees to his or her home reservation. Under generally established rules, the tribe may be able to surrender the person to the state, but the state cannot unilaterally come onto the reservation and take him or her.

See also **Criminal Jurisdiction; Jurisdiction**

F

FEDERAL ENCLAVE A federal enclave is a parcel of land under the direct or indirect supervision of the U.S. government. All of the 50 states have numerous areas where, but for federal laws such as the Assimilative Crimes Act, 18 U.S.C. § 13 (1825), state laws would have no effect. Under most circumstances, unless the federal government has given its permission, states have no power over these areas or over any buildings or structures located thereon. The federal courts normally have the authority, or jurisdiction, to deal with any civil or criminal matters arising in these places. If no federal law is applicable to alleged offenses in these areas, the federal courts invoke the Assimilative Crimes Act to let them "borrow" the applicable state laws and use them to help settle the controversy. Examples of federal enclaves include Indian reservations, military installations, national parks, post offices, and other federal property.

FEDERAL TORT CLAIMS ACT OF 1946 The Federal Tort Claims Act (FTCA) of 1946, 28 U.S.C. § 1346(b) and other parts of the U.S. Code, waives the sovereign immunity of the federal government, in some cases, in order to allow citizens or businesses to sue the government if it has committed a tort against them. A tort is a "civil wrong" other than a breach of contract that one person or company commits against another. For example, if a person driving a car does not look where he or she is going and runs into a pedestrian, the driver has committed the tort of negligence. The accident victim can then sue the motorist in a court of law for money damages for injuries the victim suffered. Sovereign powers, such as the United States and Indian tribes, cannot always be sued in their own courts. With respect to Indian tribes, only the Congress or the tribal law-making body can waive immunity and give consent to be sued. Some tribes have done this.

Until 1946, a person who had a tort claim against the U.S. government had to get Congress to pass a bill to grant him or her access to the federal courts in order to bring a lawsuit. Enacting special legislation for each case was slow and cumbersome. As part of the streamlining of the federal government in 1946, Congress passed the FTCA. This law allows the U.S. government to be sued in federal courts for specific types of lawsuits, such as for negligent acts committed by its employees or agents. This Act only gives the injured party federal court access. The injured party must still prove his or her case in court. Negligence lawsuits might be brought, for example, if a plaintiff is injured in a motor vehicle accident by a federal employee on government business or in a government vehicle, or for injuries resulting from a faulty medical procedure performed by a doctor employed by the Indian Health Service. Tribes, as sovereign nations, are still free to prohibit lawsuits against themselves in their own courts. Under the FTCA, independent contractors, such as tribally operated housing authorities and police departments, are not normally considered to be federal employees, and thus they are not covered under the Act. However, in recent years Congress has extended the coverage of the Act to employees of specific programs, such as tribally operated schools. Other federal laws deal with claims that may arise out of contracts made between the federal government and businesses.

Although it may appear advantageous for a tribe to prohibit suits against itself, this is not always the case. People may be reluctant to provide needed goods and services to a tribe if they have no legal recourse against it should problems arise. In some cases, the tribal courts offer the only forum in which to bring a lawsuit.

See also **Sovereign Immunity**

FEDERALLY RECOGNIZED TRIBE A federally recognized tribe is a group of ethnically related people who are recognized by the U.S. government as being a Native American assembly and a political entity. Such a tribe is entitled to maintain a government-to-government relationship with the United States and is eligible for various housing, health, education, and tribal government support services offered by the Bureau of Indian Affairs (BIA) and other federal agencies.

This recognition must be distinguished from the enrollment of individual persons into the membership of an Indian tribe. Strictly speaking, whereas the enrollment process deals with individuals one at a time, the recognition process deals with an entire group of people together, who form a new political entity, which may be denoted an Indian tribe.

Ultimately, the secretary of the interior has the primary responsibility for recognizing a group of Indians as a tribe for federal purposes. A state or other unit of government is free to grant its own recognition of tribal status to a group. However, the federal government is not bound to accept such state or local recognition of an Indian tribe as such. The secretary of the interior has delegated this recognition task to the BIA, which has a Federal Acknowledgment Project specifically established to handle this duty. The process is lengthy and complicated and may take many years to complete.

For a Native American group in all states except Hawaii, the first step in the recognition process is the filing of a petition with the BIA requesting recognition as an Indian tribe. By administrative decision of the BIA, it does not deal with the official federal recognition of Native Hawaiian groups as such. The group must meet a number of conditions, including these:

1. The group must be historically recognized on a continuous basis as American Indian or aboriginal to the United States. "On a continuous basis" means that there must be some evidence that the group has had recognition by society as a group with a distinct culture for an extended period of time. Just how long this period of time must be is decided on a case-by-case basis. Some of the evidence that may be considered for this condition are references to the group in newspapers or other periodicals; repeated recognition as American Indian or aboriginal by federal agencies; identification as an Indian group by scholars, anthropologists, church records, or schools; recognition by other Indian organizations, and so on.
2. The group lived and still lives in a geographically identifiable area or community, which is seen as Indian and as distinct from other groups of people, and group members are descendants of an Indian tribe that previously inhabited the area.
3. The group, as a "tribe," has maintained political influence over the members as an independent group throughout history to the present. This is a different situation, for example, from that of a large family living in a small town for several generations. Such a town is likely to be part of a county and state and to be under their domain.
4. The group should have some written document, such as by-laws or a constitution, that is used to govern its affairs. If there is no written document, there must be a statement that describes how members of this group are chosen and how the "tribe" governs itself at the time the petition is filed.
5. The group must have a membership roster of all known current members who are not already members of another North American Indian tribe. Among the evidence of membership that can

> be considered are church and school records identifying the person specifically as a member of this group, affidavits of tribal elders, and state or federal records showing such identification of the members as part of that group or "tribe."

If investigation (which could take many years) shows that there is sufficient evidence, then the BIA gives notice to the public of the petition by publishing it in the *Federal Register,* an official publication of the federal government. After that, public hearings are held where persons both for and against tribal recognition may testify and present evidence in favor of their position. The BIA and the Department of the Interior then make a decision, which may be appealed to the federal courts, if necessary.

Tribes that were terminated pursuant to a law of Congress generally would not follow this process. They would directly ask Congress to pass a new law to reestablish federal recognition of their tribe.

This long process may require input from many experts: geologists, archaeologists, historians, economists, political scientists, government officials, and many others. The hearings are extensive, and the process itself is expensive. Some people argue that the detailed requirements for recognition help ensure that only truly distinct, ethnically identifiable groups get federal recognition. Others argue that the process helps ensure that the limited "pie" of economic and other benefits available to tribes does not get spread too thin.

See also **Administrative Law; Administrative Procedures Act of 1946; Enrollment Process; Termination**

FEE PATENT A fee patent is a grant of land from the public domain (that is, public land holdings) by the federal or state governments. In the context of Indian affairs, this term generally refers to the issuance of a deed, or title, to land formerly held by the U.S. government, to individual members of an Indian tribe. Under the General Allotment Act of 1887, otherwise known as the Dawes Act, each Indian or family was granted a specific parcel of land, called an allotment. The Act applied to many of the nation's tribes. It was intended to encourage Indians to become more like non-Indians by having them take up farming or a related occupation, but it failed to take into account the different lifestyles, beliefs, or other characteristics of the tribes across the nation. The lifestyles of many tribes were simply not suited for farming or ranching.

Because the purpose of the law was to ease the transition of Indian people into "civilized" society, the land set aside for the individual or family carried some restrictions for a period of up to 25 years, which was intended to give the individual Indian time to learn how to handle financial matters as practiced by the dominant non-Indian culture. Land previously held in trust status could not be sold or mortgaged without the approval of the federal government. Nor was it subject to any local or state property taxes of any kind. At the end of 25 years from the time the land was first allotted, or some other time set by Congress, the allottee was granted a fee patent from the government. The land so given was no longer in trust status. This former trust land was now to be treated like any other non-Indian lands; it could now be sold to anyone or mortgaged without the approval of the United States. Furthermore, it was fully subject to all applicable state and local taxes.

The Dawes Act was amended in 1906 to allow the secretary of the interior to "declare" that individual allottees were competent (that is, able to handle their own business affairs), regardless of whether this was actually the case. Federal competency commissions, acting for the secretary of the interior, went to Indian country and declared many allottees competent after brief reviews. When such a finding was made, the government issued a "forced fee patent" to the allottee. The land then lost its trust status, and as was the case with ordinary fee patents, the parcels became subject to all local regulations, mortgages, and taxation. The term "forced fee patent" was used because between 1916 and 1920, such deeds were issued in especially large numbers, regardless of whether the allottees wanted them or not. Many allottees preferred that the land retain its trust status, with all the attendant restrictions, rather than be subject to state and local taxation. Forced fee patents caused the Indian land base to shrink greatly until 1934, when Congress put an end to the issuance of such deeds.

See also **Allotments; General Allotment Act of 1887**

FEE SIMPLE A fee simple is an ownership interest in land that generally has no restriction on whom the owner may sell or transfer the land to. Banks and other lenders will often make a loan to the owner of a fee simple and use the land as collateral (that is, security) by placing a mortgage against it.

In Indian law, land owned this way is distinguished from trust lands: The occupier of trust lands (an Indian tribe or tribal member) can only sell or give away interest in the land with the permission of the U.S. government. Since the "owner" cannot freely transfer interest in the land to another, lenders will usually refuse to make a loan because they cannot place a mortgage against the land. The federal government will generally not allow mortgages or other nonfederal liens to be placed on such trust lands.

See also **Trust Lands**

FRACTIONALIZED INTERESTS An interest, or title, in a piece of land that is divided among many owners is called a fractionalized interest. Much land in Indian country became fractionalized as a result of the General Allotment Act of 1887 (the Dawes Act). Under that Act and other federal laws, tribal members were each allotted a particular parcel of land. Since most Indian people did not make wills to specify who should get their land, when the allottees died, their spouses and children all inherited the land. Over several generations, hundreds of people could come to be co-owners of a specific parcel of land. Under traditional legal principles, *all* owners of undivided interests in realty must agree to sell, lease, or otherwise transfer it to a given person or entity. (An undivided interest is one in which no single person owns a physically identifiable part of the parcel.) For example, if ten people each own an undivided interest in an acre of land, no single owner can stake out one-tenth of that acre, claim it as his own, and exclude the other nine owners. This situation may make it virtually impossible to ever sell, lease, or otherwise make productive use of a piece of land. A legal proceeding known as a partition action could be brought in the courts to physically separate the ownership interests in the land, but such cases are expensive and time-consuming.

See also **Allotments; General Allotment Act of 1887**

FULL FAITH AND CREDIT CLAUSE The Full Faith and Credit Clause (Article IV, Section 1) of the U.S. Constitution provides that each state shall give "Full Faith and Credit" to the "public acts, records, and judicial proceedings" of every other state. This clause means that each state must treat court orders of other states as their own. For example, if a person who has been awarded money in a court case finds out that the debtor (the person who has to pay the money) has moved to another state, the creditor (the person owed the money) may go to the new state and have the new state treat his judgment for money as if the court hearing had taken place there. In addition, in some cases this clause requires one state to recognize and apply the law of a second state to a case in the first state. Although one state may reject the law of another state if there are serious "public policy" reasons for doing so, a court deciding a case under this clause usually recognizes only the most pressing of such reasons to disregard the laws of a sister state.

However, Indian tribes are not considered "states" within the meaning of this clause. Because Indian tribes are not states, the U.S. Constitution does not force them to recognize state court and other public proceedings in their tribal courts. Nevertheless, a tribe may make a compact (that is, an agreement) with a state to do so. For instance, tribes seeking to collect child support for their members may make a compact with their state to recognize its court divorce and child support orders. The state then would recognize tribal court orders for the same purposes. This voluntary recognition of each other's court orders is called comity.

Additionally, federal laws such as the Indian Child Welfare Act (ICWA) of 1978 may require that the states give full faith and credit to tribal court orders in certain types of cases. The Indian Child Welfare Act concerns cases dealing with the foster care placement and adoption by non-Indians of Indian children. For example, it mandates that states, territories, the United States, and *other Indian tribes* give full faith and credit to a tribal court's orders regarding placement of such children.

See also **Comity; Indian Child Welfare Act of 1978**

G

GAMING COMPACT Pursuant to the Indian Gaming Regulatory Act (IGRA) of 1988, a state and federally recognized tribe may make a gaming compact (that is, agreement) for the regulation of certain types of gambling on an Indian reservation. Such gambling typically includes video and other types of lotteries, blackjack, poker, and similar casino-style games of chance. Under the Act, tribes may operate games of chance to the extent that the state in which the tribe is located allows gambling. Before a tribe may open a casino or conduct such gaming, however, it must negotiate an agreement to do so with the state. This agreement must then be approved by the U.S. secretary of the interior. There are more than 100 state-tribal gaming compacts in effect around the country.

Both sides must work through many tough issues in negotiating a compact. Both often struggle with the jurisdictional issues. The state wants to assume criminal and civil jurisdiction over issues relating to the administration of gaming on a reservation. The tribes see such an assumption of jurisdiction by the state on their reservation as a threat to their sovereignty. The usual agreement is that a tribe must give up a part of its sovereignty to the state in order to legally conduct gaming or operate a casino. The state, in exchange for its agreement to the gaming, assumes limited jurisdiction over gaming activities on the reservation. Although states may not directly tax gaming proceeds, in exchange for their approval of a compact, they usually exact a share of the gaming profits to cover the costs of gambling regulation and administration.

Other important issues covered by gaming compacts include the location of the gambling activities, the number of lottery machines or gaming tables to be allowed the tribe, the specific types of gaming, the licensing of casino employees, the minimum age of players, the betting limits. These compacts must often be renegotiated every so many years. Because of the history of strained Indian-white relations, considerable discussion and litigation in federal court may precede the signing of a compact.

See also **Indian Gaming Regulatory Act of 1988**

GENERAL ALLOTMENT ACT OF 1887 The federal General Allotment Act of 1887, 25 U.S.C. §§ 331–334 and other parts of Title 25, allotted (that is, assigned) Indian reservation and other public lands to individual tribal members on a wholesale basis. The General Allotment Act (or Dawes Act, as it was popularly known) was the centerpiece of the assimilation era of federal-Indian relations. This law was in full force from 1887 until 1934, when Congress passed the Indian Reorganization Act (IRA). The IRA effectively stopped all further allotments of Indian or other public lands, both by actually prohibiting allotment and by extending indefinitely the trust period of land already allotted.

Congress enacted the General Allotment Act in an era when white settlers moving westward exerted tremendous pressure on it for more land to farm, to raise livestock on, or simply to sell for a profit. The increasing flow of settlers westward made it more difficult to keep Indians separated from white people, whose lifestyles were radically different from their own. The promoters of the Dawes Act claimed it was necessary to separate Indians from their lands in order to speedily assimilate them, whether they wanted to be assimilated or not, into the dominant white culture. In their view, the then-current system of Indian-white relations was not working, for the two cultures viewed land in radically different terms.

Most Native American tribes and peoples did not have a concept of individual ownership of land, evidenced by a written deed, as did the white culture. The Indian concept of land ownership was a fluid one, not limited to fixed or specific boundaries. Land was permanently owned by all members of a tribe or band. The fact that Indian families or bands did not continuously occupy the land in question did nothing, in their view, to lessen tribal control over it. The advocates of the Dawes Act, so-called Indian reformers, believed that modern civilization could come to Indians only if they owned, occupied, and worked the land as their white neighbors did. Prior to passage of the Dawes Act, some reservations were allotted, with some land being parceled out to individual tribal members and the rest being sold as "surplus" lands. However, this was done only sporadically.

The Dawes Act was the first national effort to assimilate Indians into the cultural mainstream of the day by forcing allotment upon most of the Indian tribes across the country. Under the terms of the law, each Indian man, woman, or child received an allotment of 80 acres of farm land or 160 acres of grazing land. The parcels were assigned to each person, and actual ownership of the land remained in the U.S. government for a period of up to 25 years. Indians without a tribal land base from which to choose allotments had four years in which to select an allotment from designated public lands owned by the United States.

The idea was to provide Indians time to learn how to farm or ranch and to otherwise manage their own affairs according to the standards of the white culture. However, federal help to allottees for these pursuits was negligible at best. For a number of years, Congress made no federal appropriation to carry out the purposes of the Act, that is, to provide seed, farm implements, and experts to help the Indian farmer. During some years, funds allocated for this work amounted to about $10 per allottee for assistance in assuming a farming or ranching lifestyle.

During the trust period, state and local authorities could not levy taxes on the land, nor could the allottee sell, mortgage, or otherwise transfer it to another person without the permission of the Bureau of Indian Affairs (BIA), the agency designated by Congress and the president to oversee such matters. The president was empowered to shorten the trust period to less than 25 years.

For some of the period this allotment policy was in force, some BIA officials speeded up the process by issuing forced fee patents, that is, by arbitrarily finding that the Indians were competent (that is, able to handle their own business affairs, measured by white cultural standards) and issuing them a fee patent for their land whether they wanted one or not. However, the typical process for determining competency was for a so-called competency commission to examine an allottee and then decide whether or not he or she was capable of handling business affairs. If so, the BIA then issued a fee patent (deed) to the allotment. At this point, the land was no longer in trust status and was thus fully subject to state and local taxation and regulation. The landholder could mortgage the property and transfer it to anyone he or she chose. Because many of the new landowners could not afford to pay taxes, or because non-Indians took advantage of a people not schooled in financial matters in the white world, or for other reasons, the Indian land base shrank significantly from 1887 to 1934 as the land passed into non-Indian hands. In 1887 Indians or their tribes owned 187 million acres; by 1934 that had dwindled to 48 million acres.

The law continues to be relevant today because many parcels of land in Indian country are still trust lands held for the benefit of individual tribal members. Primarily as a result of the Dawes Act, millions of acres of land on Indian reservations across the United States acquired this status, resulting in the so-called checkerboarding of much of Indian country. Today, many non-Indian parcels may be intermingled with parcels owned by a tribe or its members, either in trust or in deeded status. This checkerboard pattern causes a great deal of confusion for those trying to determine whether the tribe or the state has civil or criminal jurisdiction over a given parcel of land within Indian country.

See also **Allotments; Checkerboard Lands; Fractionalized Interests; Indian Reorganization Act of 1934**

GROUNDWATER Groundwater is water that flows in channels or accumulates in pools underneath the surface of the earth. In Indian law, the question of the rights to groundwater is especially important because many reservations are located in arid (dry) or semiarid areas. Even though the surface of the land may be dry, there may be large pools of water, or aquifers, below the surface. For example, the Oglalla Aquifer, located under a good portion of the Dakotas, Montana, Nebraska, and Wyoming, supplies millions of people in the United States with water. Under certain principles of water law as it relates to Native Americans, various tribes may have special claims to the use of such water.

See also ***Winters* Doctrine**

GUARDIANSHIP Guardianship is a relationship in which one person (a guardian) is required by law to look after and protect the personal or financial interests of another (a ward) who is unable to look after his or her own affairs because of age, inexperience, or mental infirmity. This relationship was, and often still is, used to describe the relationship between the federal government and the various Indian tribes and individual Indians as well. Indian people were not considered "sophisticated" or experienced enough to participate in the non-Indian world of commerce, and therefore the federal government assumed the role of "protector."

Although the legal framework supporting this federal-tribal relationship still exists, its underlying assumption is no longer valid. Indian-white contact is a fact of life today, and tribal members are fully capable of dealing with the non-Indian systems of finance and commerce.

See also **Ward**

H

HABEAS CORPUS Under the legal remedy or right of habeas corpus, a person who has been jailed illegally may bring a lawsuit to compel his or her release from confinement. For example, a person who has been sentenced to prison for a longer period than the statute allows can go before a judge and demand release when the jail time exceeds what the law allows. The Indian Civil Rights Act of 1968 provides that Indian tribes must extend certain rights guaranteed under the Bill of Rights of the U.S. Constitution to anyone, whether Indian or not, who is on a reservation.

For instance, the Act guarantees the right of free speech to people on a reservation. If a tribal government puts a person in jail for making a speech criticizing the tribal chairman or president, that person may bring a habeas corpus action in a tribal or federal court to obtain release from jail. The person is then brought before a judge who determines whether or not the judge who originally handed down the sentence had the jurisdiction, that is, the authority, to jail him or her. The guilt or innocence of the imprisoned person is not the issue in a habeas corpus action. Virtually all habeas corpus actions are heard by a second judge, not the judge who imprisoned the person in the first place.

See also **Indian Civil Rights Act of 1968**

HAWAII ADMISSION ACT OF 1959 The Hawaii Admission Act of 1959, Public Law 86-3, 73 Stat. 4, authorized the admission of the Territory of Hawaii to statehood. Unlike most statehood acts in U.S. history, this law explicitly recognized the trust status of nearly 2 million acres of land in the new state. In 1893, American business interests in the Hawaiian Islands, along with their allies in government positions, deposed the government of Queen Liliuokalani. The former queen was forced to cede her 2 million acres of land to the United States when it annexed the Hawaiian Islands in 1898. The federal law admitting

Hawaii to statehood established five specific trust responsibilities that the new state had concerning these lands: (1) to support schools at all levels; (2) to better the living conditions of Native Hawaiians; (3) to develop farm and home ownership among the people; (4) to develop public improvements upon these lands; and (5) to make the best public use of this ceded lands trust. Until the voters of Hawaii created the Office of Hawaiian Affairs in 1978, the state government had done very little to manage these trust lands for the benefit of the people.

HAWAII HOMES COMMISSION The nine-member Hawaii Homes Commission supervises the Department of Hawaiian Home Lands, the agency of the State of Hawaii that oversees the administration of the Hawaii Homes Commission Act of 1921. The commission oversees the management of the approximately 200,000 acres of land from the ceded lands trust. Eight members, each of whom represents an island where trust lands are located, sit on the commission. A ninth member serves as both the chair of the commission and the director of the department. The governor of Hawaii appoints all members of the commission. The governor need not consult with those citizens, that is, Native Hawaiians, whom the Act is intended to benefit before appointing the board members.

See also **Ceded Lands Trust; Hawaii Homes Commission Act of 1921**

HAWAII HOMES COMMISSION ACT OF 1921

GENERAL OVERVIEW AND BACKGROUND

The Hawaii Homes Commission Act (HHCA) of 1921, 42 Stat. 108, ch. 42, was passed by the U.S. Congress for the benefit of Native Hawaiians, ostensibly to provide them with homesteads to farm or ranch and to live on. The land for the homesteads was land that had originally been ceded, or granted, to the United States by the Republic of Hawaii upon annexation. Congress, in passing the Act, assumed a trust responsibility toward Native Hawaiians. This trust is somewhat analogous to the obligation that the federal government has assumed for other Native Americans. Congress restricted the benefits conferred under the Act to Native Hawaiians with more than 50 percent Hawaiian blood.

Part of the rationale for passage of the Act was to prevent the continuing loss of a native land base to Western private interests. The great *Mehele*, or land division of 1848, had essentially transformed a system of communal land ownership into a private property system. With the continuing erosion of the Native Hawaiian land base, the original peoples of Hawaii were in danger of cultural extinction. By the early twentieth century, Western sugar and ranching interests had become quite powerful in the Territory of Hawaii. These interests collided with Native Hawaiian interests in retaining their land base and something of their culture and customs, which, just as among other aboriginal peoples, depended on a stable and secure land base.

Among the controversial aspects of this legislation were the allowable purposes of the leases, the extent to which nonnative commercial and other private interests could get access to these lands, and the blood quantum necessary to qualify for homestead and agricultural leases. Under the guise of rehabilitating Native Hawaiians and stabilizing their land base, Congress passed the Act in 1921, granting major concessions to Western commercial interests in Hawaii.

TRUST RESPONSIBILITIES AND FEATURES OF THE ACT

Under the HHCA, before Hawaii became a state, the federal government assumed the duties of a trustee for the native peoples of Hawaii. However, in a departure from the other trust responsibilities the federal government has assumed for American Indians, Congress turned these responsibilities over to the State of Hawaii after Hawaiian statehood in 1959. It appears that the native-state relationship did not carry quite the same load of historical tension in Hawaii as it did on the U.S. mainland.

The state agency charged under the Act with carrying out the duties of the HHCA is the Department of Hawaiian Home Lands (DHHL). In theory, the department is to exercise the most exacting "fiduciary" standards. This means that the DHHL is to manage the land for the best interests of eligible Native Hawaiians. This high standard requires the department to use every means at its disposal to ensure that the lands are leased and otherwise managed to bring the greatest possible financial benefits to Native Hawaiians. Whether or not this has been or is the reality is left for the reader to decide.

Notwithstanding the fact that the Act is incorporated into Hawaii's state statutes, in most instances the U.S. Congress must approve any amendments to the Act enacted by the state legislature. The same is true of Article XII of the State Constitution of Hawaii, which deals with the Act and other matters pertaining to Native Hawaiians.

PROBLEM AREAS OF THE ACT

Unfortunately, the Act has not worked as its drafters intended. There are large numbers of Native Hawaiians who have not benefited from the Act. Several factors may account for this: First, for many years, there has been no administrative oversight of the DHHL. No outside agency, public or private, has conducted regular audits of the department's activities. Second, until recently, the Hawaiian state legislature has not allocated sufficient funds to cover the administrative costs of running the agency. Third, much of the land set aside or made available under the Act is not suitable for agricultural purposes, either farming or ranching, or for homesteading. Many of the plots are far from good roads, sewers, and other public utilities that would make them especially attractive for homesteads. Finally, perhaps, farmers and ranchers taking leases on DHHL lands pay far below the market rates for such leases.

A careful study of the problems of the Act might lead one to find striking similarities between this situation and that of the Bureau of Indian Affairs (BIA) and Native Americans on the mainland. There has been a long history of problems with the BIA's management of tribal trust lands. Many of the leases granted by the agency yield only minimal returns to the tribal owners of the parcels.

Despite these problems, the DHHL is becoming more responsive to the needs of Native Hawaiians. The state and federal courts, either through case law or statutory enactment, tend to allow Native Hawaiians greater access to the courts for allegations of poor management of the lands by the DHHL. Congress and the Hawaiian legislature are also providing increased oversight to better monitor the DHHL's activities. And in the spirit of native self-determination, there is a move toward more Native Hawaiian control of the DHHL.

HOUSE CONCURRENT RESOLUTION 108 (1953)

House Concurrent Resolution (HCR) 108 (1953) was Congress's first formal expression of its desire to end the special relationship that Indian tribes had with the U.S. government. Resolutions, even if approved by both houses of Congress, have no legal effect, and they do not bind future congresses. They are formal statements of Congress's opinion on a given issue. However, they can be quite influential.

HCR 108 became the centerpiece of congressional legislation in Indian affairs for the next ten years, part of an era of Indian-white relations, beginning after World War II and ending in the early 1960s, that is generally known as the termination era. The resolution helped to bring about such developments as the federal relocation program and the actual termination of the trust relationship with a number of Indian tribes. In 1988, with the passage of the Tribally Controlled Schools Act, Congress expressly repudiated HCR 108.

See also **Termination**

I

IMPACT AID The federal government makes monetary payments, called impact aid, to state and local units of government to compensate for the latter entities' inability to tax federally owned or controlled real estate. Typically, most local units of government derive a large measure of their income through the taxation of real property within their borders. Only that property owned by a governmental body or by nonprofit institutions, such as religious groups or other charitable organizations, is exempt from taxation. Indian reservations are federally controlled lands and are generally exempt from local property taxation. (Other examples of untaxed federal lands include military bases, national forests and parks, and federal facilities such as U.S. courthouses and post offices.) To help enable local governments to provide services for all residents in their areas, whether residing on tax-exempt lands or not, the federal government has provided impact aid, also called PILT (payments in lieu of taxation) monies.

The Johnson-O'Malley Act of 1934, 25 U.S.C. §§ 452–457, is one of the major impact aid programs. It provides funds to public school districts located near Indian lands to educate Indian children. Another example of impact aid is the Federally Impacted Areas Act of 1950, 20 U.S.C. § 238, which provides support monies to school districts that contain large blocks of tax-exempt lands. Other programs give local governments a percentage of money earned by the federal government for logging or grazing on public lands located within that state or local government's jurisdiction.

See also **Johnson-O'Malley Act of 1934**

INDIAN The term "Indian" is used to denote the legal or ethnological (racial) status of a person as a native inhabitant of North America. Indians are a distinct race of people. Whether or not an individual is legally defined as an Indian depends upon the purpose for which the definition is applied. Laws, governmental or private agencies, and other entities employ different definitions of who is an Indian. For example, a tribe may have its own definition, under its own constitution and laws, of who is an Indian or tribal member. The federal government, under a specific law or regulation, may not accept the tribal definition.

A person might be considered an Indian for one federal or state program but not for others. Generally, if a federal or state law uses the term "Indian" without definition, the entity dealing with the subject of that law is free to apply its own definition.

Federal courts normally use a two-part test to determine whether or not someone qualifies as an Indian. First, that person must be of some identifiable Indian ancestry—in other words, he or she must have some Indian blood. Second, the applicable Indian community must recognize that person as an Indian. This second factor usually comes in the form of tribal membership status.

Under federal law, each Indian tribe recognized as such by the U.S. government has the authority to determine its own membership, regardless of whether the federal government accepts that definition for certain federal programs. One typical requirement is that the person have a certain quantity of "Indian blood" by ancestry. Though ethnologically distinct from those Indians from the "lower forty-eight" United States, many federal laws include the native peoples of Alaska within their definitions of "Indian." Native Hawaiians are often covered under special federal laws apart from those that deal with programs for all other Native American peoples.

See also **Enrollment Process**

INDIAN ARTS AND CRAFTS ACT OF 1990 The Indian Arts and Crafts Act, originally enacted in 1935 and amended in 1990, is a federal law that both promotes the manufacture of Indian-made goods and offers some protection to Indian artisans against those who would counterfeit or market non-Indian-produced goods as Indian-made. The original Indian Arts and Crafts Act (IACA), 18 U.S.C. §§ 1158–1159 and 25 U.S.C. § 350 *et seq.*, was enacted by Congress during the New Deal era of President Franklin D. Roosevelt. During this period Congress began to see the value of Indian culture, and it thus tried to encourage Indian artisans to produce and market their work to the general public. The original IACA provided for the establishment of an Indian Arts and Crafts Board composed of members appointed by the secretary of the interior. The duties of the board, then as now, include promoting the sale of Indian arts and crafts through market research; offering technical assistance to tribes, artisans, and arts-and-crafts marketing cooperatives; and creating official trademarks for these individuals and groups to use in marketing their goods as Indian-made. The original Act also provided for small civil or criminal penalties for those people or organizations who knowingly and willingly either counterfeit the official arts-and-crafts trademarks or represent non-Indian-made goods as Indian-made. Because the penalties were so minor—fines were less than $5,000—it was difficult for federal officials to justify the enforcement of these laws.

The 1990 changes to the Act made it easier to prosecute civil and criminal violations of the law by removing requirements that a person or organization, such as a store, actually know that the official trademark certifying goods as Indian-made is counterfeit or that goods are falsely portrayed as Indian-made or produced. Criminal sanctions for violations of the Act were also significantly increased. It is enough, at least for civil lawsuits, that the federal government or Indian tribe simply prove that a retailer or other group is selling goods labeled as Indian-made or produced when they are actually not. Under the 1990 changes to the Act, the plaintiff need not prove that the seller was actually aware of the non-Indian origin of the goods. The Act as amended also allows Indian tribes as well as federal officials to file civil cases against a marketer of such "false" goods, on behalf of the affected tribe, Indian artisans, or Indian arts-and-crafts organizations. Nonetheless, federal officials alone continue to be responsible for prosecuting criminal violations of this Act. Changes to the IACA also provide the tribe, artisan, or other native group harmed by the counterfeiting or false claims with a court injunction forbidding the continuation of such activities and up to three times the damages suffered by these parties.

The law applies to both federally recognized Native American tribes and Native Alaskan villages. It is not clear whether the IACA applies to Native Hawaiians as well, however. Unlike most federal laws, the IACA's benefits and protection also apply to any Indian group formally recognized as such by a state legislature. (It is very rare for any federal Indian laws to embrace any Indian group that is not officially recognized by the U.S. government.)

See also **Federally Recognized Tribe**

INDIAN CHILD WELFARE ACT OF 1978 A major federal law, the Indian Child Welfare Act (ICWA) of 1978, 25 U.S.C. § 1901 *et seq.*, regulates the placement of Indian children in non-Indian homes. Before passage of the Act, there was mounting concern that many tribes were losing their identity when their children had to be placed by state or county social workers in non-Indian homes. Many Indian reservations have a high incidence of alcohol or drug abuse. In any culture, these problems in a family setting often lead to physical or psychological abuse of children, as well as to neglect of children's physical needs such as food, clothing, and shelter. Though such difficulties exist all over the United States, when Indian children are removed from Indian homes and placed with non-Indian families or institutions, they face the special problems of overcoming cultural hurdles, among other obstacles.

BACKGROUND

The initial assessment of whether or not a child is in an injurious environment, necessitating immediate removal from the home, typically rests with a social worker. Normally, within several days of removal, a judge will hold a hearing and decide whether the social worker's concerns were justified. But many social workers, even in jurisdictions on or near Indian communities, failed to understand cultural differences between non-Indian and Indian ways of life. When faced with a situation where a child had to be removed from an Indian home for his or her own safety, the child welfare agent would typically place the child with a non-Indian family, whether or not local Indian families were willing and able to furnish temporary or permanent foster care for needy Native American children, because social workers would often apply middle-class white values in making a decision on whether to remove a child from the home. The native and white cultures do not often agree on what is best for a child. For example, many Indian cultures highly value the extended family. Aunts, uncles, nieces, nephews, grandparents, and their descendants may all live under one roof, even if that means some crowding. Partly because of government policies, the standard of living on many Indian reservations is low by non-Indian standards. This may mean that large, extended families may live in older homes, with aging electrical and plumbing facilities. In many non-Indian homes, by contrast, there may typically be only a single family of parents and children residing in one house or apartment. Social workers evaluating living situations rarely, if ever, took into account the Indian extended family.

As a result of non-Indian social workers' ignorance of Native American culture, Indian children were often placed with non-Indian families, some never to be returned to their natural parents. To be sure, there are always situations where children must be permanently removed from the home because of chronic parental abuse or neglect. However, in many cases social service agencies, with the approval of the courts, did little to reunite the children with their culture. Instead, the children remained permanently in foster care or were adopted by non-Indians. State courts, which must approve any permanent placements, were no more aware of Native American traditions than were state or local welfare or social service personnel.

The population base of some tribes, especially smaller ones, was being eroded by the continual placement of such children outside their homes, in some cases hundreds of miles from their home reservation. This problem was often accelerated by the federal government's early policy of assimilating Native Americans into the mainstream of American life. Indian agents or welfare workers from various religious groups took Indian children, against the wishes of their parents, to be "civilized" in Bureau of Indian Affairs (BIA)–sponsored boarding schools many miles away from the reservation. There the children would learn about white culture. They were usually forbidden to speak their native tongues at the boarding school. In the face of these twin problems—boarding schools and non-Indian foster care or adoptive placements—some legislation was thought necessary to help stem the erosion of native American traditions. The Indian Child Welfare Act of 1978 attempts to balance the child's best interests with the continued survival of his or her tribe as a culturally distinct entity. Many child welfare laws focus first on what is in the best emotional, moral, physical, and spiritual needs of children and only second on the desires and needs of the parents. This Act is perhaps unique in attaching great importance to the self-perpetuation interests of a child's Indian tribe rather than merely focusing exclusively on the child's own interests in a good home.

THE INDIAN CHILD WELFARE ACT PROVISIONS

General

In passing the ICWA, Congress attempted to assist Indian tribes in preserving their culture by giving tribes greater participation in Indian child-placement decisions. The ICWA also recognized the failure of state governments to appreciate the importance of cultural ties to Indian children.

In essence, ICWA is a special jurisdictional law that provides guidelines as to whether state or tribal courts should decide where an Indian child should be placed. Child welfare decisions are normally the concern of the states and not of the federal government. Nonetheless, under the Constitution and the Plenary Powers Doctrine, Congress has the right to deal with the placement of children who are members of *or* eligible for membership in any federally recognized Indian tribe.

Coverage of ICWA

This Act only applies to children under the age of 18 years who are members of or eligible for membership in any federally recognized tribe. Actual enrollment, then, in an Indian tribe is not necessary for the Act to apply. For the present discussion, the term "child" means a child under the protection of the Act. The ICWA does not apply to children who are placed with one parent in divorce or legal separation cases. The Act is also inapplicable to cases where a parent's rights to the child have been permanently taken away because the child has been adjudged a juvenile delinquent. (A delinquent offense is one that would be considered a crime if committed by an adult.) All other placements of Indian children, whether permanent or temporary, are subject to the provisions of the Act. Examples include short-term foster care placements in which a child subject to abuse is temporarily removed from a home under state child abuse or neglect laws, or in which an orphaned child is placed with a family for adoption.

Jurisdiction over Child Placement Cases

With the exception of tribes located in Public Law 280 states (Alaska, California, Minnesota, Nebraska, Oregon, and Wisconsin, which are the states that Congress, in enacting PL 280, has allowed to assume criminal and civil jurisdiction over people and activities arising on some or all of the Indian reservations within those states), the tribal courts of any reservation where a child lives has the sole authority (that is, exclusive jurisdiction) over a child placement case involving the child, and the state courts have none. This is so even if the child lives with non-Indian parents or resides in a non-Indian foster home on the reservation. In Public Law 280 states, the tribe concerned must get the permission of the U.S. secretary of the interior to assume jurisdiction over ICWA cases.

If the child lives off the reservation, the presumption is that the tribal courts, not state courts, should have jurisdiction to decide the child custody issue. When a state court has reason to believe that a child might come under the provisions of the ICWA, it has a duty to properly notify the Indian tribe concerned. Usually the social service agency, in the course of its investigation, will at least have become aware of the possibility that the child has a Native American background.

The child's tribe or Indian parent or custodian then may petition the state court to transfer the case to the tribal court. The state court must then do so unless either parent objects to the transfer or there is "good cause" for the state tribunal to refuse to send the case to the tribal court. In other words, there is a preference under the Act to transfer an eligible case to the appropriate tribal court. What constitutes good cause to prevent such a transfer is often the subject of much litigation. Numerous court decisions and BIA regulations help determine just what good cause may be in a given situation. Reasons for refusing to send a case to the tribe—that is, good cause—may include the following: (1) The tribe concerned does not have a judicial tribunal in existence; (2) the child has had little or no contact with the tribe; (3) the child is more than twelve years old and does not want the case moved to the tribal court; or (4) it would be extremely difficult or cause great hardship to present the evidence necessary to decide the case in the tribal court. The child's contacts with the tribe are often at the center of the transfer dispute. Under ICWA, the tribe may voluntarily choose to decline to take the case or to be involved with it in any way. This may happen, for example, when the child has never had any contact with the tribe and neither parent has an interest in tribal intervention in the case. That decision, however, is made solely by the tribe according to its own laws and procedures. Many of the larger tribes have a special child welfare office that may investigate the case when the state court notifies it of a pending case. That tribal office may then decide to pursue the matter and to get involved. In some tribes the tribal council or chairman or president may make that determination upon the recommendation of the Indian child welfare office.

Cases in State Courts

If the case starts in a state court, that court must give proper notice to the tribe concerned so that the tribe may decide whether to seek to transfer the case or merely to intervene, that is, to exercise the right to fully participate in the state case as an interested party. The Act still governs the proceedings in state court, even if the tribe declines to assume the case or to intervene.

Regardless of state law, there must be compelling evidence presented to the court before it permanently terminates the rights of an Indian parent over his child. The same quality of evidence that is used in criminal cases, that is, that the case be shown beyond a reasonable doubt, governs this situation. Since termination of the parent-child relationship is so important and is permanent, Congress decided that there should be a high degree of certainty that this should be done. Expert testimony from a witness familiar with the customs of the tribe concerned must also be presented to prove that it would not be in the child's best interests to remain with the Indian parent or parents.

Once the decision has been made to place the child somewhere other than back with the parents, the Act provides a set of choices as to whom the child should live with in foster care or preadoptive placement, and there is an order of preference among these choices. It is preferred that the child be placed near his Indian community, if possible. The child's extended family is the first choice. Just what this means may vary from one tribe to another. The second preference is a tribally approved foster home. These homes are usually on or adjacent to the Indian reservation that approves it. Third, an Indian foster home approved by a state or county agency may be considered by the court. Last, any other institution approved by the tribe that could meet the child's needs is a possibility.

Similar preferences exist for adoptive (that is, permanent) placements of children: The first choice of placement is with a member of the child's extended family. Second, other members of the child's Indian tribe may take him or her. The last preference is to place the child with families who are members of a tribe other than that to which the child belongs. For any type of ICWA child placement, a child may be placed with a non-Indian family only if there is no other alternative.

It is important to note that the ICWA does not compel any of these families or institutions to take custody of a child. The Act only requires that the child live with the most-preferred custodian if the custodian is willing to accept him or her. These rankings were devised to carry out Congress's intention of reducing, if possible, the wholesale placement of Indian children with caregivers unconnected with the child's tribe. There are similar "good cause" provisions under the Act that allow a state court, under exceptional circumstances, to refuse to award custody of a child to one of the preferred caretakers. What constitutes good cause to deny a preferred placement of a child is somewhat similar to the criteria used to decide whether a tribal or state court should assume jurisdiction over the case.

Effect of Custody Decisions

States are not required under Article IV of the Constitution (Full Faith and Credit Clause) to treat the great majority of tribal court orders and judgments as their own. However, under the ICWA the United States itself and the states must treat tribal court ICWA child custody decisions as if they were rendered in their own state or federal courts. In other words, tribal court orders made pursuant to the Act must be given the same respect as if made by another state or by the United States. The situation often arises when a tribal court renders a decision in an Indian child custody case and the parents and child subsequently move off the reservation, even to another state. Assuming that the time has expired for challenging a tribal or state court custody decision, a party to the case who is dissatisfied with the original placement decision cannot go to another state and attempt to have that other state or tribe issue an order contrary to the original tribal or state custody decree.

CONCLUSION

The ICWA has succeeded in giving tribes a great deal of authority in making, or at least influencing, custody decisions involving Indian children. Some critics claim that judges who do not fully understand the Act may wrench children with no connection with a tribe out the care of a non-Indian family and place them in a tribal setting. How true this may be depends upon the perception of the reader. Nonetheless, the ICWA, like most laws, could be improved as the need to do so arises. In theory, at least, states may no longer unilaterally place children with families or institutions devoid of any connection to the child's tribe. Just how much influence tribes have can perhaps be measured by the increasing number of child custody cases that are appealed in state court systems where the Act is at issue. The historic struggle between state authority and tribal self-determination continues. What could be more important to the survival of an Indian tribe than its ability to perpetuate its own culture by having some input into the custody of its youngest members?

See also **Full Faith and Credit Clause; Jurisdiction**

INDIAN CIVIL RIGHTS ACT OF 1968

INTRODUCTION

After a series of congressional hearings dating back to 1962, Congress in 1968 passed the Indian Civil Rights Act, 25 U.S.C. §§ 1301–1341, which extends certain parts of the U.S. Constitution, notably the Bill of Rights, to Indian reservations. These hearings concerned the administration of justice on the reservations. There were (and are) many well-managed tribal governments; some, however, were thought to be tyrannical. Members of Congress discovered, to their surprise, that before passage of this law, a line of federal court decisions held that the Constitution did not apply to Indian reservations.

CONTENTS

Individual Civil Rights

Only one part of the Indian Civil Rights Act (ICRA) actually extends provisions of the federal Constitution to the Indian reservations. The other parts of the ICRA establish how a state can accept or relinquish jurisdiction over Indian lands within that state's borders. These civil rights extend to all persons, Indian or not, living in or merely visiting a reservation and include rights that limit the right of tribal governments to pass or enforce laws restricting the free exercise of religion, free speech, the press, or the rights to assemble and to petition the government. These rights are also found in the First Amendment of the Constitution.

Other rights that tribal governments may not limit include those found in the Fourth and Fifth Amendments, which include requiring government to produce search and arrest warrants of persons suspected of committing crimes. The tribe may not try a person twice for the same crime (double jeopardy). It cannot force a criminal defendant to testify against himself at a court proceeding (self-incrimination). The tribe cannot take a person's private property for its own use without paying the owner a fair price (eminent domain—just compensation). The tribe must give a criminal defendant due process in a trial on criminal charges, including advance notice before trial of the charges to be heard, the right to question the tribe's witnesses (confrontation), the right to subpoena witnesses that might help the defendant at the trial, a trial by a jury of at least six persons for any offense that might include jail time, and the right to have a lawyer help the defendant prepare a defense.

However, unlike in state or federal criminal proceedings, persons in Indian country who want their own lawyer must pay for that service themselves, even if they cannot afford a lawyer. In nontribal proceedings, defendants who cannot afford legal services are entitled to free counsel. Congress believed that requiring tribes to furnish a lawyer at tribal expense would be unduly burdensome to them financially.

Other civil rights that an accused has on the reservation include the right to obtain reasonable bail, the right not to be subject to cruel and unusual punishment, and a maximum possible penalty for any tribal offense of a $500 fine and six months in jail, regardless of the offense. Amendments to the original Act have raised the maximum penalties that a tribe may impose for the violation of a criminal offense to a $5,000 fine and one year in jail. However, in state and federal courts, there is no "maximum" fine or jail time except whatever the state legislature or Congress determines for a particular offense. The only limitation for states, tribes, and the federal government is that under the Eighth Amendment, the punishment must be somewhat "proportionate" to the crime committed. For example, a person found guilty of speeding could probably not be given five years in prison and a $10,000 fine.

Finally, a tribe may not pass an ex post facto (that is, after the fact) law or a bill of attainder against any person. In the former case, a tribe cannot change the legal rights of persons for acts or deeds committed before that law was passed. For instance, the tribe cannot retroactively make criminal any conduct that was previously lawful. It cannot, for instance, make a contract that was legal when it was made illegal by the passage of an ex post facto law. In the latter situation, a tribal council cannot pass a bill of attainder declaring a certain named person guilty of a crime. That person has the right to full judicial process before he or she can be found guilty of a criminal offense as previously defined in tribal laws. This includes the right to know in advance what the charges are, the right to a trial before an impartial judge, and the right to have a lawyer help with the defense. A tribal council, state legislature, or Congress cannot bypass this process by merely passing a law declaring someone guilty.

Unless stated otherwise above, all of these individual civil rights are identical to those all persons enjoy off a reservation. These civil rights are limits on what a tribal government may do with people on the reservation, just as is the case off the reservation with the federal, state, and local governments.

Other Provisions of the Act

The only remedy available for violations of the ICRA is the writ of habeas corpus. In other words, persons who think the civil rights guaranteed to them under the Act have been violated by a tribal government can only ask a federal court to release them from a tribal jail, if they have been detained there, or to return to them any property wrongfully taken from them by tribal authorities. If they have not been detained or their property has not been wrongfully seized, then there is nothing they can sue for in federal courts under the ICRA. Money damages are not available to persons suing a tribe under the provision of the Indian Civil Rights Act.

There are also provisions in the Act that address the assumption by states of both civil and criminal jurisdiction over Indian lands. The United States, under certain conditions, gives its permission for a state to assume such jurisdiction. However, an important change is that unlike under the original Public Law 280 (under which Congress has allowed Alaska, California, Minnesota, Nebraska, Oregon, and Wisconsin to assume criminal and civil jurisdiction over people and activities arising on some or all of the Indian reservations within those states), under this Act a tribe must give its consent before a state may assume such jurisdiction over it. However, with respect to civil jurisdiction, a state assuming such authority must give great weight to tribal customs in cases where preexisting tribal laws and customs conflict with state laws on the same subject. It is interesting to note that since this change was made, no tribe, except tribes in Utah, has given its consent to state assumption of jurisdiction over it. This should not be surprising, given the tension that has existed for many years in state-tribal relations. The ICRA also contains provisions for a state to give up its authority over civil and criminal matters on a reservation and to have the tribal and federal governments reassume their former authority. The ICRA also amended the Indian Country Crimes Act of 1948, 25 U.S.C. § 1152 to include assaults involving serious bodily injury as a serious offense on tribal lands over which the federal courts assume jurisdiction.

Other changes affect tribal contract approval by the Bureau of Indian Affairs (BIA). Normally, the BIA must approve any tribal contracts with attorneys before they become effective. To speed up such decisions by the BIA, the Act provides for automatic approval of tribal attorney contracts if the BIA does not make a formal decision within 90 days after the application for approval is made. Finally, in minor provisions of the Act, Congress directed the U.S. secretary of the interior to republish certain materials pertaining to the legal status of Indian tribes, materials that have been out of print for many years.

THE INDIAN CIVIL RIGHTS ACT AS OF 2000

Differences between the ICRA and Civil Rights off the Reservation

Congress deliberately did not apply all civil rights under the Constitution to Indian tribes. To do so would have seriously undermined the government-to-government relationship between the tribes and the federal government. For instance, the Fifteenth Amendment to the Constitution, which prohibits the government from denying the right to vote on account of race, gender, national origin, and so on, was not made applicable to the tribes. Since the tribes are regarded as sovereign nations, such an imposition would seriously diminish the tribes' right to govern themselves and possibly to remain in existence as distinct tribal entities. For example, if a tribe were required to allow non-Indians living on the reservation the right to vote and to hold tribal office, this would have the effect of allowing non-Indians to determine the affairs of a tribal nation composed of people with an ethnic background different from that of non-Indians.

Although many tribes may no longer have very many members who are "full-blooded" in an ethnic sense, the body of tribal membership nonetheless often still retains a distinct language, culture, and customs apart from those of Americans who are non-Indian. In reality, this is little different from the case of a U.S. citizen, for example, living permanently in France, Turkey, or Israel. No one would seriously question the right of those governments to exclude the permanent American residents from citizenship and the right to participate in the political process of those nations. Native Americans hold dual citizenship both with the United States and with their tribe, just as people from many other nations hold citizenship in two countries.

A second major difference in the civil rights of people on the reservation from those off the reservation is that unlike local, state, and federal governments, tribes are not prevented from establishing or maintaining an "official" or tribal religion. In many tribes, religion or spirituality is intimately connected with the culture, mores, and way of life generally. Some tribes are theocratic, that is, the political and religious or spiritual leaders are one and the same. Such a constitutional requirement to completely separate church and state would seriously disrupt such tribes.

The Act in Operation

As already mentioned, generally, habeas corpus is the only remedy a person has if the tribal government violates his or her rights. In practice, this often means that the Act has no real teeth in it. Habeas corpus is generally available only to those, Indians and non-Indians alike, who are detained in jail by a tribe, or in certain cases, to those people with child custody disputes where the tribe itself is involved. But mindful of Congress's intention of maximizing tribal self-autonomy, the federal courts have imposed the requirement of going first to the tribal courts. Therefore, if a person is being illegally held in a jail by order of a tribal court, that person has to first go through the tribal court, and only if that fails can he or she then go to federal court afterward. Only if a delay in going through tribal court would cause irreparable harm do federal courts allow a claimant to go there first.

If habeas corpus will not solve a problem, such as employment discrimination by a tribe, a tribe's refusing to enroll a person, or a tribe's taking of private property without paying for it, then there is sometimes no other remedy in federal court. State courts would have no authority over the dispute, either. Therefore, it is quite possible that for most violations of a person's civil rights under ICRA, there is no relief at all. Another example would be a case in which a person was jailed for a week but was not given a jury trial as requested. By the time a federal court was able to hear the request for a writ of habeas corpus, the person would already be out of jail.

In spite of potential abuses under ICRA, a person may not be totally without long-term solutions to problems. Depending on the circumstances, the tribal legislative body might be persuaded to change the law or tribal members may run for office to effect a change in the policy causing a problem. In extreme cases, Congress or the BIA might be persuaded to reduce or cut off funding for the activity infringing upon people's civil liberties. Despite some abuses, Congress has had to balance the individual rights of people on the reservation with tribal concerns with self-determination and self-government.

There have been some attempts by individuals and groups to persuade Congress to pass legislation that would allow claimants to go into federal courts on ICRA claims or to require tribal courts to waive their sovereign immunity and hear such claims. Given Congress's reluctance to interfere with tribal self-determination, these efforts have not gotten very far. However, claimants may have remedies for violations of their civil rights that are not of the type listed in the ICRA but that are found in other federal civil rights statutes, such as 42 U.S.C. § 1983. Except as covered by these different statutes, the federal courts have consistently held that it is up to Congress, with its plenary power over Indian affairs, to strengthen the ICRA if it so desires.

See also **Bill of Rights; Civil Rights; Habeas Corpus; Public Law 280: Indian Self-Sovereignty**

INDIAN CLAIMS COMMISSION In 1946 a special federal panel was established by the Indian Claims Commission Act of 1946, 60 Stat. 1049, to hear and resolve outstanding claims by Indians and tribes against the U.S. government. This panel, the Indian Claims Commission (ICC), was originally to have a life of only ten years. Congress extended its life several times until 1978, when it ceased to exist and all of its remaining cases were transferred to the U.S. Court of Claims. Generally, the tribes hired their own lawyers to present the claims, and U.S. Justice Department attorneys defended the government against the tribes. Despite the government's trust obligation toward the tribes, their attorneys usually resisted the claims by every legal means, partly contributing to the long delay in settling the claims. It was not unusual for claims to take more than 20 years to settle, an exceptionally long period of time even for complex legal cases today. If the ICC ruled in favor of the tribe or individual claimant, Congress then had an obligation to appropriate the funds to pay the judgment against the government. Typically, a percentage of the award was deducted for attorney fees and some administrative expenses connected with the case.

Congress created the ICC in part to find a more efficient way of evaluating claims against the government and in part to speed the termination of the government's involvement in Indian affairs. Some supporters of the law creating the commission viewed the ICC as a vehicle to settle long-standing Indian claims once and for all and to speed the process of "getting out of the Indian business."

Until 1946 Indian tribes or tribal members normally had no recourse against the federal government for the wrongful seizure of Indian lands, underpayment for those lands, or any other wrong perpetuated against them. Unlike state courts, federal trial courts may hear only those cases that Congress by law allows them to hear. That is why federal courts are called courts of limited jurisdiction. Therefore, unless a tribe persuaded Congress to pass a special law permitting it to sue the government, it had no redress for any wrong the United States may have committed against it. Over the years, Congress had indeed passed a number of such special laws permitting these lawsuits. That same year, Congress also enacted the Federal Tort Claims Act of 1946, which gives Indian tribes, as well as the general public, permission to sue the government, in federal court, for certain types of claims against it.

Under the law creating the ICC, tribes or members had until 1951 to file any claims that arose (that is, became known to them) prior to 1946. Any claims that arose after the ICC was created were to be filed with the Court of Claims, a special federal tribunal with expertise in evaluating claims that a person or entity has against the government. There are a number of Indian claims cases still pending in 2000.

See also **Federal Tort Claims Act of 1946**

INDIAN COMMERCE CLAUSE The Indian Commerce Clause (Article I, Section 8, Clause 3) of the U.S. Constitution grants Congress the authority to "regulate Commerce with foreign Nations, and among the several States, and with the Indian Tribes." This provision has been interpreted and cited numerous times by the U.S. Supreme Court as primary authority for Congress's right to regulate Indian affairs. In the late 1800s, after Congress ended treaty-making with the tribes, the Court stated in *United States v. Forty Three Gallons of Whiskey,* 93 U.S. 188, 195 (1876) that "[a]s long as the Indians remained a distinct people with an existing tribal organization, recognized by the political department [Congress and the president] of the government, Congress has the power to say with whom, and on what terms, they shall deal." As late as 1973, the Supreme Court still held this view in *McClanahan v. Arizona State Tax Commission,* 411 U.S. 164 (1973), which dealt with the taxation of Indian people.

According to those Court decisions and numerous others, Congress may regulate nearly every aspect of tribal life, from housing and education to employment and more. There are other bases of federal power over Indian affairs, but the Indian Commerce Clause remains the most important. Even though the clause speaks of commerce with Indian *tribes,* it has been interpreted to include dealings with individual Indian people as well and it also permits the federal regulation of non-Indians doing business on an Indian reservation or with the tribes themselves. The Bureau of Indian Affairs is the primary federal agency representing the federal government on the Indian reservations.

See also **Plenary Powers Doctrine**

INDIAN COUNTRY A parcel of land or territory that has a legal connection with Native Americans is called Indian country. A finding that land is indeed Indian country is very significant because such a finding generally operates to prevent a state or local government from exercising civil or criminal jurisdiction over that land. Until 1948, many federal laws contained different definitions of the term "Indian country." In that year, in order to bring some consistency to the term's legal meaning, Congress wrote the current definition of "Indian country," which is found at 18 U.S.C. §§ 1151–1152. Although this definition is contained in the U.S. Code title dealing with crimes, it applies to civil (noncriminal) jurisdiction as well. Generally, the term applies to all land, whether under the supervision of the federal government or a tribe, that has been set aside primarily for Indian use and occupancy. With minor exceptions, the term generally does not apply to land located in Alaska or Hawaii. Under the terms of this section, Congress defined three types of land that qualify for the legal designation as Indian country.

The first is "all land within the jurisdiction of the United States government, not withstanding the issuance of any patent or any right-of-way running through the reservation." This is land within the borders of an Indian reservation, and this is probably the most widely understood meaning of this phrase. It generally also includes fee simple as well as trust land. Whether Indian or non-Indians own the fee, or nontrust, land is immaterial for the purposes of this term. However, in applying federal liquor laws, privately owned fee land in what is considered a "non-Indian community" is not considered Indian country.

The second type of land considered to be Indian country is "all dependent Indian communities within the borders of the United States, whether within the original or subsequently acquired territory thereof, and whether within a state or not." If an Indian community has come to take on Indian country status, it does not matter whether or not it is located within one of the original thirteen states or even within one of the fifty states. A "dependent Indian community" means land set aside by the federal government for the use and occupancy of Indians, whether in the confines of an Indian reservation or not. Some examples include Indian schools operated for Indian children or Indian housing projects in which only tribal members and their families may live. It is not uncommon for some tribally owned housing areas or schools to be located outside the reservation. Nonetheless, the area in which they are located is considered to be Indian country. For the purposes of this term, it is not enough that the land is used or occupied primarily by Indians. There must be some federal or tribal supervision of those lands and activities conducted thereon.

The third type of Indian country is "Indian allotments, the Indian title to which has not been extinguished [canceled], including rights of way running though the same." Any lands held in trust for an Indian tribe or individual, regardless of whether or not the reservation still exists, is considered to be Indian country.

See also **Allotments; Trust Lands**

INDIAN COUNTRY CRIMES ACT OF 1948 The Indian Country Crimes Act of 1948, 25 U.S.C. § 1152, one of the major federal laws dealing with crime in Indian country, has its origin in the earliest days of the United States, when Indian affairs commanded much more of Congress's time than it does today. Also known as the General Crimes Act, this law provides for federal criminal jurisdiction for crimes committed in Indian country under certain circumstances. Only minor changes in the wording of the Act have been made in the last 100 years.

This law extended federal jurisdiction and the application of federal criminal laws to Indian country. Generally, the law provides that the same federal criminal statutes that apply to crimes committed at federal facilities, such as post offices, military installations, and national parks and monuments, also apply in Indian country. The Act was intended to cover crimes committed by Indians against non-Indians and crimes committed by non-Indians against Indians. Although on its face the law appears to be quite broad, language in the Act itself, other federal laws (such as the Major Crimes Act of 1885), and court decisions have created exceptions to the statute that substantially narrow its reach in Indian country.

One exception is created by the "Indian against Indian" clause. Showing some respect for inherent tribal sovereignty, Congress exempted internal tribal cases from the Act. Any offenses committed by one Indian against the person or property of another Indian must be handled, under the terms of this law, by the tribe. Most of the changes to the Act were passed by Congress in an era when tribes handled their own affairs.

A second exception to coverage under the Act concerns crimes committed in Indian country that are punished by the tribe itself. Other federal laws and U.S. Supreme Court decisions have left tribal courts with the authority to punish Indians for misdemeanor offenses. Tribal courts have no authority under this Act, or any other, to punish non-Indians for any crimes committed on their lands.

The third exclusion is known as the *McBratney* or non-Indian exception, so named for the U.S. Supreme Court case of *United States v. McBratney*, 104 U.S. 621 (1881). That case held that because a tribe's interest in regulating its own affairs was not directly affected when one non-Indian committed a crime against another non-Indian in Indian country, the state in which the crime was committed had jurisdiction over the case. The reasoning of the *McBratney* court in carving out the non-Indian exception to the Act is a substantial departure from the Canons of Construction (the set of rules developed by the U.S. Supreme Court to guide themselves and the lower courts when they need to interpret or determine the legal effect of a certain statute, treaty, or executive order) in Indian law cases. Nonetheless, this exception still stands today.

See also **Major Crimes Act of 1885; *United States v. McBratney***

INDIAN EDUCATION ACT OF 1972 Several federal laws help to meet the educational needs of Native Americans. The Indian Education Act (IEA), 20 U.S.C. §§ 241aa–241ff and other parts of

Title 20, provides some funds for local school districts for the education of Indian children. Unlike some other federal laws dealing with Indian education, the IEA has a broad definition of "Indian": No residency or blood quantum requirements appear in that definition. As a result, the IEA funding is available to both reservation and urban Indians, the latter group of people perhaps living hundreds of miles away from their home reservation.

INDIAN FINANCING ACT OF 1974 The Indian Financing Act of 1974 consolidated numerous federal funding sources for tribal economic development into one fund. Prior to passage of this law, the government had attempted to financially assist Indian-owned enterprises. However, these programs have been scattered throughout the federal bureaucracy. Congress, realizing that reservation economic development is important to the cause of Indian self-determination, enacted the Indian Financing Act of 1974, 25 U.S.C. § 1451 *et seq.* Congress understood that in order for self-determination to have any meaning, individual tribal members and tribes as governmental entities must be able to foster local economic development.

The Act attempts to streamline the process for both tribal members and their governments to secure both technical assistance and funding for the operation of businesses on the reservation. Congress initially provided $50 million for a revolving loan fund (that is, one in which new loans are made as borrowers pay back current loans). This law provides for several different types of loans, but there are several features common to all of them. For example, there are restrictions on how much of the loans can benefit non-Indians and on the percentage of Indian ownership participating businesses are required to have.

INDIAN GAMING REGULATORY ACT OF 1988 Congress enacted the Indian Gaming Regulatory Act (IGRA) of 1988, 25 U.S.C. §§ 2701–2721, to define the extent to which certain types of gambling (called Class III games) may be conducted on trust lands or within the boundaries of an Indian reservation. The Act was a response to the U.S. Supreme Court decision in *California v. Cabazon Band of Mission Indians,* 480 U.S. 202 (1987), which favored Indian self-determination over state interests and opened the door for Indian tribes to run whatever gaming operations they chose, regardless of what types of games of chance a state allowed and without any state regulation. Federal law puts certain types of gaming under federal and state control. A regulatory agency, the National Indian Gaming Commission, was established to oversee Class II and Class III gambling activities in Indian country.

IGRA establishes three classes of gaming: Class I games are social games played solely for prizes of minimal values or traditional forms of Indian gaming used in conjunction with celebrations or ceremonies. These types of games are not covered at all by the federal Act, nor are they under the jurisdiction of the commission or of any state or local government. The conduct of these types of games remains a purely internal tribal matter.

Class II gaming includes such games as bingo or pull tabs but does not include any game of chance played on electronic or electromechanical devices or on slot machines. Class II games are under the purview of the Act and are subject to oversight by the commission and by the tribe. However, they are not subject to state regulation. Class I and II games are thus not the subject of negotiation of tribal-state gaming compacts. Which games are considered Class II games has sometimes been decided by the federal courts.

Class III gaming is the catchall category, and it includes all other types of gaming, including poker, blackjack, lotteries, horse or dog racing, and electronic or electromechanical games. This category of gaming is the most intensively regulated under the Act and by the commission. IGRA requires tribes and states to negotiate compacts before the tribes can offer Class III gaming on Indian trust lands or reservations.

See also **National Indian Gaming Commission**

INDIAN HEALTH CARE IMPROVEMENT ACT OF 1976 The Indian Health Care Improvement Act of 1976, 25 U.S.C. §1601 *et seq.*, is intended to improve the health care services provided to Native Americans. The formal Indian health care delivery system is of recent vintage. The Indian Health Service (IHS), the primary care provider for American Indians, was established only in 1955. Congress, somewhat concerned with the health of Native Americans, enacted this law to permit Medicare and Medicaid reimbursement for treatment in IHS facilities. The statute also provided that the IHS may contract with urban Indian health service organizations to provide services to Indians who do not live on or near an Indian reservation. It may not always be economically feasible for the government to construct and staff a clinic and hospital to serve a small number of Native Americans in a given area. As a result, many urban Indians may have been underserved by not having health care available off the reservation. The federal obligation to provide such services to Native Americans has its origins in treaty rights and the federal trust responsibility.

INDIAN HEALTH SERVICE

The Indian Health Service (IHS), an agency of the cabinet-level U.S. Department of Health and Human Services, is the primary federal agency responsible for carrying out the U.S. government's treaty and trust obligations to provide health care to members of federally recognized tribes. To meet its responsibilities, the IHS operates numerous clinics and hospitals located on the various Indian reservations and in some cases, in large metropolitan areas such as Albuquerque, New Mexico.

All facilities are staffed with such professionals as medical doctors, dentists, nurses, counselors, technicians, and other health care professionals and support staff. Many of these employees are commissioned officers in the U.S. Public Health Service, which directly oversees the IHS. In reality, because of limited budgets and the large backlog of unmet health needs in Native American communities, the quality of health care often suffers.

The agency struggles to meet the medical needs of its clients as best it can, but some people nevertheless question whether the federal government is adequately meeting its trust and treaty obligations. Those responsibilities began in the nineteenth century under treaty provisions that required the government to send a doctor, nurse, or other health care provider to the reservation. The local Indian agency superintendent or agent was responsible for finding a health care professional willing to serve on the reservation.

See also **Treaty; Trust Responsibilities**

INDIAN HUNTING AND FISHING RIGHTS

OVERVIEW

From the earliest times American Indians, like all other indigenous people, lived off the land, hunting, fishing, and gathering crops for food. Because of their importance to tribal sustenance, these activities often had religious overtones as well. Congress and the executive branch have long realized the importance of such activities, and the courts consider the right to do these things and to regulate these activities to be an inherent right of any sovereign nation, and in particular, they consider Indian hunting and fishing rights to be vested rights of Native Americans, especially in Indian country.

All governments have some right to regulate the affairs of their citizens. Many of the early reservations were established by treaty. In order for the United States to acquire more lands for settlement by non-Indians, they often treated with local Indian tribes to persuade them to cede (that is, give up their claims on) some of their territory. In some regions, such as the southeastern United States, the Indians were at a disadvantage in the treaty-making process because they were faced with forced removal by the government if they did not voluntarily agree to surrender their lands. The removal of the Cherokee from the Carolinas to what is now the state of Oklahoma is one such example. Ordinarily, the treaties with those tribes that remained on a portion of their lands did not contain specific clauses discussing fishing, hunting, or gathering rights. In areas of the country where such rights were especially important to the tribes, such as the Northwest, the treaties often contained specific clauses reserving these rights to Indian nations in perpetuity.

By the 1870s, the United States held a military advantage over the Native Americans. As a result of the shift in the balance of power from Native Americans to the federal government, by 1871 Congress had declared an end to the treaty-making process with Indian tribes. Consequently, a number of reservations were either created, expanded or reduced in size, or eliminated altogether, either by act of Congress or by an executive order of the president of the United States.

INTERPRETATION OF TREATIES AND OTHER AGREEMENTS

Recognizing the importance to Indians of these rights, both as a matter of survival and as an attribute of tribal sovereignty, the courts applied the Canons of Construction (a set of rules developed by the U.S. Supreme Court to guide themselves and the lower courts when they need to interpret or determine the legal effect of a certain statute, treaty, or executive order) in many cases involving conflicts over hunting and fishing rights between Indian tribes and non-Indians. The Supreme Court, beginning with its decision in the case of *United States v. Winans,* 198 U.S. 371 (1905), has usually found that even on lands that long ago passed out of Indian hands, Indian hunting, fishing, and gathering rights still exist.

The inequities between the tribes and the government in the treaty-making process and the trust obligations that the government has toward Indian tribes have persuaded the courts to apply the canons in Indian hunting and fishing cases. A complete recitation of all of the court cases that have shaped and defined the extent of Indian rights in this field is beyond the scope of this article. Nonetheless, by the application of these rules of interpretation by the courts to numerous case, a number of settled rules have evolved.

Many of these rights apply, regardless of whether the land in question acquired Indian country status through treaty, statute, or presidential order or was part of the pre–United States ancestral homeland of the Indian tribes. The courts have recognized that the right to hunt and fish (henceforth, this term also includes gathering rights, such as to take grains or other things naturally growing on the land) is one of the attributes of inherent tribal sovereignty. Even if a treaty, statute, or other government order does not mention these rights, the aboriginal rights to do these things may nonetheless still survive, despite the silence of these documents.

When the courts applied the Indian law canons in dealing with hunting and fishing rights in lands that are part of an Indian nation by treaty or agreement, they interpreted those rights as the Indians would have understood them when the treaties or agreements were drawn up. In many instances, there was a significant language barrier between the Indians and the government negotiators. Indian people of those times simply were not accustomed to the legalisms used by non-Indians of their day. It was highly unlikely that Indians would have freely bargained away their hunting, fishing, and gathering rights. Early court decisions, such as *Winans,* acknowledged the government-to-government relationship between the tribes and the United States. Those courts interpreted various provisions in treaties and executive agreements as the grant of hunting and fishing rights *from* tribes *to* the government, not a grant *of* rights *to* tribes *from* the federal government. This is a very important distinction because the courts give some meaning to the concept of inherent tribal sovereignty in that only those rights that were bargained away by treaty or expressly limited or eliminated by Congress under the Plenary Powers Doctrine will be considered lost. Therefore, the hunting and fishing rights that the Indian people originally had are not lost to them unless Congress says otherwise in legislating in Indian matters. Congress has rarely done so. In fact, in one of the major jurisdictional statutes passed by Congress in the latter half of the twentieth century, Public Law 280, which opened the door to state regulation of reservation activities in some states, Congress expressly preserved existing Indian rights in this area. In some cases, the courts have decided that these rights are not lost even after Congress has chosen to terminate the tribal-federal relationship altogether.

Additionally, depending on the parties to a hunting and fishing rights case, the terms of a treaty or statute may be ambiguous or may be interpreted in more than one way. For example, some treaty clauses reserved to the tribes the rights to take fish in their "usual and accustomed grounds and stations." Does this mean that the rights to fish in these places are lost if the land passes out of Indian hands or if fishing is not conducted there for a period of time? How much fish may a tribal member take? Who may take a quantity of fish: an individual tribal member or a tribal fishing entity? These are all questions that numerous federal (and some state) courts have answered by applying the rules of interpretation. The courts tend to interpret these ambiguous treaty and statutory provision liberally, in favor of expanding Indian rights in this area. If Congress has not limited or extinguished those rights, they still exist. In few other areas of Indian law is an understanding of history so important.

THE EXTENT OF INDIAN HUNTING, FISHING, AND GATHERING RIGHTS

On-Reservation Rights and Regulation

As a general rule, tribes have the full authority to regulate and manage wildlife resources located on their reservation, including regulating the rights of Indians, members of the tribe or not, as individuals. This authority is an essential part of a tribe's self-rule, and the state has very little authority to regulate the management of wildlife resources on Indian lands within a reservation. However, a narrow exception permits state regulation of fishing if that is necessary to ensure the continued propagation of a species of fish. The burden of proving this is on the state agencies: They must show a court why state regulation in Indian country is necessary.

A second significant exception to tribal control, and one that limits true tribal self-government, is the so-called *Montana* exclusion. The U.S. Supreme Court, in the case of *Montana v. United States,* 450 U.S. 544 (1981), ruled that as a general rule, states, and not tribes, may regulate hunting and fishing activities by non-Indians on non-Indian lands. Many reservations are in fact, "checkerboarded"; that is, they contain non-Indian-owned parcels of land interspersed with tribal or individual Indian trust lands. Only when the affected tribe can show a court that state regulation of such hunting and fishing activities will adversely affect the tribe's health, welfare, safety, or self-governance will such state authority be excluded. For example, if non-Indians overfish a location within the reservation, and the state does not deal with that problem, then the tribe may be able to take over the regulation of fishing in that location. It may be argued, of course, that any state regulation of activity within Indian country is a threat to tribal self-rule, but the *Montana* court ruled otherwise.

The matters just discussed deal with the tribes' rights to regulate these activities, not with their rights to undertake these activities. As a general rule, both a tribe and its individual members have the right to hunt and fish, with tribal licenses, anywhere on the reservation, unless some treaty or other federal regulation or law has limited such rights. The question then arises: To what extent may the tribe or individual tribal member exploit these resources on non-Indian-owned land on a reservation? That question must be decided by the courts on a case-by-case basis.

Off-Reservation Rights and Regulation

Less clear, perhaps, is the situation in which these rights are guaranteed by treaty or federal law but the land over which the controversy rises is, at the time of the controversy, located off a reservation. This has been the subject of much dispute in the northwestern United States, where hunting and, particularly, fishing remain important mainstays of the regional economy.

From the latter half of the nineteenth century into the 1930s, Indian lands passed into non-Indian hands at a prodigious rate. The controversy often comes to a head in situations in which non-Indian lands have, over a period of time, come to be located far from an Indian reservation, so that land to which Indian hunting and fishing rights are still attached may be many miles from an Indian reservation. Nonetheless, with the exceptions stated earlier, both individual Indians and their tribe have the right to fish from these non-Indian lands. The tribe, however, must prove that this land was included in a treaty or that the right to fish or hunt there was preserved by aboriginal title or by congressional or executive statutes or agreements. If that is the case, then Indians have the right to an easement (that is, a right to cross) over non-Indian and even public lands to gain access to the fishing area.

The regulation of hunting and fishing on off-reservation areas is even less clear. Generally, tribes may regulate the hunting and fishing rights of their members, even on off-reservation areas to which such rights attach through treaties or other federal regulation. This constitutes a rare exception to a state's right to regulate matters or concerns off a reservation. Off a reservation, Indians are subject to state regulation just like all other citizens. For hunting and fishing matters off-reservation, non-Indians would be subject to state control, as would Indians.

In certain northwestern tribal fishing and hunting areas, federal treaties and laws give rise to both concurrent state and tribal control, even over non-Indian fishing and hunting grounds. That, however, is the exception rather than the rule.

OTHER ISSUES

Quantity

Another issue that frequently arises is the quantity of fish or animals that may be taken pursuant to Indian rights. Unfortunately for all parties concerned, the issue is ultimately decided by the courts. It is rare for Indian and non-Indians to agree on these matters without court intervention. Over a period of time, the courts have developed a number of tests to balance the rights of both Indian and non-Indian consumers of such natural resources. It must also be realized that the rights guaranteed to the various Indian tribes also allow them to use modern methods to take their share of fish, animals, or produce.

Federal Regulation and Just Compensation

Regardless of whether these rights occur on or off a reservation, Congress, under the Plenary Powers Doctrine, could abrogate treaty rights or change federal statues or executive agreements at any time to reduce or eliminate Indian fishing and hunting rights. This doctrine enables Congress to give federal authorities the jurisdiction or authority to regulate Indian rights, even to the point of excluding tribal or state authority in this area. Generally, however, Congress has left the regulation of these affairs to the tribes themselves. However, if Congress chose to significantly reduce or eliminate these rights, the Just Compensation Clause of the Fifth Amendment to the U.S. Constitution would require the federal government to compensate the affected tribe for the loss of their interests. The sole exception to the Just Compensation requirement is if the fishing, hunting, or gathering rights are grounded on aboriginal or original title to the lands concerned.

The Supreme Court ruled, in *Tee-Hit-Ton Indians v. United States,* 348 U.S. 272 (1955), that Congress does not have to compensate Indians for the loss of these rights where Congress or the president have not explicitly recognized them by statute, treaty, or executive agreement. Nonetheless, at times Congress has chosen to grant compensation anyway. Conversely, in *Menominee Tribe v. United States,* 391 U.S. 404 (1968), the Court held that these rights recognized by treaty, statute, or presidential order are to be considered valuable property rights. As such, if Congress chooses to reduce or eliminate these rights altogether, it must compensate a tribe (not an individual tribal member).

CONCLUSION

With the increasing complexity and sophistication of tribal governments, Indian tribes are more willing than ever to assert their hunting, fishing, and gathering rights, long dormant in many cases, in the courts. Until recent times, few Indian tribes possessed the resources or expertise to effectively deal with these issues. An ever greater number of tribes are establishing their own natural resources agencies to regulate and manage these matters. Given the litigious nature of U.S. society, the future will find more cases in federal and state courts to balance tribal interests with those of state and local governments and their citizens.

See also **Canons of Construction; *New Mexico v. Mescalero Apache Tribe;* Plenary Powers Doctrine; *United States v. Washington; United States v. Winans***

INDIAN LAND CONSOLIDATION ACT OF 1982

The Indian Land Consolidation Act of 1982, 25 U.S.C § 2201–2211, attempts to solve the problem of "fractionalized" land interests on reservations. Since the enactment by Congress of the General Allotment (Dawes) Act of 1887, many parcels of trust land in Indian country have come to have many co-owners. With so many owners, these fractionalized land interests severely diminished the economic value of the property. Under traditional principles of law, the consent of all the owners of undivided interests is needed to sell, transfer, or otherwise lease the land. It is usually very difficult (and sometimes impossible), time consuming, and expensive to get all of the owners to agree to this. As a result, the land generates little or no income for its owners. In the event that the land was leased or sold, often each owner received as little as a few cents per year. Because of this fractionalization, much of the land could not be put to a use that would benefit its owners or the tribe itself.

Congress attempted to help tribes consolidate their land interests into usable parcels by enacting the Indian Land Consolidation Act of 1982. The heart of the Act is a provision that requires that when a tribal member owning a small interest in trust land dies, that ownership escheats, or automatically passes to the tribe. Under the law, a "small interest" is one that amounts to less than 2 percent of the total acreage or that earned an average of less than $100 annually over the five years prior to its transfer to the tribe. Other provisions of the law allow tribes to exchange their land interests with those of individual tribal members.

However, in the case of *Babbitt v. Youpee,* 519 U.S. 234 (1997), the Supreme Court ruled that the escheat part of the law violated the Just Compensation Clause of the U.S. Constitution, which requires that any governmental entity that takes a private interest in land or other property must pay the former owner a fair price for that allotment. When Congress enacted this Act, it did not appropriate any monies for tribes to pay owners for such fractionalized interests. Most tribes do not have funds available for this purpose. Nonetheless, the law still has some value as it provides a framework in which tribes may exchange real estate parcels with their members to increase the usefulness of tribal land holdings that can be used for tribal farming, ranching, or other enterprises.

See also **Fractionalized Interests; General Allotment Act of 1887; Just Compensation Clause**

INDIAN LAW RESOURCE CENTER The Indian Law Resource Center, a legal and human rights organization based in Helena, Montana, provides free legal assistance to Indian tribes, Alaska Native communities, and Native Hawaiian communities. The legal representation offered by the Indian Law Resource Center focuses on five areas of vital importance to all Indian communities: (1) land rights; (2) legal reform and human rights; (3) environmental protection; (4) native sovereignty and self-government; and (5) the international protection of human rights.

Most Native American, Alaskan, and Hawaiian communities cannot afford legal representation to protect their rights and otherwise advance their interests. Lawsuits that help shape and test the rights of Indian peoples are time consuming and expensive. Such non-Indian interests as corporations and governmental entities are usually in a far better position to absorb the expense of court cases. Organizations like the Indian Law Resource Center must prioritize and allocate their resources among the many requests that they receive for legal assistance.

INDIAN PREFERENCE The term "Indian preference" is generally applied to the practice of hiring Indians instead of non-Indians for jobs with certain organizations. Currently, the only legally recognized preferences exist within the Bureau of Indian Affairs (BIA), the Indian Health Service (IHS), tribal governments themselves, and entities that do business with these organizations. Courts do not find such preferences to be improper racial discrimination on the basis that singling out Indians for special consideration is not racially based but, rather, is derived from the political relationship between tribes and the U.S. government.

Such preferences are based on the long-standing congressional policy of granting ever increasing self-governance to Indian people through their tribal governments. The BIA wields tremendous authority over the lives of Indian people, especially those living on or near reservations. For much of the bureau's long history, it employed very few Indians. There were almost no Indians in positions at the highest levels, the policy-making levels, of the agency.

To rectify the situation, over the years Congress and the executive branch, by statute and by executive order, have encouraged such an employment preference. The rationale implicit in self-governance is to have the people governed by their own. Because the BIA effectively governs Indian people, the agency should be staffed by those people it is to supervise. Self-governance is further encouraged by allowing tribes to give employment preference to their own members or other Indians over non-Indians for tribal programs. Likewise, the IHS, though not a governing body, provides its services exclusively to Native Americans. The courts reason that it furthers the interests of Indians to employ and promote Indians over non-Indians. The courts believe that because cultural and religious practices play a part in health care, those most familiar with them should deliver health services to the people and thus help preserve tribal cultures.

It is important to note, however, that such preferences are not legally recognized in any other federal, state, or local governmental agencies, which do not direct all of their resources toward Indian people. The factor determining whether such preferences are allowed is whether they would preserve tribal identities as such and promote Indian self-government.

A lesser known preference deals with BIA contracts for goods and services to be provided either to the bureau itself or to tribes or individual Indians. Federal statutes require that as far as possible, the bureau choose contractors who employ Indians or buy Indian-made products in carrying out their agreements. The BIA also gives preferences to Indian-owned businesses as well.

Other federal laws also permit or allow tribes to require that private businesses located on or near an Indian reservation give preference in hiring or promotion to tribal members as a condition of doing business there. (What constitutes "near a reservation" so as to trigger an employment preference may be the subject of a lawsuit in court.) Such employment preferences do not apply to any private business that is not near a reservation or that does not have any contract with an Indian tribe or similar entity. In this latter situation, Indian people are not legally treated any differently than are non-Indians.

See also **Buy Indian Act of 1908; Indian Self-Determination and Education Assistance Act of 1975; *Morton v. Mancari***

INDIAN PROBATES The process of determining who inherits certain types of property from a member of a federally recognized Indian tribe is called by the generic term "Indian probates." This question is really one of jurisdiction, that is, of which court has the authority to determine who gets the property. Under modern probate law, if a person leaves a will, a state court will determine if the will was properly made without fraud and then will distribute the property to whomever the deceased (testator) named in the will. If the testator does not leave a will, all states have rules as to which of the decedent's relatives inherit the property. These rules, called intestate succession, take the place of a will.

State courts have jurisdiction over intestate (that is, without a will) decedents, Indian and non-Indian alike, if they live outside a reservation and their property is also off-reservation. However, if the private nonrestricted property is on a reservation or if the decedent lived on a reservation, regardless of race, tribal courts or the Bureau of Indian Affairs (BIA) have the authority, to the exclusion of state courts, to determine the inheritance of a decedent. Typically, if a tribal court has authority over the property of a tribal member, the tribe may have its own rules as to the disposition of that property where the member dies intestate. Otherwise, the tribe may follow the law of the state where the tribe is located.

The rules are somewhat different when a deceased tribal member owned an interest in trust or tribal property, whether real or personal. Such tribal property could include not only land but also, for example, shares of stock in a tribal manufacturing business. In most of those cases, federal law provides that regardless of where the member lived, the BIA must conduct administrative law proceedings under the federal Administrative Procedures Act of 1946 to determine the heirs to that property, regardless of whether the member died with a will or not. However, Congress has enacted special probate laws for certain tribes, such as the Five Civilized Tribes (the Cherokee, Chickasaw, Choctaw, Creek, and Seminole Indians settled in Indian Territory after 1830).

In many situations, an administrative law judge will apply the law of the state where the tribe is located to determine who inherits the property. However, if state law conflicts with federal law in these probate cases, the latter will prevail. This special judge will notify all potential heirs of the proceedings and will then conduct a hearing to determine the validity of the will, if there is one, and who should inherit. One or more of these judges are located at each BIA Area Office.

Generally, federal law only permits members of the particular tribe from which the property comes to inherit that property, regardless of the wishes of the decedent. This is especially true with respect to tribal land allotments. Congress intended for trust property to benefit tribal members only, and not non-Indians. To allow non-Indians to inherit such property would further erode the tribal Indian land base.

If any member is dissatisfied with the judge's decision, they may appeal that decision to the three-member Board of Indian Appeals, a special tribunal under the secretary of the interior. This board's decision is the final one for the Department of the Interior. Further review of that board's decision may be made by a U.S. district court.

See also **Administrative Procedures Act of 1946**

INDIAN REORGANIZATION ACT OF 1934

The Indian Reorganization Act (IRA) of 1934, 25 U.S.C. §§ 461–479, also known as the Wheeler-Howard Act, was the centerpiece of the so-called Indian New Deal during the administration of President Franklin D. Roosevelt. The Act had several provisions and was intended to increase self-governance and to foster the economic independence of Indian tribes. Prior to this time, the Dawes Act (General Allotment Act) of 1887 and the general neglect by the federal government of its trust obligation toward Indians led to the massive breakup of Indian landholdings and severely weakened tribal governments. By 1928, when a federally sponsored survey of Indian tribes revealed appalling governmental indifference and neglect of Native Americans, Indian landholdings were only a fraction of what they had been in the late nineteenth century. More than 80 percent of the tribal land base had passed out of Indian hands by 1934.

Indian reformers were able to convince the president and Congress that changes were needed in the way the government dealt with Native Americans. Indian Commissioner John Collier worked many months to secure passage of the bill and its adoption by the Indian tribes. The IRA gave the tribes two years to accept or reject it. The Bureau of Indian Affairs (BIA) actively pushed tribes to come under the provisions of the Act.

The Act accomplished a number of things. The first major provision of the IRA immediately ended the national policy of allotment of Indian lands, regardless of whether a tribe adopted the Act. Under the Dawes Act, the landholdings of Indian tribes were severely reduced when land owned by the tribes were divided up by the government and parceled out to tribal members. After a period of years, the land would be subject to local property taxes. Many allottees could not afford to pay them, and thus many of the allotted parcels passed out of Indian hands. In some cases, unallotted Indian lands had been declared "surplus" by the government and were then put up for sale. The Act stopped any further sale of such land, and it returned unsold surplus land to the tribe itself.

The Act also authorized the secretary of the interior to work with the tribes to consolidate their landholdings. Often, tribal land parcels were interspersed with deeded lands, and this "checkerboarding" reduced the economic value of the tribal land base. For example, it would be difficult to run a profitable cattle-grazing operation without worrying about trespass onto nontribal parcels if there was not one large parcel where the cattle could freely roam. The Act authorized the secretary of the interior to work with the tribes to try to end checkerboarding of lands by exchanging parcels of land with non-Indian landowners.

Another part of the Wheeler-Howard Act made federal loans for economic development available to IRA tribes. Once the IRA tribe became federally chartered, it was eligible for these loans. Only those tribes that adopted the Act were eligible for these economic development loans, which during the Great Depression of the 1930s meant much to many of the tribes. This is largely irrelevant today, however, for numerous federal programs in such areas as agriculture, economic development, education, and housing are available to any federally recognized Indian tribe. In the days prior to the IRA, such loans were generally available only to individual tribal members, not the tribal entity itself.

The Act gave the tribes two years to vote on whether they wanted to opt out of the Act. To opt out, a majority of the adult tribal members had to vote against adoption. Those members who failed to vote were considered to have consented to the Act. More than 250 elections were held under the Act, and all but 77 tribes voted to be covered under the Act. Today, about half of the federally recognized Indian tribes have IRA constitutions. The largest non-IRA tribe is the Navajo Nation, in the southwestern United States.

Those Indian tribes who came under the IRA had a period of time to enact a tribal constitution and to become incorporated, much like a corporation or city. Many of these constitutions contained boilerplate language; that is, they were identical to one another except for the name of the tribe and other particular details. The newly incorporated tribes had many of the same powers as any modern corporation: to buy and sell property, to sue and be sued in court, and so on. Additionally, they had some powers of self-government, usually exercised by an elected tribal council. To a limited extent, tribes have some measure of home rule in their own internal affairs. In other words, they may exercise any governmental power not denied them by federal law. The American concept of the separation of powers into the traditional three branches of government was not necessarily followed. It was not uncommon for the tribal council not only to act as a legislative body but also to possess executive and judicial functions as well.

Besides the ending of the land allotment policy, the most significant aspect of the Act was probably that of restoring some measure of self-government to those tribes that adopted the Act. Before the coming of the Europeans, the Indian tribes had complete authority over their own affairs. With the military and political subjugation of the Indian nations, the BIA came to exercise nearly total control over every aspect of Indian life on the reservation. This can best be seen as analogous to the colonial administration of the British Empire after the mid-1800s. British colonies such as India were subject to total control by the English monarch in London. Similarly, in Indian country, every expenditure made, every employee hired, was subject to approval of the BIA. Many tribes were not financially able to hire their own lawyers.

Even under the IRA, the secretary of the interior still has to approve the contract of any attorney that the tribe wants to hire. Since passage of the Act, although some of a tribes' decisions—such as the amendment of the constitution itself and the enactment of tribal laws—are still subject to BIA approval, that agency generally has adopted a hands-off attitude unknown in the past. It is probably rare today for the BIA to veto the enactment of tribal legislation. Although tribes have an increased measure of self-government, however, the BIA still exercises considerable authority over them, even after the Indian self-determination period, which began in the 1970s.

The IRA also mandated, for the first time, an Indian hiring preference within the BIA. Qualified members of Indian tribes were to be hired, if possible, for job vacancies within the bureau. The U.S. Supreme Court, in *Morton v. Mancari*, 417 U.S. 535 (1974), ultimately found this practice to be constitutional.

The Act is not without its critics, however, both as to its adoption by the tribes and its effect upon them. The major criticism of the ratification process is the pressure the bureau exerted on the tribes for their approval. Among other questionable tactics, those tribal members who failed to vote were counted as having voted yes. Other critics contend that the IRA has done little to better the lot of either the tribes themselves or individual members. Additionally, some commentators questioned whether non-Indian forms of government should be imposed upon Native Americans. The Wheeler-Howard Act was drafted with minimal input from Indian tribes. That was a typical practice in its day.

See also **Allotments; General Allotment Act of 1887; Indian Reorganization Act (IRA) Tribe**

INDIAN REORGANIZATION ACT (IRA) TRIBE

Federally recognized Indian tribes that chose to be covered under the terms of the Indian Reorganization Act of 1934—so called Indian Reorganization Act (IRA) tribes—became eligible for federal economic development loans, which was a major incentive to become an IRA tribe. That incentive is largely meaningless today, however. Federally recognized tribes are eligible for many types of federal loans and assistance today in such areas as agriculture, housing, and natural resources conservation.

IRA tribes were required to adopt a constitution before they could receive a federal charter as an IRA tribal corporation. Many of these constitutions contained boilerplate language; that is, they were identical to one another except for the name of the tribe and other particular details. IRA-chartered tribes have many of the same powers as any modern corporation: to buy and sell property, to sue and be sued in court, and so on. Additionally, they have some powers of self-government, usually exercised by an elected tribal council. To a limited extent, tribes have some measure of home rule in their own internal affairs. In other words, they may exercise any governmental power not denied them by federal law. The American concept of the separation of powers into the traditional three branches of government was not necessarily followed. It was not uncommon for the tribal council not only to act as a legislative body but also to possess executive and judicial functions as well.

Typically, non-IRA tribes are informally structured, perhaps without an elected tribal council, three separate branches of government (that is, executive, legislative, and judicial), or a constitution. They may have few members, a very small land area, and exercise few governmental powers. For instance, some non-IRA tribes, instead of operating their own tribal courts, if they even have one, may rely on a Bureau of Indian Affairs Court of Indian Offenses, also known as a *Code of Federal Regulations (CFR)* court. These special courts deal only with minor criminal offenses enumerated in the *Code of Federal Regulations,* and their procedures are delineated in that same code. By contrast, an IRA tribe has the complete authority in most states to set up its own courts, define what types of cases it may decide, and establish the procedures under which the court operates.

See also **Indian Reorganization Act of 1934**

INDIAN SELF-DETERMINATION AND EDUCATION ASSISTANCE ACT OF 1975 In 1975 Congress passed the Indian Self-Determination and Education Assistance Act (ISDEAA), 25 U.S.C. § 450 *et seq.* and elsewhere in the U.S. code, to implement its tribal self-determination policy. The Act somewhat loosens the tight grip of the Bureau of Indian Affairs (BIA) and several other federal agencies, such as the Indian Health Service (IHS), on the daily life of Indians and their tribal governments. Prior to passage of this law, the BIA and other federal agencies minutely regulated the delivery of educational, health, and a myriad of other services to the Indian people. The BIA, for example, operated a number of boarding schools, some for many years, with little meaningful input from tribal members or the tribal governments themselves. Some of these schools are still in existence.

Although this law deals primarily with the delivery of educational services, nearly all other federal support to Native Americans is also within the purview of the Act. Such services include agriculture, health care, law enforcement, and other programs in support of tribal government.

Essentially, the ISDEAA permits the tribes themselves or any group chartered by the tribe's governing body to assume the responsibility for delivering federal services to tribal members. Contracting organizations other than the tribe itself must meet certain requirements before they are eligible to enter into such agreements with the federal government. Elementary and high schools located on a reservation are among the most common organizations that have so-called 638 contracts (named after the number of the Indian Self-Determination and Education Assistance Act, Public Law 93-638). Where the BIA itself operates boarding or day schools for Indian students, it oversees every detail of their operation. Under the Act, the tribes and local tribally chartered schools contract with the BIA for the former to take over school operations. The BIA or other agency allocates a fixed sum to the contractor, which must then furnish the services to the tribe.

This law also strengthens the Johnson-O'Malley (JOM) Act of 1934 by requiring all off-reservation schools that receive federal funding for the education of Indian children to involve Indian parents in decisions over how those funds shall be used. Local committees of Indian parents have considerable authority over how local schools may spend JOM monies.

The Act is not without its critics, however. Although tribes and allied organizations now deliver these services using their own employees, buildings, and equipment, the federal government still retains significant oversight over these contracts. The government must approve each contract and must be provided with data regarding accounting practices, equipment, personnel, and other important details of the proposed contract. If the government is not satisfied with the agreement, it may reject it despite local community support. The contractor may, under the Administrative Procedures Act of 1946, appeal that rejection to the highest levels of the executive branch and ultimately to the federal courts. Such appeals, of course, are lengthy and expensive.

Some critics see the law as one step back toward the termination of federal responsibility for Indian services. They reason that the next step beyond turning over the running of federal programs to the tribes is to someday end that assistance to the tribe entirely. Nonetheless, the current trend is to expand the number of federal programs to be operated by Indian tribes.

Later amendments to the law established a pilot project for ten tribes to take over the activities previously conducted for them by the BIA and IHS. In addition to those already mentioned, these endeavors include resource conservation, land use planning and zoning, and others. Many tribes have only limited 638 contracts with the government. These agreements must be negotiated one at a time. These tribes chosen for the pilot program administer all federal services themselves. Additionally, unlike the usual 638 contracts, the tribes chosen for this program have much more latitude in designing or altering their programs to meet the needs of their people and in reallocating the funds among the different programs. These 638 contracts are similar to block grants, in which recipients may use the funds in nearly any way they wish, subject only to some very limited restrictions.

See also **Administrative Procedures Act of 1946; Johnson-O'Malley Act of 1934**

INDIAN TAXATION What types of taxes Indian tribes may levy against people, property, and places and what taxes Indians or tribes may be subjected to by various types of governmental entities may differ from the rights and obligations of other organizations or individuals in the United States.

As a general rule, Indian people are subject to most of the same federal taxes as are other citizens and residents of the United States. The Supreme Court, in the leading case of *Squire v. Capoeman,* 356 U.S. 1 (1956), for federal tax purposes reversed the usual rules of construction in Indian law cases. Normally, when a particular law may be interpreted in one of several ways, courts will interpret it in a way to protect Indian rights and in a manner favorable to Indians. However, when a federal tax law is subject to legal interpretation, the courts will narrowly construe it so as to avoid giving that law the effect of granting a tax exemption. In other words, unless Congress clearly states in a law that it intends the law to grant a tax exemption to Indians, the courts will not interpret it as such.

Congress, however, has exempted tribes, along with state and local governments, from most federal taxes. Until 1982, there were generally no specific laws on that subject, but federal agencies, notably the Internal Revenue Service, treated federally recognized tribes as states for tax purposes. The Indian Tribal Governmental Tax Status Act of 1982, 26 U.S.C. § 7871 made this policy a matter of federal law.

When dealing with the question of whether states may tax Indians, tribes, or activities occurring in Indian country, the rules are quite different, however. Recognizing that the power to tax is the power to destroy, Congress and the federal courts have tried to protect Indian tribes from state intrusion. History shows that state governments have a long record of hostility toward Indian tribes. Therefore, the Canons of Construction apply to the question of the applicability of state tax laws in Indian country. The general rule is that states ordinarily have no authority to tax Indians located on or commercial activities taking place in Indian country. See, for example, *Bryan v. Itasca County,* 426 U.S. 373 (1976), and *McClanahan v. Arizona State Tax Commission,* 411 U.S. 164 (1973). For instance, Indians do not pay state taxes for income earned or for goods bought on an Indian reservation. States seeking to apply their tax laws to Indian country normally have the burden of proving that Congress gave them the authority to do so. One of the issues that has been heavily contested in recent years is the authority of states to tax cigarettes sold on a reservation. In following the general rules of interpretation, the courts have allowed states to tax only those sales made to non-Indians.

Tribal taxation of people, property, or activities on their reservation presents yet another issue. As a general rule, Indian tribes, as sovereign nations, have the authority to tax. The power to tax is part of the inherent sovereign doctrine. This power is essential to any government, for without it, no government could function. Congress has not taken away the power of tribes to tax, so a tribe retains that authority until Congress chooses to do away with it. Until recent times, few tribes levied their own taxes. Today, as tribes are continuing to develop their economies and the demand for tribal services is increasing, the power of tribes to tax is becoming more of an issue between the tribes and the states. Court decisions have also given tribes the authority to levy taxes on non-Indians and nonmembers who voluntarily do business on a reservation.

Some critics have argued that tribal taxation of non-Indians or nonmembers amounts to taxation without representation because these groups cannot vote in tribal elections or otherwise take part in tribal government. However, it must be remembered that states tax nonresidents for a wide variety of activities. For instance, nonresidents of a state must pay sales taxes on goods they purchase within that state. Residents of one state who commute to work by driving their vehicle into another state may have to pay a commuter tax to drive their car in the second state. The federal government taxes the income of noncitizens, who generally cannot vote in either state or federal elections.

The phrase "Indians not Taxed" found in Article I of the U.S. Constitution has no real application at the current time. Before Congress generally conferred U.S. citizenship on Indians in 1924, the phrase had some relevance to the apportionment of seats in the U.S. House of Representatives. Since Indians were not generally subject to any form of taxation at the founding of the United States, they were excluded from the population count when Congress allocated seats in the House to each state.

See also **Canons of Construction**

INDIAN TITLE The term "Indian title" denotes the extent of legal interests owned by Indians in a particular parcel of land. Since the earliest history of the United States, whenever non-Indian settlers moved closer to Indian territory, the courts found it necessary to define the extent to which Native Americans owned their lands. Several legal principles emerged over the centuries. First, "Indian title" is a mere right of possession. Individual tribal members or a tribe itself only have the right to occupy and use the lands in question. They do not actually own it. Second, legal ownership is vested in the United States. Only the federal government can authorize Indians to sell or otherwise transfer land to which they have Indian title. The federal government could, if it chose, give legal ownership of the lands to the Indian tribe or its members. Third, the U.S. government acquired legal ownership of Indian lands by "discovering" and conquering the Indian peoples through a show of superior military force. The term "Indian title" is generally synonymous with "aboriginal title."

See also **Aboriginal Possession or Title; Trilogy Cases**

INDIAN TRIBAL GOVERNMENTAL TAX STATUS ACT OF 1982 Prior to passage of the Indian Tribal Governmental Tax Status Act of 1982, 26 U.S.C. § 7871, federal agencies such as the Internal Revenue Service as a general rule treated federally recognized tribes as states for federal tax purposes. The Act codifies the government's policy of treating Indian tribes like states for tax purposes and makes it clear that tribes enjoy many of the privileges that states do. For example, tribes do not have to pay federal taxes on their purchases of goods or services, and they can issue tax-exempt government bonds to construct buildings or encourage economic development on the reservation.

See also **Indian Taxation**

INDIAN WATER RIGHTS

INTRODUCTION

Under the *Winters* Doctrine, which originated in the U.S. Supreme Court case of *Winters v. United States*, 207 U.S. 564 (1908), tribes and tribal members enjoy special privileges with respect to the use of water found on Indian lands, whether above or below ground. In most cases, the right to use water is vital to the economic value of land. Indian water rights differ substantially from those of non-Indians. To understand such differences, it is first necessary to briefly discuss water rights as they apply to non-Indians. There are two different water allocation and use systems in effect in the United States.

Riparian Rights

The term "riparian rights" refers to the rights of the owners of land through which a stream or river runs. All owners of land upon which water flows or stands, on the ground or underground, share the water in times of scarcity. The prior use of water does not create special rights. This rule of water allocation is generally followed by the states east of the Mississippi River. Water is generally more plentiful there than in the West, and as a result, there is little litigation on the subject. The *Winters* Doctrine would presumably be followed should there should there be a scarcity of water for prolonged periods of time and should Indian lands be affected in a water-use dispute.

Prior Appropriation

The second major system of water allocation and usage is known as prior appropriation. There are four basic rules to prior appropriation, which generally applies to the states west of the Mississippi River: (1) "First in time, first in right"—that is, the first person to divert an amount of water from a source may continue to take the same amount of water as long as the source is available and as long as he or she continues to own those water rights.

The date the water is actually first used is called the priority date. Subsequent users are called junior appropriators; they get to take whatever is left over. (2) These rights are property in the truest sense, just as is real estate or personal property. These water rights can be sold or transferred, either together with or separately from the land the water flows through. In other words, the water rights need not go with the land, so they could be transferred to someone other than the landowner. (3) If there is not enough water to go around, the senior appropriator—that is, the person to first acquire the water rights—may use his or her entire share, even if that means that all junior appropriators get no water at all. Finally, (4) a person with water rights who fails to use them after a period of time loses those rights. All questions under prior appropriation principles, where no Indian land is involved, are determined by the law of the state where the water is located.

To illustrate how this works, assume that three farmers live on a stream. A is the first to divert water from a stream, and he continually does so for a number of years. B and C, in turn, use a share of water from that same stream. A drought nearly dries up the stream, leaving too little water to fully satisfy the needs of all three farmers. During the dry period, A may use up to the quantity of water he initially diverted from the stream years earlier, even if there is none left over for B and C. Moreover, appropriators may sell their water rights or a part of them to anyone whenever they choose.

Indian Water Rights

There are some differences between Indian water rights and prior appropriation rules. First, Indian water rights are generally governed by federal rather than state law. Second, Indian water rights are not lost, as are appropriated rights, through nonuse. Such water rights are considered "reserved." Third, the quantity of water that may be taken under Indian rights is not limited to that which may have first been taken when the Indian reservation was established. Unlike under prior appropriations rules, the quantity of water is not limited to the amount first taken, if it is limited at all. In other words, the amount of water to be used is not confined to what was first claimed.

Indian water rights concern not only lakes, ponds, streams, and rivers in or flowing through Indian country, but underground water therein as well. Several questions are often at the center of water disputes between Indian tribes and their neighbors: First, how much water is available to the Indian tribe under the *Winters* Doctrine? Second, for what purposes may the water be used? Third, shall disputes be decided in the federal courts or in the state courts? This is often crucial. History has shown that state courts are often more hostile to the rights of Indians than are federal courts. Fourth, to whom or to what entities may tribes or tribal members transfer part or all of these water rights? Fifth, to what extent may tribes manage and regulate the use of water resources? Sixth, who may represent Indian interests in legal disputes? The date in which water rights accrue or inhere in the tribe is usually the date Congress established the reservation or otherwise set aside the land for the use of a tribe. This date is not usually subject to much controversy.

Quantity of Water Available

The allowable quantity of water usage under the non-Indian prior appropriations system is fairly well defined by the quantity initially used by the claimants. Congress could not foresee how much water Indian reservations would need when it created them. Modern industrial and recreational uses were not fully contemplated either by Congress or by the Supreme Court in the *Winters* case.

Indeed, most Indian water rights cases, from *Winters* to recent times, have tended not to quantify Indian privileges so that the amount of water used may expand with modern needs of the reservation. Quantification would not normally be in the best interest of a tribe, for it would be locked into a specific amount of water regardless of its expanding needs, which may occur because of a growing populace, increased commerce, industry, and the like. Non-Indian water users, on the other hand, would generally prefer quantification of Indian rights in order to know with some certainty just what competing water rights they have and to be able to plan for their future needs. It is important to realize that not all water disputes end up in the courts. Both sides may negotiate the quantity for both Indian and non-Indian users and then sign a formal agreement.

The standard most often cited for quantifying water rights is "practically irrigable acreage," which of course deals largely with agricultural issues, as opposed to recreational uses or industrial needs such as manufacturing. Among the decisions to be made in determining what this standard means is whether the land is of sufficient quality to maintain crops and whether the cost of supplying water therein is reasonable. To answer these questions requires an analysis of economics, history, and science. The specific amount of water a tribe is entitled to varies with each tribe. For example, the courts or Congress would probably not condone a desert tribe's attempt to use unlimited amounts of water to irrigate a crop that requires huge amounts of water—rice, for example—if the tribe had no prior history of rice cultivation. Furthermore, if the cost of bringing water to a tribe for rice crop irrigation far outweighs whatever economic benefit irrigation might bring the tribe, this large cost factor might prevent quantification of the water rights. Conversely, if a tribe had a history of cultivating fish and growing certain crops, the water needed to sustain both the crops and the fish harvests would be considered in arriving at a quantity of water, even if this may seem unjustified to non-Indian neighbors. It is important to realize that because Native Americans as identifiable economic, political, and social groups predate white settlement in the United States, tribal priority dates are usually much earlier than those of non-Indian settlers and other users of water from the same aquifers, lakes, rivers, and other water sources.

There is no one quantification standard for all uses. To actually determine a quantity is time consuming and expensive and involves a great deal of scientific work. Of course, quantification may mean that a tribe may not have enough water to expand its economic activities beyond what can be sustained by the amount of water negotiated with non-Indian users or imposed by the courts. Unquantified water rights cannot be sold. However, the tribe may have a larger amount of water available for use when the need arises if it chooses not to measure the extent of its water rights. Unfortunately for the tribe, the decision as to whether to quantify or not may be forced upon it, especially if a serious dispute arises between a tribe and a non-Indian water user when both share the same water source.

The Use of Reserved Water

The basic rule under *Winters* is that enough unappropriated water is reserved to the tribe to accomplish the purposes for which the federal reservation was created. In other words, the reasons given by Congress or the president for setting aside the lands, often found in its committee reports, and the language of the laws or executive orders themselves are all important. The purposes for which the reservation was established must be determined for each tribe individually. Not all tribes raised crops and livestock; some depended on fish for their livelihood. To determine what the water on Indian lands may be used for, one must look at the specific reasons the reservation was established, the tribe's past use of water, the express language of the legislation or executive order setting aside the land, and current conditions of the tribe.

In practical terms, however, the courts generally give a wide latitude to tribes in determining the activities for which such waters may be used. Lands were typically set aside to enable Indians to become self-sustaining and "civilized." Of course, tribes may engage in a wide range of activities to become self-sufficient, including logging, fishing, environmental uses, and even recreational uses, such as operating fishing or skiing resorts for profit.

The quantity of water available and its legitimate uses are not without limits, however. The courts have determined that tribes can use only enough water to fulfill the purpose for which the reservation was created. In times of scarcity (which is nearly always for the water-starved West) the courts would probably not allow tribes to recklessly squander water allocations. Even if there might be alternative means to fulfill the purposes of the tribe, it does not necessarily follow that the tribes would have to give up their water rights. In essence, the tribes may use their share of water for any lawful purpose. The key to the *Winters* Doctrine is flexibility. Indian tribes change with the times, just as non-Indian cultures do. For reasons to be discussed later in this entry, relatively few tribes, if any, currently use all of their reserved water.

Jurisdiction over Water Rights Cases

Indian water rights are federal rights and are determined under federal law. Without special federal legislation, disputes over Indian rights would be decided in federal court. In 1952, however, Congress enacted a law allowing disputes over water rights (including those involving Indian rights) to be decided in state courts. It is important to realize that this law did not remove the authority of federal courts to hear such cases. As a result, federal and state courts have what is commonly called concurrent jurisdiction over such cases. This means that either the state or federal courts in a given case may decide the case and that its decision is legally binding on all parties to the case. Even if a state court hears such a case, it must apply federal and not state law in deciding the case because Indian water rights are federal rights. Both the existence of these federal rights and the trust responsibility compel the U.S. government to represent the tribe in state courts in these cases.

This 1952 law, also known as the McCarran Amendment, was something of a setback for Indian rights. State courts have been more hostile to Indian rights, whereas federal courts have been more protective of them. State courts are likely to interpret *Winters* rights more narrowly, perhaps, than would the federal courts. State court judges are generally subject to election by the voters of the district in which they live, whereas federal judges are appointed for life by the president. Only Congress can remove a federal district (trial) judge from office, and it has very rarely done so. As a practical matter, then, federal judges who make unpopular decisions in Indian rights cases or any other case are protected from ultimate removal from office as a result of those decisions.

There seems to be a preference by the federal judiciary to have state courts decide these cases. Generally, the federal courts will not assume responsibility for the case (at the trial level, at least) unless one of the following conditions are met: (1) A state government voluntarily gives up its authority to decide the case. (2) The arguments for and against dismissal of the case in the federal court are about even. (3) The federal case is so far along in the process that it would be wasteful of judicial resources to refer the case to a state court, only to start the case over from the beginning.

Transfer of Water Rights

Generally, tribes are able to transfer (that is, lease or sell) their reserved water rights in conjunction with the lease of reservation lands. Problems usually arise when land allotted to tribal members passes to non-Indians, such as when the land is converted from trust to deeded status. Tribal lands allotted to individual tribal members carry with them all reserved water rights, which of course have a priority date from the date the land was set aside by the federal government for Indian use. The question of exactly what water rights remain attached to former reservation lands acquired by non-Indians has not been fully settled by the courts. At least one court has ruled that a non-Indian purchaser of what was once tribal land also acquires limited *Winters* rights.

On occasion, when tribes and non-Indian water users are able to settle their disputes by agreement, as opposed to litigation, that agreement may contain specific provisions about whom the tribe may sell or lease its unused water rights to. This problem is especially a concern where tribes possess water rights senior to the rights of users who need high volumes of water (for example, large cities such as Denver or Los Angeles). Courts often have to decide these matters. In some instances the tribes are restricted to selling surplus water to specified entities or locations (for example, they might only be allowed to sell to on-reservation users).

Tribes and individual tribal landowners may only sell or lease these rights if the rights have first been quantified; after all, one can only sell or lease what one knows one has. If the rights have not been determined as a specific amount, they cannot be sold or leased. Therefore, Indian water rights that have not been quantified may be less valuable to the tribe.

Tribal Court Jurisdiction over Water Management Issues

Unfortunately for the tribes, it is not at all clear whether it is the tribe or the state that has regulatory authority over water management issues. For many years, the vast majority of water projects, such as irrigation and drinking-water systems, have been built and managed by either the federal or the state governments. The tribes have generally been left out of both the operation of these projects and the settling of any disputes with respect to water usage or system operation.

Further confusing the issue is the passage in the 1970s and 1980s of major water quality legislation by Congress. Congress typically delegates the enforcement of these laws to the states, even for tribal lands located in the state. The general trend of recent court cases, troubling for tribal sovereignty, is to deny tribal oversight of non-Indian water users within an Indian reservation.

Representation of Indian Interests

The federal government, not tribes, holds the legal title to Indian water rights. In addition, the federal government has a long-standing trust responsibility to look out for the best interests of the tribes. Therefore the federal government has the primary responsibility of representing Indian tribes in court whenever these water rights are threatened. History has shown, nonetheless, that the federal government has been less than diligent in adequately representing Indian interests in the courts or otherwise.

The courts have allowed tribes, however, to hire their own lawyers in any case where an Indian tribe believes that their representation by the federal government is less than adequate. As a practical matter, this is not often very helpful to the tribes. Many Indian tribes operate on a very limited budget, and water rights litigation is very time consuming and expensive. Attorneys' fees make up a major portion of the expense of any litigation or negotiations. The lawyers may put in thousands of hours on a case over many years. Despite the fact that the outcomes of such cases are of tremendous importance to any tribe involved, few tribes are in a position to be able to afford counsel.

CONCLUSION

Indian water rights cases will continue to be controversial, especially as competition for water increases in the dry western states. Non-Indians must continue to deal with the fact that Indian tribes often have valuable rights to water, even if the tribes do not use all of the water to which they are entitled. Because these cases tend to be complex, both non-Indian and Indian water users may make greater attempts to negotiate solutions to these questions.

See also **Trust Responsibilities; *Winters* Doctrine**

INDIVIDUAL INDIAN MONEY ACCOUNT

Income from the sale or lease of trust lands allotted to tribal members and money from the sale of timber or other natural resources harvested from these lands are deposited in individual Indian money accounts, also known as IIM accounts. These monies are generally managed by the Bureau of Indian Affairs (BIA) for the benefit of individual tribal members who own an interest in trust lands. Typically, because these lands have such a long history of being fractionalized (that is, of ownership being divided among many people), the lease income accruing to individual tribal members may be less than a few dollars per year. Over several generations, many people inherited an interest in a land parcel, so the lease income spread among many landowners may be small indeed. The BIA has the authority to decide whether or not account owners may withdraw these funds for their own use. In that respect IIM accounts are vastly different from savings accounts, from which the account owner can withdraw funds at will.

IIM accounts are highly controversial because of the way the BIA has managed them: It has admitted that it is unable to fully account for all of the IIM accounts in its care. More than 150,000 IIM accounts exist, together worth more than $100,000,000. As a result of investigations over the handling of these accounts, Congress enacted the American Indian Trust Fund Management Reform Act of 1994 (TFMRA), 25 U.S.C. § 4001 *et seq.* This law is designed to reform the procedures by which the IIM funds are managed and to ensure that they earn a fair rate of interest for the benefit of the account holders. To accomplish that, the Act established an Office of Special Trustee for American Indians. The trustee is aided by a staff of financial experts trained in investment and money management. The trustee's job is to reform the administration of these accounts over a period of time. After that is done, under the terms of the Act, the office will cease to exist.

As part of current congressional policy to give Indian tribes an increasing role in the management of their own affairs, TFMRA also allows a tribe to elect to manage its members' IIM funds itself. Indian tribes did not have this option prior to the passage of this Act.

See also **Fractionalized Interests**

INFRINGEMENT TEST In the absence of federal law concerning a particular issue, courts use the infringement test to determine whether state or tribal courts have jurisdiction over a particular type of civil dispute, that is, action for debts, negligence, land use, and so on. That test was first enunciated in *Williams v. Lee,* 358 U.S. 217 (1959), which concerned a non-Indian merchant trying to collect on a debt owed to him by Indians for goods sold on the Indian reservation.

When a state proposes to regulate an activity occurring on or near Indian country—which means, of course, that the federal government has not already decided to deal with such matters under the Plenary Powers Doctrine—courts must decide whether the tribe or state should oversee the issue in question. The relevant question is whether state regulation would infringe on (or violate) a tribe's right to govern itself. Tribes, as sovereign nations, have a limited right to govern themselves, much as a state or nation does. Without such rights, tribes would cease to exist as effective governments. Any state regulation of matters in Indian country that would tend to violate the tribe's right to self determination is generally not allowed.

Examples of state regulations that would be unlawful in Indian country include the taxation or licensing of retail stores and merchandise located on trust lands; negligence cases arising between Indians in Indian country; and marriages, divorces, and child custody cases concerning tribal members. The key to the infringement test is whether state control of these activities would tend to undermine the authority of tribal courts over reservation matters.

However, the test is not without limitations. Even without federal law on the subject, not all activities that arise in Indian country are immune from state jurisdiction. If the conduct of non-Indians does not affect tribal interests, then it is possible the tribe does not have the authority to deal with the matter. The infringement test has been weakened in recent years. If two non-Indians are involved in a traffic accident on the reservation, for example, the state may exercise jurisdiction over lawsuits stemming from the accident. It would be difficult to say that the tribe does not have an interest in regulating traffic safety of all who travel within reservation borders, but current court decisions give short shrift to tribal interest in such cases as these. Domestic relations (family law) matters where no Indian person is involved might not be tied sufficiently to tribal interests to trigger tribal court jurisdiction.

In recent years, however, there has been some shift away from the infringement test to the preemption test, in which the question of jurisdiction to deal with criminal cases is governed by entirely different rules and which is more restrictive of tribal authority in Indian country. Nonetheless, the infringement test is still used by many courts to decide jurisdictional disputes in civil matters.

See also **Jurisdiction; Preemption; *Williams v. Lee***

INHERENT SOVEREIGNTY The principle of inherent sovereignty, a fundamental Indian law principle created by the courts, holds that those powers of self-government that have not been negotiated or taken away by Congress are retained, or reserved to the tribes. This rule has its origin from the founding of the United States in the late 1700s. At that time, Indian tribes were sovereign nations, with complete powers of self-government and control over their own lands. When the federal government made treaties with these nations, only those rights that were negotiated were changed. The tribes retained all other attributes of self-government not mentioned or discussed in the treaties. This principle is closely related to and a part of the Canons of Construction in Indian law, which hold that uncertain or ambiguous interpretations of treaties, laws, and the like should be interpreted in favor of the tribes. The principle of inherent sovereignty is also closely connected with the Reserved Rights Doctrine but deals more closely with jurisdictional issues over persons and over the particular types of cases that tribal courts can legally hear. Cases concerning "reserved rights," on the other hand, deal with such things as fishing, hunting, and water rights rather than with the power of a tribe to regulate activities in Indian country. Notwithstanding the Canons of Construction, the courts have not always adhered to the inherent sovereignty principles developed over many years of resolving disputes in Indian law cases.

For instance, until recent times inherent self-rule has dictated that Indian tribes have the authority both to define what acts constitute crimes and to try and punish those people who commit crimes on a reservation. Unless a treaty expressly provided that the state or federal government was to deal with these matters (which was rare), criminal matters were handled by a tribe as one of its powers of self-government. Congress, of course, had the power to limit tribal self-government, and it did so from time to time. In criminal justice matters, Congress passed the General Crimes Act of 1948 and the Major Crimes Act of 1885, which eliminated tribal authority over felonies on a reservation, tribal self-rule notwithstanding. Supreme Court cases, until *Oliphant v. Suquamish Indian Tribe,* 435 U.S. 191 (1978), generally followed the inherent sovereignty principle and did not deny the tribes the authority to try and punish non-Indians for misdemeanor crimes committed on a reservation. *Oliphant,* however, reversed course and, ignoring the long-established inherent sovereignty principle, found that tribes could not punish non-Indians for crimes committed on a reservation. This case is a good illustration of the fact that these doctrines of law are subject to change by the U.S. Supreme Court. The more tribes organize their court systems and assert long-dormant powers of self-rule, the more people will raise legal challenges to the Inherent Sovereignty Doctrine.

See also **Canons of Construction; Reserved Rights Doctrine**

INJUNCTION

An injunction is a court order requiring a person to do something, preventing a person from doing something, or ordering a person to discontinue some course of action. A court order may be distinguished from a judgment, which orders a party to a lawsuit to pay money to another person or entity. An injunction does not order one to pay money; rather it orders one to do or not to do a certain thing.

One type of injunction, called a restraining order, orders a person not to have contact with a victim of domestic abuse. Other types of injunctions order someone to stop causing noise in a neighborhood or to stop dumping toxic waste in a landfill. Other recent examples of injunctions have required schools to desegregate, or companies to stop false advertising or to stop infringing on another company's patents.

Many tribes may also have provisions in their legal code allowing their courts to issue injunctions, sometimes in any case and sometimes only in certain types of cases. Except for disputes of an emergency nature, where permanent damages may occur if the injunction is not granted immediately, all parties to a dispute are entitled to due process. This means that they are entitled to a hearing before an impartial judge to determine whether the injunction should be issued. Depending on the specific nature of the problem, injunctions may last for a few weeks or for many years.

IROQUOIS CONFEDERACY Also known as the Iroquois League, this federation of the Mohawk, Onondaga, Seneca, Oneida, and Cayuga Indian tribes was located in the northeastern United States. The league's methods of power sharing predated those of the U.S. government. It was composed of delegates from each tribe who met from time to time in a common council to decide issues of interest to all of the tribes. This confederacy lasted for at least several centuries, dying out during the mid-1700s. Many historians believe that the basic constitutional structure of the U.S. government is taken directly from the structure of the league. The two systems of government have much in common, including delegates elected by their respective tribes, the power to bind member states or tribes to decisions made by a council or congress, and the ability of both to admit new members as the need arose. The U.S. government also incorporated some other features of the league into its own structure, such as provisions for removing someone from office and the separation of military and civil offices.

J

Johnson and Graham's Lessee v. William McIntosh (1823)

Johnson and Graham's Lessee v. William McIntosh, 21 U.S. (8 Wheat.) 543 (1823), was the first of the Trilogy Cases. In this case, the U.S. Supreme Court for the first time discussed the validity of land transfers made by Indian tribes before the American Revolution. Johnson, one of the plaintiffs, possessed a piece of land that Indian tribes had originally sold to various speculators; the land was later sold to Johnson. These Indians sold the land before the Revolution. McIntosh, one of the defendants, received a federal patent, or title, to the same land, which the federal government itself had acquired by treaty after it had defeated the tribes in battle. The Court was called upon to decide who owned the parcel of land, and in doing so, it carefully analyzed and rationalized how the U.S. government came to have the ultimate power to regulate the transfer of Indian lands.

Johnson dealt with the ownership of the land, as opposed to any type of jurisdiction, that is, the power of a government to apply its laws over that land. Moreover, this decision only discussed land title derived directly from the Indian tribes, as opposed to land held pursuant to federal law or executive order. Chief Justice John Marshall, the author of this case, applied the European doctrine of discovery, which holds that the nation that "discovers" so-called uninhabited lands has the ownership rights to it. The Court held that "discovery" of the lands alone gave title, or the right of possession and economic use, to the discoverer. The Court also found that Indian tribes had originally held possession of the land through Indian, or aboriginal, title. Marshall defined the Indian inhabitants as the "rightful occupants of the soil, with a legal and well as just claim to retain possession of it."

However, when such lands were discovered, the tribes of necessity gave up a large portion of their sovereignty, or power of self-rule, to those who discovered the lands. Marshall reasoned that the tribes retained the right of possession of the land, subject to legal title in the discoverer, which in most cases was the U.S. government. One who has legal title to land may sell or otherwise transfer it, while mere possessors usually may not. The tribes therefore could not sell or otherwise dispose of the lands without the approval of the government. Only the discoverer, usually the United States, could extinguish or end the Indian tribes' right of possession of land (which it has done many times by treaty or congressional legislation).

The case dealt only with lands originally held by original Indian title, as opposed to land held by treaties, executive orders, or other federal reservations of land for Indian use. Tribes could not on their own sell land to third parties. It should also be realized that the Court did not question or discuss the morality of divesting Indian tribes of self-rule. Nonetheless, the case is a cornerstone of Indian law, used to "legitimize" American land titles, many of which originated from Native Americans. The case ultimately came down to the fact that according to the doctrine of discovery, a superior show of force was enough to defeat native sovereignty.

See also **Doctrine of Discovery; Trilogy Cases**

JOHNSON-O'MALLEY ACT OF 1934

The federal Johnson-O'Malley Act of 1934, 25 U.S.C. §§ 454–456, was passed during the Indian New Deal of the 1930s to encourage the U.S. government to contract with public and private agencies to provide services to Indians. During this era of Indian-white relations, Indian reformers attempted to reduce the grip the Bureau of Indian Affairs held on virtually every aspect of the lives of reservation Indians. The Johnson-O'Malley Act also meant to help provide educational, medical, and other services to Indians in rural areas, where it was difficult for the federal government to do so. Under the law, the secretary of the interior has great flexibility in contracting with state and local governments, as well as with private institutions, to supply services to Native Americans. An interesting modern provision of this Act gives parents of Indian children in local schools some input into educational decisions made by schools that receive federal funds pursuant to the Act. Local committees of Indian parents have the power to approve or disapprove of school programs funded under the Act. Few other federal programs provide for such a high degree of local control by the citizenry, as opposed to public officials.

JUDGMENT

A judgment is a final order of a court, usually expressed in writing, that directs a person, corporation, or other entity to do or not to do something. A judgment is also a court decision that determines the rights of two or more parties in a lawsuit and ends the dispute. It is the court's final determination of the rights of the parties in matters submitted to it.

Examples of judgments include decisions awarding one person money from another in a small-claims action; evicting a person from a residence for nonpayment of rent, when requested by a landlord; or finding that an insured person is covered by his or her insurance company on a particular claim. In many cases, a person or company dissatisfied with a court's judgment may appeal that decision to a higher court, which will review the case to determine whether the lower (that is, trial) court made the correct decision.

See also **Declaratory Judgment; Judicial Review**

JUDICIAL REVIEW

The term "judicial review" has two primary meanings: first, the appeal of a trial court's decision to a higher court, as allowed by a tribal, state, or federal constitution or statutes; second, the power of the courts to decide whether or not an act of a legislature or public official is unconstitutional and therefore void.

APPEAL OF COURT DECISIONS

Generally speaking, the right to appeal a trial court's decisions is defined by a particular statute or set of statutes that say which types of decisions may be appealed. For instance, certain minor criminal cases or disputes involving small sums of money may not be appealable. Judicial review statutes or constitutional provisions also define the types of cases that may be appealed, the time limits for bringing an appeal, the procedure to follow, and most important, which types of higher courts may hear a particular appeal.

The types of court systems used by each government differ considerably. Small tribes and state governments may have only one level of appeals courts. A person who is dissatisfied with the trial court decision may have only one higher court, typically called a supreme court, to appeal that decision to. Large states and tribes may have a three- or four-tiered appeals court system. For instance, a person appealing a trial court decision in New York State may go through three or more levels of appeals courts before getting to the highest court of New York. Many tribal governments, however, have only one level of appeals courts, if appeals are allowed at all. There is no federal constitutional or statutory requirement that tribes must provide a person the right to appeal either civil or criminal cases to higher tribal courts.

It is important to remember that the right of appeal does not allow for a complete retrial of the case. In the trial court, live witnesses testify, and a judge or jury or both consider various items of evidence, such as documents, photographs, and so on. In the higher (or appellate, as opposed to trial) court, a judge or judges only consider what is called the "cold" record in making a decision. In other words, the appeals court judges review a word-for-word transcript of everything said at the trial, the evidence actually considered by the lower court, and the legal documents filed with the lower court. They do not listen to any live witnesses or consider any new evidence or matters not considered by the trial court. Depending on the rules, the appellate court may or may not hear verbal arguments by the lawyers or parties to the case. The parties usually submit precise, written legal arguments, called briefs, to the court to try to help it reach a decision.

Even though a person, corporation, or other entity (called the appellant) may have appealed to the highest state court, there still may be the possibility of appeal to the federal courts. Certain state court decisions may be reviewed by the federal courts. According to some recent U.S. Supreme Court cases, there are some situations in which a person who is dissatisfied with the decision of the highest tribal court of appeals may appeal that ruling directly to the federal courts.

Appeal of Actions of a Legislative Body or Public Official

There is no statement in the U.S. Constitution—nor in many state or tribal constitutions—that expressly gives the courts the role of interpreting statutes or laws or of reviewing the actions of public officials to determine whether or not they are constitutional. In the earliest days of the United States, the courts did not have this power. The issue first arose in the case of *Marbury v. Madison,* 5 U.S. (1 Cranch) 137, 2 L.Ed. 60 (1803), in which the U.S. Supreme Court asserted its power to review the actions of public officials and the laws passed by the Congress for their constitutionality.

Ultimately, the question of judicial review has been and remains a test of the public's faith in the integrity and fairness of the judicial system. If the president, a state governor, a tribal chairman, or some other public official chooses to ignore a court ruling declaring an action or law to be illegal, there is little the courts themselves can do about it. The courts do not maintain a police or military force. For example, although many public officials disagreed with the courts over the school desegregation decisions of the 1950s and 1960s, they nonetheless obeyed, albeit grudgingly, such court decisions.

Each tribe, whether through laws or court decisions, individually decides the scope and extent of its judicial review. Some tribes may give their courts no power to review actions of the tribal council. Others may have as extensive a review power vested in their courts as exists in the state or federal systems of government. As already noted, federal courts have only limited power to review the decisions of tribal officials and the acts of tribal councils or legislative bodies.

JURISDICTION The term "jurisdiction" refers to the authority by which courts decide cases and have the power to require persons and legal entities such as corporations to obey their decisions. The term also denotes the geographic area over which a government may enforce its laws. There are several types of jurisdiction, some of which are listed as separate articles in this book.

1. *Civil jurisdiction:* the power of a government, through its courts and administrative agencies, to decide civil disputes, such as landlord-tenant cases, contracts, personal injury cases, and so on.
2. *Criminal jurisdiction:* the power of a government, through its courts and law enforcement agents, to apprehend, arrest, and detain persons suspected of committing crimes and to have the courts determine the guilt or innocence of the persons accused of criminal acts.
3. *Subject matter jurisdiction:* the authority of a court to try certain classes of cases. For example, in many states, so-called small-claims courts can try civil cases where the claim does not exceed a certain dollar amount. In criminal matters, traffic or magistrate courts may only have the authority to try misdemeanor cases.
4. *Personal jurisdiction:* the authority of a court to require that the parties to a criminal or civil case abide by its decisions, whether the parties are natural persons or corporations or other business entities. For example, if a court has personal jurisdiction over a person sued in a personal injury case, then once that person (the defendant) is properly served with a notice to appear (also called a summons), he or she is subject to all lawful orders of the court in which the dispute is to be heard. If the defendant fails to obey such orders, he or she could be jailed for contempt of court. If the plaintiff (the person bringing the lawsuit) wins the case, the court can make the defendant pay the plaintiff an amount of money awarded by the court to the plaintiff.
5. *Concurrent jurisdiction:* the authority that one sovereign government may share with another over a particular type of case arising in a given geographic region.
6. *Exclusive jurisdiction:* the power of the courts of one sovereign government alone to decide criminal or civil disputes that arise in a defined geographic region.

Jurisdiction should not be confused with venue. "Jurisdiction" refers to a court's authority to decide a certain type of case or its power to compel persons or entities to abide by its orders and decisions. The term "venue" refers merely to the geographic place where the case is actually tried.

For instance, a state district court may have the authority to try cases in all of the counties the district serves. Many states are divided into one or more districts, and each district may be composed of a number of counties. These district courts have the authority to try all types of cases, both civil and criminal, regardless of the dollar amount of the civil dispute or whether a criminal charge is a felony or misdemeanor. However, state statutes may require that a divorce or other civil case be tried in the county where the defendant lives. It is common in most states for criminal cases to be tried in the county where the crime occurred. The place, or venue, where a case is actually tried is independent, then, of the power of the court to try a particular type of case.

Before a court may make a valid decision in a case, a decision that can be considered binding upon all parties to the controversy, it must have both personal jurisdiction over the parties in the case and subject matter jurisdiction over the type of case to be heard. If either type of jurisdiction is lacking, then the person against whom the judgment or order is directed does not have to obey it. Normally, with regard to personal jurisdiction, a person or legal entity can voluntarily agree to be subject to a particular court for resolution of a dispute. (Such an agreement is also known as a waiver.) For example, if a debtor from tribe A owes money to a creditor located on the Indian reservation of tribe B, the creditor may file a suit in the proper court at tribe B. The debtor may voluntarily agree to be subject to tribe B's power to decide the case, rather than risk being obliged to pay any additional expenses the creditor might incur trying to get jurisdiction over the debtor.

With regard to subject matter jurisdiction, however, only a legislative body, such as a tribal council, may grant its courts the power to try certain types of cases. The parties involved in a case cannot confer subject matter jurisdiction on a court.

See also **Civil Jurisdiction; Concurrent Jurisdiction; Criminal Jurisdiction; Exclusive Jurisdiction**

JUST COMPENSATION CLAUSE The Just Compensation Clause of the Fifth Amendment of the U.S. Constitution requires that any governmental entity or authorized private organization—such as a public utility—pay an owner a fair price for any property taken for public use. In Indian country, the most recent application of the Just Compensation Clause was the Indian Land Consolidation Act of 1982, 25

U.S.C. 2201–2210. Under that Act, tribes tried to take small parcels of land, which generate little income, in order to combine them into larger, economically viable parcels to be used by the tribe, and not the individual members, to further tribal enterprises.

When a government exercises its right of eminent domain (that is, its right to take private property for public use) by "condemning" a parcel of land, any dispute is usually not over whether the property is being used for a legitimate public purpose but, rather, over how much the government should pay the owner for it. The government will negotiate with the owner to try to come up with a mutually agreed fair price for the land. If the two parties cannot agree, then they might submit the dispute over the property's value to a neutral third party, called an arbitrator, who then issues a decision binding on everyone. If the parties cannot come to an agreement and do not submit the dispute to an arbitrator, then a lawsuit becomes necessary. In that case, either a judge or a jury must decide what a fair amount would be for the property. Among the factors a judge or jury considers in arriving at a fair value for the property is its income-producing potential and the recent selling prices of similar parcels in the area.

In Indian country, most proceedings involving just compensation have dealt with land that has been flooded as part of dam building and other water projects or with rights-of-way for public utility services. Some cases arise out of treaty rights, such as, for example, the Sioux Nations' claims to the Black Hills of South Dakota. Although the 1868 Fort Laramie Treaty guaranteed that land to the Indian people, the government eventually opened it up to settlement by non-Indians. The Sioux Nations claimed that the government took (or in effect, condemned) the land by failing to reserve it for the Indian people. In 1980, the U.S. Supreme Court determined that among other things, the Just Compensation Clause of the Fifth Amendment required that the United States compensate the Indian people for the loss of that land.

See also **Eminent Domain; Indian Land Consolidation Act of 1982**

K

KULEANA A kuleana is a small plot of land in Hawaii granted or sold to Native Hawaiians in fee simple. The term "fee simple" means that the owner can sell or otherwise transfer ownership of the land to whomever he or she chooses. Many of these parcels still exist today. These parcels of land are similar in some of their characteristics to allotments held by many Native Americans. Unlike those trust allotments, kuleanas may be subject to mortgages or other liens. However, these fee simple plots are limited in size to land actually cultivated by the Native Hawaiians plus a small plot, no more than a quarter-acre, for a house. Gathering and water rights often came with the ownership of a kuleana.

In response to Western (that is, non–Native Hawaiian) influence, the Land Commission, a government agency of the Hawaiian monarchy, sold these parcels to Native Hawaiians. These lands are often mixed in with the ahupua'a. An ahupua'a is an economically self-sufficient, triangular parcel of land that starts at a point on a mountaintop and runs down to the seashore, spreading base downward. The economic usefulness of the kuleanas (like allotments in Indian country) is reduced by several factors.

First, many of these kuleanas, whose origin dates to the 1850s, have many owners. In other words, the ownership of these plots is fractionalized, that is, divided up among many co-owners. Each owner has the right to use and develop the land, but there is little incentive to do so when the title is so clouded or unclear, making an owner feel that his or her legal interest in the land is only temporary. The great legal expense of clearing the title to the property may be out of proportion to the value of an individual kuleana.

Second, many kuleanas may be accessed only by indirect roads in very poor condition. However, many rights-of-way or easements exist allowing owners to gain or improve access to their kuleana.

Third, since dozens of people might have an ownership in the kuleana, it is likely that none of them has used the land for many years, subjecting it to adverse possession. This means that a nonowner, by occupying the land, might eventually be able to acquire legal title to it. The holdings of large landowners such as developers and sugar plantations might surround the kuleana. Those large landowners might acquire it by adverse possession, either by cultivating this land next to their own or by simply showing that it has not been used by its legal owners for many years. Thus, these large landowners may absorb these plots.

See also **Deeded Lands; Trust Lands**

KULEANA ACT OF 1850 The Kuleana Act of 1850, found at 2 Revised Laws of Hawaii § 2120 *et seq.* (1925 ed.), a law of the territorial legislature of Hawaii, granted fee simple title, access to the mountains and the sea, and water rights to residents of an ahupua'a. The term "fee simple" means that the owner can sell or otherwise transfer ownership of the land to whomever he or she chooses. The Act was meant to make those subdivisions of an ahupua'a, or kuleana, economically viable by allowing the occupants to gather certain materials—such as firewood, wood for houses, and thatch—and to have access to streams. Additionally, the Act also awarded fee simple titles to tenants of these plots. The size was limited to a house lot of up to one-quarter acre plus the land under cultivation by the tenant. The Act still survives, significantly modified by the legislature and the courts. This law helped to establish the riparian water rights doctrine in what is now the State of Hawaii.

See also **Ahupua'a; Kuleana; Riparian Rights**

L

Lacey Act of 1900 (Amendments of 1981)

The federal Lacey Act, 16 U.S.C. §§ 3372(a)(1); 3373(d)(1)(B); and 3378(c)(2,3), helps support the enforcement of tribal hunting and fishing laws. The Lacey Act, as amended in 1981, makes it a federal crime to acquire, sell, or otherwise possess any fish, wildlife, or plant in violation of tribal or federal law. The Act plays an important role in the enforcement of tribal fish and game laws.

Prior to enactment of the 1981 amendments to the Act, tribal courts found it almost impossible to enforce their fish and game ordinances, or any other laws carrying a criminal penalty, against non-Indians. The U.S. Supreme Court, in the case of *Oliphant v. Suquamish Indian Tribe,* 435 U.S. 191 (1978), removed the jurisdiction of tribal courts to try non-Indians for any criminal offenses. Reservations located in most non–Public Law 280 states cannot call upon state authorities for help because many of these states have little or no jurisdiction over criminal offenses in Indian country. A non–Public Law 280 state does not have congressional authority to decide, in its own court system, civil and criminal cases arising in Indian country in that state.

This Act and its 1981 amendments expressly allow federal authorities to prosecute violators of tribal fish and game laws, whether Indian or not, in federal courts. Because the Lacey Act gives the federal courts concurrent jurisdiction with the Indian tribes over these matters, the tribes are not prevented from prosecuting Indian defendants who are accused of violating these laws. Other provisions of the Act make it clear that it does not alter the existing federal-tribal relationship. States do not gain any regulatory jurisdiction over tribal hunting and fishing issues as a result of the passage of the Lacey Act or its 1981 amendments.

Legal Services Corporation

The Legal Services Corporation (LSC) is a federally chartered (organized) corporation that oversees the operation of offices throughout the United States providing basic legal services for those low-income individuals who need but are unable to afford them. Many offices serve primarily minority clients, such as Native American, Hispanic, and black individuals. However, these legal services are provided on the basis of the client's income, assets, and debts, not race.

The types of cases these offices handle include (1) landlord-tenant disputes; (2) denial of welfare or other benefits to an individual by a federal, state, or local agency; (3) criminal cases in tribal, state, or local courts for defendants who cannot afford to hire their own lawyers; and (4) at some offices, divorce and other domestic relations (family law) cases. Some cases that these offices have dealt with resulted in major changes in federal or state law.

Each office employs one or more attorneys, secretaries, paralegals, and other staff members. Before taking a case, the local office must first determine whether the client's income makes him or her eligible for legal assistance and whether that office handles the type of problem the client has. Many of the offices are located on or near Indian reservations and are popularly known as the "legal aid" office.

The U.S. Congress regularly makes an appropriation to fund the LSC. The LSC then uses a formula to determine how much money each office or program will get for the next year. For budgetary and philosophical reasons, the LSC limits the types of cases local staff attorneys may accept. For instance, they cannot take most personal injury cases against a private person or lawsuits against a tribe. Because of very heavy caseloads, some offices will not take divorce or child custody cases. In recent years, the funding of the LSC has often become quite politicized, with both political parties using the hearings on funding to enunciate their philosophy on welfare and related topics.

***Lone Wolf v. Hitchcock* (1903)** In *Lone Wolf v. Hitchcock*, 187 U.S. 553 (1903), the U.S. Supreme Court ruled that Congress could change or abolish treaties without the consent of the Indian tribe affected. *Lone Wolf* concerned a treaty concluded between the United States and the Kiowa and Comanche Tribes. As was typical of the treaty process, the tribes agreed under certain conditions to relinquish lands to the United States in return for certain benefits. One section of the treaty provided that before these lands would be opened up for white settlement, three-fourths of all adult men living on the reservation had to agree that the land could be opened. Some years later, pursuant to the treaty, more than 400 Indian men purportedly signed such an agreement. Some tribal members alleged fraud by the government in securing Indian agreement to opening the land. Congress passed a law to abrogate the treaty—there was considerable disagreement as to whether the signatures supporting changes to the treaty were fraudulently obtained—and the law was then put into effect.

The question was whether Congress could unilaterally change the terms of a treaty without the approval of the other party to that treaty—the Kiowa and Comanche Indian Tribes, in this case. The Supreme Court held that Congress may unilaterally cancel or modify treaties without the approval of the Indian tribes. The Court based its decision on earlier court decisions that held that Indian tribes are in effect "domestic dependent nations"—without full political independence such as that possessed by foreign nations. As such, the tribes are dependent on the government for their protection, and in some cases for their sustenance. Therefore, according to the Court, Congress had complete, or plenary, authority to decide what was in the "best interests" of the Indian tribe.

The *Lone Wolf* decision is still binding today. Its significance for present times is that it weakened the Indian tribes' ability to use the treaties to hold the U.S. government accountable for its conduct with regard to the preservation of tribal resources such as land and natural resources. Congress, therefore, can change any term of a treaty or abolish it entirely, without the approval of the tribe so affected.

See also **Plenary Powers Doctrine; Treaty**

***Lyng v. Northwest Cemetery Protective Association* (1988)** In *Lyng v. Northwest Cemetery Protective Association*, 485 U.S. 439 (1988), the U.S. Supreme Court denied protection against commercial and recreational intrusion on lands considered sacred in Native American religious beliefs. The *Lyng* case concerned the proposed construction of a forest service road across public lands considered holy by several northern California Indian tribes. The lower federal courts found that the construction of the road would seriously impair or destroy tribal members' ability to practice their religion. According to the trial court, the proposed road would cut across forest service lands considered sacred for many centuries and used for hundreds of years for religious ceremonies by area Indian tribes. The lower tribunal also found that there were no other ancestral lands available that were of a comparable spiritual value to the area's Indian people.

At the time the U.S. Forest Service was planning the road, Congress had already enacted the American Indian Religious Freedom Act of 1978, 42 U.S.C. § 1996, which required federal agencies to take American Indian religious practices into consideration when developing land use policies in areas of importance to Native Americans. Unlike many laws, this Act was merely a joint resolution of Congress; that is, it was an expression of Congress's feelings on the subject of Native American spirituality. At that time, there were no powers of enforcement in the statute.

Despite the feelings of Congress on such issues and despite the findings of the lower courts, the Supreme Court in the *Lyng* case declined to require the government to show a compelling government interest in construction of the roadway. Generally, under the First Amendment's freedom of religion guarantees, the government must show a compelling reason why it should be able to do something that would have the effect of preventing a person or group from practicing its religion. For example, if a state outlaws drugs, and a group uses drugs as a sacrament in its religious rites, the state would need to show a court some strong reason why it should outlaw those drugs, since that would prevent the group from practicing its faith. Generally, the courts have found that states have a compelling interest in maintaining the health and safety of their citizens. Therefore, banning the use or sale of certain drugs does not violate a person's constitutional freedom to practice his or her religion, even if certain groups may be restricted by the state's action. This is called, in legal terms, a "balancing test": The rights, interests, or needs of the government are weighed against those of the citizens.

Unfortunately for the tribes, the majority of the justices in the *Lyng* decision were not convinced that building the road would, in fact, prevent them from practicing their religion. Therefore, the Court never applied the balancing test to determine whether the government's need for the road was compelling. Despite the Forest Service's victory, they never built the road. However, the *Lyng* decision remains today as a serious impediment to Indians who challenge government actions that may interfere with the practice of their religion.

See also **American Indian Religious Freedom Act of 1978**

M

MAJOR CRIMES ACT OF 1885

The Major Crimes Act (MCA) of 1885, 18 U.S.C. § 1153, is one of the primary laws granting federal courts the power to try Indian defendants for certain major crimes (felonies) enumerated in the Act. Among the specific offenses covered under the Act are murder, rape, aggravated assault, burglary, robbery, and certain other offenses committed against persons under 16 years of age.

Some commentators have suggested that this law was passed in response to public outcry over the U.S. Supreme Court's decision in *Ex Parte Crow Dog*, 109 U.S. 556 (1883), which held that tribes have the sole authority to punish any crimes committed in Indian country by one Indian against another. Other critics believe that the Act resulted from a campaign by the Bureau of Indian Affairs to extend federal authority on Indian reservations. Over the years, the number of crimes covered under the Act has grown from seven to more than a dozen.

The Act only applies when the defendant is Indian, although the victim may be Indian or non-Indian. However, there are a number of different definitions of the term "Indian" in various federal laws, and the lower federal courts have not agreed upon a definition of who is Indian for the purposes of this law. (The MCA itself does not define the term.) The general rule is that the defendant must be enrolled in a tribe that is federally recognized at the time of the crime, must have some percentage of Indian blood, or perhaps, must be considered to be Indian by the local Native American community. The factors that must be present for the Act to apply are these: (1) The crime is one listed in the MCA, (2) it was committed in Indian country, and (3) the accused is Indian.

At first glance, the Act appears to strip the tribes of any power to try these cases. However, under the doctrine of inherent sovereignty, tribes still have the authority to punish Indians for committing these acts, if their own laws provide for punishment. Tribes have concurrent jurisdiction (that is, joint jurisdiction) with the federal government to punish Indians for these offenses. However, the Indian Civil Rights Act of 1968 as subsequently amended limits the maximum penalty that tribes could mete out to Indians to one year in jail and a $5,000 fine for each offense. As a practical matter, then, tribes have limited ability to punish those who commit crimes within their territory, the MCA and tribal sovereignty notwithstanding.

Recent studies suggest that the incidence of serious crimes on Indian reservations is on the increase. Although under the MCA, tribes share some authority with the federal government in the punishment of serious crime on a reservation, most Indian nations are not in a position to adequately address these concerns. Although the Double Jeopardy Clause of the U.S. Constitution does not prevent both federal and tribal prosecutions for the same offense, some federal officials assign the prosecution of these crimes a low priority. Non–Public Law 280 states are powerless to prosecute these offenses, unless both the defendant and victim are non-Indian. Alaska, California, Minnesota, Nebraska, Oregon, and Wisconsin are the states that Congress, in enacting PL 280, has allowed to assume criminal and civil jurisdiction over people and activities arising on some or all of the Indian reservations within those states. A fine and a year in jail (if a tribe even maintains a jail) is inadequate punishment for serious offenses. Therefore, it is possible that a person subject to the MCA may never be prosecuted at all.

See also **Blood Quantum; Indian**

MANKILLER, WILMA PEARL (1945–) Wilma Pearl Mankiller, the principal chief of the Cherokee Nation of Oklahoma, is the first woman to head a large Indian tribe. Born on the Cherokee Indian Reservation in Oklahoma, she was raised in California, where her family moved pursuant to the post–World War II federal Indian relocation program. While in college, Mankiller became an activist, championing Indian causes, notably Indian self-determination. She eventually made this her life's work and moved back to Oklahoma. Despite great personal adversity, Mankiller was elected the deputy chief, and in 1985 she became the chief executive (principal chief) of the Cherokee Nation.

***MCCLANAHAN V. ARIZONA STATE TAX COMMISSION* (1973)** *McClanahan v. Arizona State Tax Commission*, 411 U.S. 164 (1973), is the last of three U.S. Supreme Court cases dealing with the authority of a state to extend its civil jurisdiction to the Navajo Indian Reservation. The State of Arizona withheld income taxes from the paycheck of Rosalind McClanahan, a Navajo living on the reservation. At the time of this case, she earned all of her income on the reservation. Although in earlier times, the U.S. Supreme Court was often all that stood between Indians and unfriendly state governments, *McClanahan* is part of a trend toward weakening the legal test courts use to determine whether or not, absent congressional approval, states may assume civil or criminal jurisdiction over Indian lands.

Williams v. Lee, 358 U.S. 217 (1959), also involved the authority of the state in matters arising in Indian country. That case involved a non-Indian trader who tried to collect a debt in state court against a Navajo couple who bought goods from him on the reservation. The *Williams* Court fashioned an "infringement test," which asked, absent federal law, whether the "state action [suing in state court over a reservation transaction] infringed on the rights of reservation Indians to make their own laws and be ruled by them." This test was generally supportive of Indian rights, inasmuch as most activities that occurred on the reservation tended to tip the balance of power toward tribal and against state jurisdiction. *Williams* still generally followed the rule first enunciated in *Worcester v. Georgia,* 31 U.S. (6 Pet.) 515 (1832). *Worcester* held that, absent federal law, states have no authority over activities arising in Indian country.

After reviewing treaties and applicable federal laws, the *McClanahan* Court ruled in favor of the Navajo Nation, finding that the state had no jurisdiction to tax income earned by Indians on the reservation. Despite the victory for tribal sovereignty in this case, however, the ruling represented a considerable weakening of Indian self-rule. The *McClanahan* Court ruled in favor of the Navajo Nation not because of a concept of inherent tribal sovereignty, as was first stated in *Worcester* more than a century earlier, but, rather, because a scheme of federal laws and treaties preempted state taxation over activities on the reservation. In other words, after *McClanahan,* when the Court allocates power between the tribes and the states over reservation activities, it no longer asks only what inherent rights of self-government a tribe might have to surrender. Additionally, it asks whether or not federal regulation is so extensive that states are precluded from regulating the same matters the federal government is involved in.

When adjudicating state-tribe conflicts, the Court is no longer primarily concerned with what part of tribal powers of self-government (which all nations possess) a tribe gave up to the federal or state government. Instead, the Court now looks to see how pervasive federal regulation is in the area that the state seeks to control. This is the preemption test, which is still in use. What powers does the federal government permit a tribe or state to exercise in Indian country? The courts place far less emphasis on the natural right of a tribe, as a nation, to govern itself.

See also **Infringement Test; Preemption; *Williams v. Lee; Worcester v. Georgia***

MERIAM REPORT OF 1928 The Meriam Report, concluded in 1928, reported the results of a survey carried out at the request of the secretary of the interior. This was the first comprehensive survey by the federal government of the health, economic, political, and cultural conditions of the American Indians on reservations. It is important because it provided valuable historical data on the Native Americans of that era. By making public the poor conditions suffered by many Native Americans, the report helped bring about the passage of the landmark Indian Reorganization Act of 1934 and greater respect for Indian culture.

See also **Indian Reorganization Act of 1934**

***MONTANA V. UNITED STATES* (1981)** In *Montana v. United States,* 450 U.S. 544 (1981), the U.S. Supreme Court defined the extent to which tribes could regulate non-Indian activities on privately owned land within the reservation. Although this case concerned the ownership of a riverbed running through a reservation, its most significant feature is that it severely reduced inherent tribal sovereignty by limiting the extent to which tribes may regulate the conduct of non-Indians on the reservation.

The *Montana* case considered whether an Indian tribe could regulate hunting and fishing activities of nonmembers (Indian or non-Indian) on land they owned in fee. The term "in fee" means that the owner can sell or otherwise transfer ownership of the land to whomever he or she chooses. This decision, in concert with *Oliphant v. Suquamish Indian Tribe,* 435 U.S. 191 (1978), ignored and reversed the Canons of Construction (rules to guide courts in their interpretation of treaties and federal laws) and the accepted principles of inherent tribal sovereignty. Decades of earlier court cases had found that under the principles of inherent tribal sovereignty, tribes retain all those powers of self-rule not expressly taken from them by act of Congress.

The *Montana* Court found that because Congress never explicitly granted the tribe the power to regulate the hunting and fishing activities on non-Indian-owned private lands within a reservation, the tribe had no power to do so. This amounts to a reversal of the long-accepted judicial doctrine of inherent sovereignty. Now, under the *Montana* decision, in order for a tribe to exercise civil authority over the activities of non-Indians on private lands within a reservation, it must prove one of two things: (1) It may show that the private landowner entered into some voluntary relationship with the tribe. An example of this would be the acquisition of a tribal license to do business on the reservation or the signing of a contract or lease with the tribe itself or a tribal member. (2) Or it may show that some important tribal interest is involved in the regulation of activities on this type of land. The tribe must prove that such regulation is necessary to protect the health or economic welfare of tribal members or to preserve the political integrity of the tribe. For instance, the tribe might want to regulate or restrict the activities of a non-Indian building a garbage dump or construction business on land surrounded by Indian farming or ranching enterprises.

Before *Montana,* the burden was usually on the private landowner to prove that the tribe lacked the power to regulate these matters. Now, inherent tribal sovereignty notwithstanding, the tribe must prove that it has the power to regulate the civil conduct of non-Indians. Perhaps implicit in the Court's decision is its skepticism that tribes possess the ability to meaningfully regulate such conduct.

See also **Canons of Construction; Inherent Sovereignty; *Oliphant v. Suquamish Indian Tribe***

MORTON V. MANCARI (1974)

In *Morton v. Mancari,* 417 U.S. 535 (1974), the U.S. Supreme Court ruled that the Bureau of Indian Affairs (BIA) could give an employment hiring and promotional preference to members of a federally recognized Indian tribe over non-Indians. Several non-Indian BIA employees brought a lawsuit on behalf of themselves and other non-Indian BIA employees alleging that such preferences were repealed by federal equal opportunity statutes and that such preferences also violated their due process rights under the Fifth Amendment to the U.S. Constitution.

The Court reasoned that Congress had given Indians some preference in hiring in the Indian service (the BIA) for more than a century pursuant to federal statutes and executive orders. The preference at issue in *Morton* was that enacted by Congress in 1934 as part of the Indian Reorganization Act (IRA). The policy of Congress, as set forth in the IRA, was to establish a mechanism by which Indian tribes would assume an increasing responsibility to govern and manage their own affairs, both politically and economically.

In the 1930s (and to a slightly lesser extent today), the BIA wielded tremendous authority and influence over the daily lives of the Indian people. Congress felt that it was important, through BIA employment, to give Indian people an even greater voice in the management of their own affairs. From the beginnings of the BIA in the 1820s to the 1970s, the agency was staffed at all levels largely by non-Indians. According to the Court, Congress wanted Indian people to run the agency that dominated their own lives.

The Court upheld these preferences with respect to the BIA and indirectly with respect to tribal governments and private businesses on or near reservations. The Court ruled that federal equal opportunity laws contained specific exemptions that would allow preferential treatment for Indians in these areas of employment.

The BIA employees also claimed that such special treatment for Indians violated their constitutional right not to be subject to "reverse discrimination" on account of race. The Court rested its decision to allow Indian hiring preferences in this case largely on the Indian Commerce Clause of the U.S. Constitution. That clause gives Congress the right to regulate Indian affairs. Additionally, the *Morton* decision found that such preferences were not racially based, that is, based on whether a person was Indian or non-Indian. Instead, the Court held that the preferences were based on a political relationship between tribal governments and the federal government, a relationship that is as old as the United States itself. The Court decided that such employment preferences within the BIA were tied rationally to Congress's intent to strengthen tribal government.

The significance of this case is that the Supreme Court, in the face of increasing protections against both public and private employment discrimination, specifically upheld certain laws actually permitting special employment treatment for a certain group of individuals, that is, Indians. However, no other ethnically distinct group of people in the United States has a distinct political relationship, as sovereign to sovereign, with the U.S. government. Nor does this case grant Indians employment preference in any other federal governmental agency. Other federal legislation and court cases have granted some additional limited preferences to Indians in the context of contracting to provide goods or services to the BIA or tribal entities.

See also **Indian Preference**

MORTON V. RUIZ (1974) In *Morton v. Ruiz,* 415 U.S. 199 (1974), the U.S. Supreme Court ruled that the Bureau of Indian Affairs (BIA) must give some public notice before limiting welfare benefits to members of a federally recognized tribe. In the *Ruiz* case, the BIA denied Ramon Ruiz, a member of an Indian tribe, subsistence benefits because he did not live on his home reservation, even though he only lived 15 miles away. *Ruiz* had the effect, in many cases, of requiring federal agencies offering programs to Indians to formally publish rules of eligibility through the Administrative Procedures Act of 1946, a time-consuming process. In this particular case, however, the Court found that the internal BIA rule that denied benefits to off-reservation tribal members was invalid because the BIA had failed to follow its own procedures for publishing such notice. Additionally, according to the *Ruiz* decision, the

BIA had continually told Congress that off-reservation Indians were provided benefits from congressional appropriations.

A later court decision, *Lincoln v. Vigil*, 508 U.S. 182 (1993), retreated somewhat from the *Ruiz* decision that changes in eligibility requirements must be published. However, *Ruiz* remains somewhat important today, if only to serve notice to such agencies as the BIA that they must abide by their own rules and be more aware of their trust responsibilities toward their clientele.

N

National Congress of American Indians

The National Congress of American Indians (NCAI), an early Indian rights advocacy organization, was founded in 1944 in an attempt to counter a growing movement in the U.S. Congress to end the special federal, or trust, relationship between the government and Indian nations. The NCAI has grown from an organization of about 100 people to more than 250 federally recognized American Indian and Native Alaskan tribal organizations. Along with a number of other Indian rights advocacy groups, the NCAI seeks to promote federal programs for Indian education, health care, and economic development. It also works for the preservation of native American treaty rights, cultures and religions, and natural resources, among other issues. To accomplish these goals, the NCAI lobbies federal policy makers on issues important to Native Americans and produces a number of publications to keep its members and the general public informed on Indian rights issues.

National Farmers Union Insurance Companies v. Crow Tribe of Indians (1985)

National Farmers Union Insurance Companies v. Crow Tribe of Indians, 471 U.S. 845 (1985), a major U.S. Supreme Court case, determined the extent of federal court review of tribal court decisions. The case that triggered the appeal process involved a personal injury on the Crow Indian Reservation in Montana. A tribal member sued a school on the reservation for injuries he received there. The school was a political subdivision of the state, and 85 percent of the student body were tribal members. The defendant school failed to respond to the summons, and as a result, the Crow Tribal Court awarded the plaintiff monetary damages. The tribal court had an appellate court available to review lower-court decisions, but it was not used in this case.

The insurance company for the school sued the tribe in federal district court, alleging that the tribal court had no jurisdiction, that is, authority, to decide a case arising out of a personal injury that concerned a state agency. As a general rule, tribes exercising their powers as sovereign nations have the authority to settle disputes that arise on their reservations, whether or not one of the parties is non-Indian. There are some exceptions to this, however. The Supreme Court, in deciding this case, found that tribal governments, as sovereign nations, must be given the first opportunity to decide the question of jurisdiction.

The Court reasoned that to allow dissatisfied litigants to immediately contest all decisions of tribal courts in federal courts without going through the tribal court appeals process would contravene Congress's policy of Indian self-determination. Although under the Plenary Powers Doctrine, federal courts and Congress have the right to define the scope of tribal court jurisdiction, the *National Farmers* Court decided that dissatisfied parties to a tribal court case must first "exhaust tribal remedies" before asking the federal courts to review a case. This means that an unhappy tribal court litigant must appeal the case up to the highest appeals court of a tribe before he or she will be allowed to file the case in a federal district court for review. Only if the tribal court has no appellate court available or for one of several other very limited reasons may a party ask the federal district court to directly review the case. The Supreme Court also reasoned that full tribal court judicial review would make for a more detailed record for the federal courts to examine.

NATIONAL INDIAN GAMING COMMISSION The federal agency that regulates much of the gaming on Indian reservations in the United States is the National Indian Gaming Commission (NIGC). The NIGC came into existence when Congress passed the Indian Gaming Regulatory Act of 1988, 25 U.S.C. §§ 2701–2721. Under the terms of this law, games of chance other than those that are traditional to an Indian tribe come under the regulation of the NIGC. The NIGC is composed of three members, two of whom must be members of a federally recognized tribe. The commissioners serve for three-year terms and may only be removed by the U.S. president or secretary of the interior, and only for a good reason, such as neglect of duties, fraudulent conduct, and so on. The NIGC's primary goal is to help assure that Indian gaming does not fall under the control of organized crime, which was of great concern to Congress when it passed the Indian Gaming Regulatory Act.

The major duties of the commission are to investigate the fitness of applicants to either work in or manage gaming operations for Indian tribes. The NIGC must also review and approve the terms of management contracts that tribes offer to persons hired to run these operations. Additionally, the NIGC may inspect and otherwise monitor Indian gaming operations to ensure that they comply with applicable federal laws. To finance its activities and those of its staff, the NIGC assesses fees to be paid by those gaming operations under its authority.

See also **Indian Gaming Regulatory Act of 1988**

NATIVE AMERICAN GRAVES PROTECTION AND REPATRIATION ACT OF 1990

The federal Native American Graves Protection and Repatriation Act (NAGPRA) of 1990, 25 U.S.C. §§ 3001–3013, offers some protection to the human remains, burial objects, and other items associated with funeral rites that were (and are) conducted by native peoples in what is now the United States.

BACKGROUND

Prior to the enactment of NAGPRA, most states and the federal government accorded little respect or human dignity to the remains of the ancestors of the native peoples (American Indians, Native Hawaiians, and Native Alaskans) in what is now the United States, as evidenced by the fact that many museums, scientific organizations, and private and public collections of Native Americana contained both human remains and related artifacts dealing with burial ceremonies.

Some of the organizations that acquired these items came by them though fraud or outright theft from Indian burial grounds. Even if nineteenth-century official federal policy did not encourage grave robbing, it at least condoned such conduct by its agents or private citizens. Until the latter half of the twentieth century, few, if any, states had laws that dealt with the sanctity of Indian human remains. Many people then held notions of racial superiority and did not regard Indians, let alone Indian deceased, as fully human. Indians, both dead and alive, at best were treated as scientific curiosities. Especially in the nineteenth century, Indian remains and burial artifacts were treated as oddities; some were part of circus "freak shows." The remains of white people were not subjected to the same lack of simple respect.

The common law of England, carried over to the United States, accorded dignity and respect to the remains of non-Indian peoples. Even those persons who died as paupers were often given a simple funeral ceremony, and state or local governments often provided a grave marker. Under these funerary laws, the remains of non-Indians could only be exhumed, or dug up, for compelling reasons, such as to rebury the person in another location or to perform scientific tests either to identify the remains or to try to solve a criminal case. The law did not extend such regard for the inherent dignity of human remains to native peoples, however. Some archaeologists and other scientists who learned about a culture from its past displayed a shocking insensitivity to the cultural mores of native peoples. Although museums and other organizations do serve a valuable role in educating the public about the history of native communities, many of these groups may have no idea how the remains and funerary objects they display were initially obtained from native burial grounds.

To balance the needs of scientific inquiry with the dignity of the human past, a number of states have passed legislation protecting unmarked burial sites, and a few have passed some sort of repatriation legislation. (Repatriation is the process by which the remains of a person and related objects are returned to his or her relatives, tribe, or other native organization.)

In the late 1980s, it was discovered that the Smithsonian Institution, a collection of federally operated museums and scientific research organizations, had acquired more than 18,000 human remains over many years. Grave robbing for commercial and scientific purposes was a fairly common practice in the nineteenth century, and the practice lasted well into the twentieth century. Increased public awareness and indignation over such affronts to the dignity of human remains led Congress to enact the National Museum of the American Indian Act of 1989, 20 U.S.C. §§ 80q1–80q15, also known as the Museum Act. For the first time at the national level, this law made the Smithsonian Institution accountable to Native Americans for its continued possession of such items. The Museum Act required the Smithsonian to inventory its holdings and to return remains and other funerary objects to the known descendants or to the Indian tribe or other native organization to which they belonged. Many native organizations have special reburial ceremonies for remains that are returned to them.

PASSAGE OF THE ACT

NAGPRA was passed shortly after the enactment of the Museum Act. NAGPRA has several features that distinguish it from most state laws on the subject of the identification and return of human remains and funerary objects. Its scope is fairly broad, for it applies to all museums, colleges, and universities that receive *any* federal funding and that might have human remains or funerary objects associated with Native Alaskan, Native American, or Native Hawaiian peoples. The federal funding criterion alone is enough to bring nearly every such institution within the Act's scope, since few exist today that do not receive federal monies to pay for some aspect of their operations. However, NAGPRA does not apply to the Smithsonian Institution because that agency is dealt with under the Museum Act just discussed.

NAGPRA is one of the few federal enactments in the field of Indian law that deals with all native peoples of the United States, whether they be of American Indian, Native Alaskan, or Native Hawaiian origin. The Department of the Interior is the main federal agency charged with the enforcement of the Act. Normally, the Department of the Interior deals with American Indian issues, and it often considers Native Alaskan issues. Rarely (though the trend is increasing) does it concern itself with Native Hawaiian issues.

The Act also applies to archaeological digs or any other work that may involve the moving or excavating of earth on federal and tribal lands. The law applies to all tribal lands, whether privately held or not. Some reservations have large tracts of land within their borders that are not owned in trust for a tribe or its members and that may be privately owned by non-Indians. Such privately held land is still covered under the Act.

On its face, NAGPRA does not apply to privately held lands located outside Indian country. For example, non-Indians may, over the years, have acquired lands that are not on a reservation and that no longer have any connection to an Indian community. The land's geographic area may have no remaining economic or cultural ties with an Indian tribe or community. Land that is no longer considered to be Indian country is not subject to the terms of this Act. (The question of whether a particular parcel of land is considered to be "Indian country" often carries with it legal and economic implications and may need to be settled in the courts.) Any other federally owned land—such as national forests or parks, military bases, or other federal installations—is within the purview of the Act whether or not it has any connection to Native Americans of any origin.

Most land in the United States is owned by state and local governments or private individuals and organizations and does not come within the scope of NAGPRA. Some critics see this as a major shortcoming of NAGPRA. For instance, a developer building a hotel on privately owned land may have no obligations under NAGPRA to identify and preserve any Native human remains found there. Even an archaeologist specifically looking for ancient human remains on private land outside of Indian country has no obligation to report a find. As a practical matter, however, if the human remains and associated funerary objects find their way to a museum or other organization to which the Act applies, that entity must notify the affected tribe. A state law might deal with these situations, but NAGPRA does not.

The Act requires several things of covered organizations. First, any organization that may have human remains or artifacts associated with native burial rights must inventory those items and make reasonable attempts to ascertain their origin. NAGPRA does not require the holders of such remains to undertake new scientific studies to do this. The museum or other organization may use any and all existing records and documentation to do the inventory. Second, the organization must notify any Indian, Native Alaskan, or Native Hawaiian organization shown to have a connection to the remains and other items. The native organization may then request and receive the human remains and associated items for reburial according to the group's customs. The descendants of the person, as well as the native organization, may claim the remains.

The Act also established a review committee, composed of representatives of native organizations who are appointed by the secretary of the interior, to oversee the inventory, identification, and repatriation process and to attempt to mediate any resulting disputes between the parties. In other words, if an institution covered under NAGPRA refuses to return a person's remains, the person's descendants or Native American group may appeal to this committee. If the parties cannot reach an agreement, they may file a lawsuit to settle the issue.

When any remains or associated objects are discovered on federal or tribal lands, either by accident or as the result of an archaeological dig, the work must stop until an investigation is made. If the remains may be culturally affiliated with a particular native group, the group must be consulted before the work may continue. If no agreement can be reached about the conditions for continuing or stopping the work, a court may be called upon to make a decision. Even though this may pose a hardship to those conducting activities on federal or tribal lands, the NAGPRA nevertheless shows a strong interest on the part of the federal government to protect the dignity of the deceased.

This Act has not been without controversy, however. There have been disputes between museums and tribes over the issue of returning human remains and funerary objects. Some museums, colleges, and universities have had these items in their collections for decades. Other groups who possess human remains claim they are needed for scientific study. Conversely, Indian tribes and other native organizations claim that proper respect for the dead, long accorded to the remains of non-Indians, should now be given to native cultures. Although many disputes can be settled through negotiation, other cases require the courts to make a decision. NAGPRA is one more step toward increasing recognition by the U.S. government that Indian people are more than just curiosities of a bygone era.

See also **Alaska Native Claims Settlement Act of 1971; Hawaii Homes Commission Act of 1921; Indian Country; Native Hawaiian**

NATIVE AMERICAN RIGHTS FUND The Native American Rights Fund (NARF) is a nonprofit legal organization whose objective is to defend and promote the legal rights of Indian individuals and tribal organizations. Founded in 1970 and based in Boulder,

Colorado, NARF provides legal representation to Indian individuals and tribes in several areas: (1) the protection of tribal natural resources, (2) Indian self-determination, (3) religious freedom, and (4) human rights issues. NARF also lobbies for the passage of legislation that respects the legal, political, and cultural rights of Native Americans. Through negotiation or litigation, NARF attempts to hold state and federal governments accountable to Native American groups for promises made to them either by treaty or legislation. NARF also publishes a newsletter and maintains an Indian legal reference library.

NATIVE HAWAIIAN A Native Hawaiian is a descendant of the aboriginal people who, prior to 1778, occupied and exercised sovereignty in what is now the State of Hawaii. The precise definition of a Native Hawaiian depends on the purpose for which the definition is being used. For example, the State of Hawaii Office of Hawaiian Affairs defines a Native as "any descendant of not less than one half part of the races occupying the Hawaiian Islands prior to 1778." The Hawaii state law that deals with subsistence hunting and fishing defines a Native Hawaiian thus: "any descendant of the races occupying the Hawaiian Islands prior to 1778." Some federal laws, such as the Native American Graves and Repatriation Act of 1990, define a Native Hawaiian as one who "is a descent of the peoples who, prior to 1778, have occupied and exercised sovereignty over what is now the state of Hawaii." The term "Native American" is also a fluid one with no single, exact meaning. Again, one must look to the purpose for defining that term as well. Like Alaska Natives and American Indians, cultural ties to families, ancestors, and the land form a part of the Native Hawaiian identity. Under current federal Indian law, the United States does not have a trust responsibility toward Native Hawaiians. No federal agency currently recognizes Native Hawaiian groups as political entities with powers of self-government. However, Native Hawaiians are slowly being included in more federal legislation dealing with Indian issues, however. One example is the Native American Graves Protection and Repatriation Act of 1990, 25 U.S.C. §§ 3001–3013. This law provides that cultural artifacts associated with the funeral rites of America's native peoples be returned from museums and other places to the families of the deceased or to the native groups to which they belonged. As public awareness of Native Hawaiian efforts to obtain self-determination and sovereignty increases, the definition of Native Hawaiian will take on increased importance. The federal population census taken in 2000 included, for the first time, an ethnic category for Native Hawaiians.

See also ***Rice v. Cayetano***

NATIVE HAWAIIAN STUDY COMMISSION

In 1980 Congress established the Native Hawaiian Study Commission (NHSC) in response to the movement by Native Hawaiian leaders to secure money for lost lands and a restoration of the political power of Native Hawaiians. The officially stated purpose of the NHSC was to study the culture, needs, and concerns of Native Hawaiians.

Native Hawaiians lost much of their lands and self-rule when prominent American residents of Hawaii, with the help of the U.S. government, overthrew the Hawaiian monarchy in 1893. Congress did not mention the events of 1893 when it created the commission, undoubtedly to avoid any legal responsibility for possible reparations owed the native peoples. However, a reading of the legislative history of the law creating the panel suggests that the NHSC was to inquire into the extent of the federal government's involvement in the 1893 overthrow of the Hawaiian monarchy.

President Jimmy Carter appointed the nine members of the NHSC, three of whom were from Hawaii. One can only speculate as to why a commission created to study local conditions in Hawaii had so few members from that state. The commission held a number of hearings and took testimony and written statements from hundreds of people. In 1983 the commission issued its final report, and the non-Hawaiian majority found that the U.S. government was without blame in the overthrow of the monarchy. The Hawaiian members prepared a minority report that disputed these findings.

Later historical analysis questioned the validity of the commission's majority report. But despite the problems associated with the final report, the data the commission compiled helped give the public a more complete picture of the educational, health, and social service needs of Native Hawaiians. To this day, Native Hawaiians still work toward regaining a measure of self-determination for their people.

NATIVE TOWNSITE

Native townsites are a form of land ownership in Alaska, dating to 1891, that enabled Native Alaskans to obtain title to public lands. This form of land title was governed by several federal township acts, all of which were repealed in 1976. No new townsites could be created after that time, but the 106 townsites then in existence were preserved. These township laws were originally designed to give Native Alaskans title to individual parcels of land rather than to grant self-government to the residents of those areas. Over the years, however, federal regulations and court decisions have permitted nonnatives to live in such townsites.

The federal townsite acts provided a scheme whereby those interested in establishing a townsite asked for federal approval to survey the exterior boundaries of the proposed town. After the survey was done, the secretary of the interior appointed a trustee, often a federal employee, to supervise the process of subdividing the townsite. Once that process was completed, the trustee issued deeds to the owners of the individual lots. The title to any townsite land not subdivided was held by the trustee until such time as someone might request that those lands be subdivided. These deeds carried restrictions against transfer similar to those imposed on Indian allotments in Alaska and the rest of the United States.

Much of the law in Alaska relating to this form of land ownership changed with passage of the Alaska Native Claims Settlement Act of 1971 (ANCSA) and other laws. Nonetheless, townsites still exist and have contributed to the complicated pattern of civil and criminal jurisdiction over lands occupied by all Alaskans.

See also **Alaska Allotment Policy; Allotments**

New Mexico v. Mescalero Apache Tribe (1983)

New Mexico v. Mescalero Apache Tribe, 462 U.S. 324 (1983) is a leading hunting and fishing case that makes clear the limits of state jurisdiction over hunting and fishing in Indian country. The Mescalero Apache Tribe's reservation is what is known as an executive order reservation, having been created not by treaty but by a succession of presidential orders in the 1870s and 1880s. More than 95 percent of its lands were Indian owned at the time of *New Mexico v. Mescalero Apache Tribe.*

The tribe, in partnership with the federal government, has developed considerable hunting and fishing resources on the reservation. To manage these assets, the tribe created an elaborate regulatory scheme of agencies and ordinances and a system for licensing hunters and fishermen. The State of New Mexico, which contributed little to the development of these natural resources, sought to regulate the hunting and fishing activities of non-Indians on the reservation.

The U.S. Supreme Court, in balancing tribal, state, and federal interests in such control, used a preemption analysis to find that the state had no real interest in regulating non-Indian participation in these matters on the reservation. The Court acknowledged that tribal sovereignty, that is, the infringement test, was no longer the key factor in analyzing such cases. Nonetheless, the Court found that permitting New Mexico to impose its regulatory powers over tribal control of this area would effectively eliminate tribal control.

This case is a recent example of the Court's application of the preemption test to determine whether the states or tribes shall regulate particular activities on reservations or elsewhere in Indian country. Using this test, the Court found that federal and tribal regulation of hunting and fishing matters were so extensive so as to preclude state regulation.

See also **Infringement Test; Preemption**

O

OFFICE OF HAWAIIAN AFFAIRS The Office of Hawaiian Affairs (OHA), an agency of the State of Hawaii, was created by the state constitution in 1978. Its main purpose, as its name suggests, is to work for the betterment of the social and economic conditions of Native Hawaiians and of Hawaiians generally. For the purposes of the OHA, a Native Hawaiian is a person with 50 percent or more of Hawaiian blood, and a Hawaiian is a person with any amount of Hawaiian blood.

The OHA is the central state agency responsible for coordinating the various programs and activities relating to native peoples in Hawaii. This agency is also charged with reviewing the impact (economic, social, or legal) that other state agencies' programs may have on Native Hawaiians and with finding and applying for grants and donations for programs to better the lot of native peoples in Hawaii. It may also make contracts, invest monies it receives, and do other things to further its mission.

This office, however, does not administer Hawaii Homes Commission Act lands and other property. The OHA is independent of all other branches of state government. It receives most of its operating funds from the Hawaiian legislature. Income from the ceded lands trust provides some other monies. Because of this funding mechanism, the independence of the OHA is somewhat curtailed.

The OHA is governed by a nine-member board of trustees, each of whom must be of Hawaiian ancestry. The members are elected from the state at large by Native Hawaiian or Hawaiian voters. In other words, the board members are elected to their posts by those people whom the OHA is to serve. The board must have one trustee from each of the islands of Hawaii, Kauai, Maui, Molokai, and Oahu. The other four trustees may live anywhere in the state.

The OHA's goals may be somewhat comparable to those of the various state agencies (often named "Office of Indian Affairs" or "Indian Affairs Commission") found in many states with sizable Native American populations. These organizations work both with Indian and non-Indian citizens and with governmental agencies to solve mutual problems and to try to end the long-standing distrust that Native Americans and non-Indians often have for one another. Most of the state offices are headed by a single official, who is usually appointed by the governor. However, unlike those state offices, the OHA is run by an elected body and has some independence from other branches of the state government.

See also **Ceded Lands Trust; Hawaii Homes Commission Act of 1921;** ***Rice v. Cayetano***

OFFICE OF HEARINGS AND APPEALS

The Office of Hearings and Appeals (OHA), a quasi-judicial office within the U.S. Department of the Interior, hears appeals from the decisions of certain boards or agencies within the department. The OHA was established in 1970. The secretary of the interior has given it the power to make rulings in cases that the secretary, as the head of the department, had to hear in the past. Its officials make what are called final agency decisions. Any party to a legal dispute who is dissatisfied with an OHA final agency decision may, in many instances, bring the case into the federal courts for final resolution. The OHA reviews the decisions of, among others, the Board of Indian Appeals and the Board of Land Appeals. These latter agencies consider such issues as disputes arising from the probate of the estates of reservation Indians, the transfer of Indian trust lands into deeded status, and similar matters.

See also **Administrative Law**

OKLAHOMA INDIAN WELFARE ACT OF 1936

The federal Oklahoma Indian Welfare Act (OIWA) of 1936, 25 U.S.C. §§ 501–509, extends the reach and benefits of the Indian Reorganization Act (IRA) of 1934 to most Indians living in the State of Oklahoma. In modern times, Oklahoma Indians have much the same relationship with the federal government as do Native Americans in other states. Earlier in the history of the United States, however, this relationship was quite different. For example, some Oklahoma Indians were not subject to the General Allotment Act of 1887 (the Dawes Act). Oklahoma tribes and their members owned their lands outright and in some cases had the authority to sell and transfer their realty without federal approval. In the late 1800s, Congress expressly removed tribal powers of self-government from Oklahoma Indian tribes when they refused to sell some of their land to the government. Tribal courts in many instances were abolished, and the tribes could not exercise civil or criminal jurisdiction over their lands.

When Congress passed the IRA, it excluded Oklahoma Indian tribes from the Act's reach. In 1936, by enactment of the OIWA, Congress extended the benefits of the IRA to Oklahoma's Native Americans. However, because Congress had earlier passed special laws dealing with the organization of the Osage Tribe, it was excluded from the OIWA. Those tribes that organized themselves under OIWA could reestablish tribal courts and be eligible for the same types of technical and financial assistance programs as are all other tribes under the IRA. The OIWA helped tribes that organized under the Act to secure the same government-to-government relationship that all other Indian tribes in the country have with the United States.

See also **Indian Reorganization Act of 1934**

OLIPHANT V. SUQUAMISH INDIAN TRIBE (1978)

An important U.S. Supreme Court case, *Oliphant v. Suquamish Indian Tribe,* 435 U.S. 191 (1978), forbids tribal courts from exercising jurisdiction over non-Indians who commit crimes on an Indian reservation. The Suquamish tribe, which is based on the Port Madison Indian Reservation in the State of Washington, at the time of this decision had fewer than 50 members, and tribal lands comprised barely one-third of the reservation's acreage. Nonetheless, the Suquamish had a fully functioning tribal court with jurisdiction to try all cases of misdemeanor, regardless of the race of the accused.

The case was decided at a time when the executive and legislative branches of the federal government were implementing Indian self-determination policies. These policies included greater tribal responsibility in such areas as the adoption of Indian children, education, and law enforcement. Prior to this time, the Bureau of Indian Affairs and other federal agencies had assumed major authority over these activities, even at the local level.

The Court, in a 6 to 2 decision, overruled the federal district and circuit courts, both of which had decided that the tribe did indeed have the authority to try non-Indians for misdemeanor offenses. Much earlier, through the Major Crimes Act of 1885 and the Assimilative Crimes Act of 1825, Congress had given the federal courts in most states the jurisdiction to try all persons charged with committing felonies in Indian country. The *Oliphant* case is noteworthy because it reversed decades of settled law—from *Cherokee Nation v. Georgia,* 30 U.S. (5 Pet.) 1 (1831), to *McClanahan v. Arizona State Tax Commission,* 411 U.S. 164 (1973)—holding that the ability to maintain law and order is an inherent part of tribal sovereignty. In other words, the ability to maintain the public peace by punishing lawbreakers is an essential aspect of self-government. Take away that police power, and little is left. The early cases just cited adopted a policy of inherent sovereignty. Federal law presumed that tribes had all powers of self-government except those that Congress, under the Constitution and the Plenary Powers Doctrine, chose to withdraw. The *Oliphant* majority instead chose to apply a theory of affirmative delegation. That is, it held that Indian tribes would only have those powers of self-government, at least in law enforcement matters, that Congress chose to bestow upon them. The Court used congressional silence on the specific question of tribal criminal authority over non-Indians as justification for its position of affirmative delegation. The *Oliphant* Court believed that if Congress had wanted tribes to have criminal court authority over non-Indians, it would have specifically said so. As already noted, this was a radical departure from the concept of inherent sovereignty.

The decision was puzzling to many observers in light of the fact that within several months, this same Court handed down two other Indian country decisions that seemed to reverse course yet again and bolster tribal sovereignty. *United States v. Wheeler,* 435 U.S. 313 (1978), and *Santa Clara Pueblo v. Martinez,* 436 U.S. 49 (1978), both once again upheld the concept of inherent tribal sovereignty. *Wheeler* held that the Double Jeopardy Clause of the Fifth Amendment to the Constitution did not protect a person from both federal and tribal criminal prosecution for the same criminal act. Implicitly, tribes were accorded the respect of separate political entities. In *Wheeler,* the Court decided that the tribes retained all powers of self-government except those removed by Congress.

The *Santa Clara* case involved a pueblo member, married to a nonmember, who claimed tribal enrollment for her children. The pueblo laws only recognized as members those children who claimed Indian blood through their father. The plaintiff brought a federal lawsuit against the tribe, claiming sexual discrimination. The Court, in another victory for tribal sovereignty, indirectly upheld the pueblo's enrollment laws, deciding, among other things, that the Indian Civil Rights Act of 1968 does not waive the sovereign immunity of a tribe and subject it to suit in federal courts in such cases. The Court decided that the ability to regulate tribal membership is an important aspect of sovereignty.

Perhaps the disparity among these three cases can be explained by a point particular to the situation in *Oliphant.* The Court may have been bothered by the fact that a tribe with fewer than 50 members would have authority over 40 times that number of people. The Court may also have been trying to rein in the tribes in an era of increasing federal recognition of their powers of self-government as distinct political entities. In any event, given the makeup of the Suquamish tribe, the Court could have limited the effect of its ruling to tribes in a similar situation, that is, where there was a high proportion of non-Indians to tribal members living on a reservation. Instead, the Court gave the ruling nationwide effect, so that it applied to tribes ranging from the Navajo Nation, which encompasses land in four states and has a population of more than 200,000, to the smallest of tribes.

As a result of the *Oliphant* ruling, tribal courts lost a major portion of their sovereignty. Non-Indians accused of committing misdemeanors in Indian country located in most of the United States now have to be tried in federal courts. In practice, such cases are not given a high priority by local federal prosecutors laboring under heavy workloads. Therefore, much minor crime goes unpunished. Tribes only have the remedy of excluding chronic troublemakers from the reservation, a punishment of questionable effectiveness.

See also **Criminal Jurisdiction; Inherent Sovereignty**

P

Plenary Powers Doctrine The Plenary Powers Doctrine gives Congress almost complete authority to make laws regulating nearly every aspect of life in Indian country. The doctrine was first enunciated in 1886 by the U.S. Supreme Court in *United States v. Kagama,* 118 U.S. 375 (1886).

Historically, Congress had legislated extensively in the field of Indian affairs long before *Kagama.* Congressional authority in Indian affairs derives from the Indian Commerce Clause (Article I, Section 8, Clause 3) of the U.S. Constitution. During the early part of the 1800s, Indian affairs were more like foreign relations and military concerns than they are today. Early dealings between the U.S. government and the Indian tribes were largely government-to-government treaty-making activities concerning matters of territory, trade, and national defense.

In the early 1800s, however, Indian-white contact increased, not always with favorable results for anyone concerned. This was a period of extensive westward expansion. White settlers exerted great pressure for more access to Indian lands and for protection from Indian attacks. Congress obliged and began to exercise increasing military and civilian control over Indian people, treaty obligations notwithstanding. (In fact, the U.S. government unilaterally violated most of the treaties that it signed with Indian tribes.) In 1885 (a year prior to the *Kagama* case), Congress enacted the Major Crimes Act, which gave the U.S. courts jurisdiction to punish criminal acts committed by Indians against other Indians in Indian country. The constitutionality of this Act was challenged in *Kagama:* The plaintiffs held that the Act was outside of the law-making authority granted to Congress under the Indian Commerce Clause. The Court ruled that Indian nations stood as "domestic dependent nations" and that they were in a ward-guardian relationship with the U.S. government. Therefore, the government, according to the Court, has some responsibility to provide for the well-being of the tribes. Thus, the Plenary Powers Doctrine came into being, giving Congress nearly total authority to regulate every aspect of life for Indian people, even in matters that do not deal with commerce or economic matters.

Although Congress still has tremendous authority to regulate nearly every aspect of Indian life on the reservation, its power is not absolute. Congress's dominion over Indians is subject to judicial review. If a law is challenged in a lawsuit, the federal courts may review it to determine whether it is "tied rationally to the fulfillment of Congress' unique obligation toward the Indian people." In other words, the courts may be asked to determine whether Congress's enactments carry out its trust responsibility to care for the Indian people. In practice, Congress leaves much authority to the various tribes to govern their own affairs.

See also **Trust Responsibilities; *United States v. Kagama***

PREEMPTION The legal doctrine of preemption holds that on matters of national scope, federal laws take precedence over state and local laws. The legal basis upon which the Supreme Court adopted such a policy in Indian affairs rests on two parts of the federal Constitution. The Supremacy Clause (Article IV, Clause 2) of the Constitution declares that treaties and federal statutes are the "supreme law of the land," and the Indian Commerce Clause (Article I, Section 8, Clause 3), gives Congress the right to regulate Indian affairs.

The essential reasoning behind this principle is that some areas of policy are best dealt with at the national level. For instance, if each state tried to regulate air pollution, we would have 50 sets of laws dealing with a single national issue. It would be nearly impossible for businesses to cope with such regulation, and the problems of air pollution might never be properly addressed. Other examples of preemption include federal laws regulating all aviation issues and most bankruptcy matters.

However, preemption may be partial: The federal and state governments work together in some areas. For instance, both the federal and state governments regulate workplace safety and the environment. Partial preemption means that states may adopt stricter, but not looser, standards than does the federal government. California, for example, has one of the strictest laws in the country regarding allowable exhaust emissions from cars and trucks. New vehicles sold there must comply with the stricter California law rather than the less-strict federal regulations. Sometimes this can be a burden on a person or company doing business in a particular state.

In Indian affairs, the Supreme Court has held that under the Indian Commerce Clause (Article I, Section 8, Clause 3) of the U.S. Constitution, the federal government has a near monopoly on the regulation of issues pertaining to Native Americans. In Indian affairs, however, federal preemption is, in most respects, total. Congress and the president have sole authority to regulate the sale of Indian lands, management of trust assets, and the extent of state jurisdiction in Indian country.

See also **Indian Commerce Clause; Jurisdiction; Plenary Powers Doctrine; Trust Lands; Trust Responsibilities**

PRIOR APPROPRIATION DOCTRINE Prior appropriation is one of the two systems of water allocation and usage in the United States. It originated in the United States to address water allocation in the generally dry states west of the Mississippi River. (The other major principle governing water use in the United States is the riparian rights principle, which applies to the wetter eastern states and which was part of the English common law that carried over to the United States when it became independent of England.) There are four basic rules to prior appropriation: (1) "First in time, first in right"; that is, the first person to divert an amount of water from a source may continue to take the same amount of water as long as the source is available and as long as he or she continues to own those water rights. The date the water is actually first used is called the priority date. Subsequent users are called junior appropriators; they get to take whatever is left over. (2) These rights are property in the truest sense, just as is real estate or personal property. These water rights can be sold or transferred, either together with or separately from the land the water flows through. In other words, the water rights need not go with the land, so they could be transferred to someone other than the landowner. (3) If there is not enough water to go around, the senior appropriator—that is, the person to first acquire the water rights—may use his or her entire share, even if that means that all junior appropriators get no water at all. Finally, (4) a person with water rights who fails to use them after a period of time loses those rights. All questions under prior appropriation principles, where no Indian land is involved, are determined by the law of the state where the water is located.

To illustrate how this works, assume that three farmers live on a stream. A is the first to divert water from a stream, and he continually does so for a number of years. B and C, in turn, use a share of water from that same stream. A drought nearly dries up the stream, leaving too little water to fully satisfy the needs of all three farmers. During the dry period, A may use up to the quantity of water he initially diverted from the stream years earlier, even if there is none left over for B and C. Moreover, appropriators may sell their water rights or a part of them to anyone whenever they choose.

Some states, such as Colorado, have an extensive administrative system for actually allocating water among competing users. This system divides the state into a number of water districts, each of which has a staff of specially trained administrative law judges (referees, or water masters), water engineers, and other professionals. The decisions of the so-called water masters on who gets how much water may be appealed to the state courts.

See also **Indian Water Rights; Riparian Rights**

PUBLIC LAW 280

BACKGROUND

Public Law 83-280 (67 Stat. 588, codified at 18 U.S.C. § 1162; 25 U.S.C. §§ 1321–1326; 28 U.S.C. § 1360), usually called simply Public Law 280 (PL 280), marks the limits of state authority in Indian country. Congress passed this major law in 1953. It is a clear legislative expression of Congress's intention to terminate its relationship with Indian tribes and merge them into the mainstream of daily life by subjecting both tribes and individual Indians to state civil and criminal law. Discussion over the law occurred during the beginning of the termination era of the Truman and Eisenhower administrations, when the federal government wanted to get out of the "Indian business" by eliminating its trust responsibilities in such areas as land management and social services. Congress and several states were also concerned with the lack of so-called law and order on some reservations. Passage of the law represented a compromise between abandoning the Indians completely and maintaining them as federal wards.

Congress had ceded federal jurisdiction to states before, but only on a case-by-case basis. PL 280, by contrast, allowed states to assume legal authority over the tribes at any time. The law pleased no one. Tribes resented and feared additional state intrusion into their affairs. States resented the continuance of federal protection and services on the reservation. Additionally, for many states, the question of payment or reimbursement for the costs of assuming jurisdiction—for example, the costs of providing schools or police, fire, and court services—was the foremost concern.

THE ARGUMENTS

Proponents of State Jurisdiction

During this period, Congress was considering various bills to transfer federal responsibility for Indian people to other governmental agencies or private bodies. Congress had two separate but related goals: The first was to eliminate federal responsibility to tribal governments, and the second was to relieve the United States from any special obligations to individual Indian persons. Arguments were advanced that Indians, all citizens since 1924, should be treated as were all other Americans. Existing federal laws regulated Indians' use of firearms and livestock and their possession and use of alcohol as well as other facets of daily life.

It was widely felt that the transfer of jurisdiction had to be addressed generally, rather than by the shotgun approach of the past. The lack of state jurisdiction, either civil or criminal, in Indian country was cited as hindering commerce on the reservations. On the civil side, banks would not lend money on real estate that was held in trust because trust lands could not be mortgaged. Often, property on the reservation could not be repossessed. Off-reservation businesses would not cash the checks of reservation residents, claiming that nothing could be done to compel payment if the check was bad.

On the criminal side, state law enforcement officials claimed that a person who committed a crime could flee to the safety of the reservation. Moreover, federal jurisdiction was limited in some cases, and if the state did not have the authority to prosecute, and the tribe lacked an adequate law enforcement system, a wrongdoer would not be held accountable for his or her actions. Proponents of this legislation claimed that even when the tribe did have a workable system, tribal judges were either related to defendants or were so biased one way or the other so as to make the impartial administration of justice impossible. However, the same could be said for state judges, especially in rural areas, where judges were familiar with many members of the local community. Proponents of PL 280 argued the need for uniformity and equal rights, obligations, and privileges for all inhabitants of a given state. PL 280 was originally intended to address the issue of law and order on the reservations, not civil jurisdiction.

Opponents of PL 280

Understandably, many Indian tribes were outspoken in their opposition to any additional state jurisdiction over their lands. Indian tribes and state and local governments have had long-standing political, cultural, and economic differences. These unresolved disagreements have led to mutual distrust. For example, some white people, failing to understand native culture, viewed Indians as lazy because some did not punch a time clock. Conversely, some Indian people saw whites as greedy and unfeeling and unwilling to try to understand or appreciate Native American society.

Especially on the criminal side, tribes and individual tribal members feared increased discrimination against them in the state courts. Indians saw federal restrictions on state criminal authority and on taxation of Indian property and other limitations on state jurisdiction as the their only protection from wholesale state domination. The tribes did not want a repeat of the disastrous removal policies of the early 1800s in the southern states.

For their part, some states expressed concern over the cost of providing law enforcement and judicial services to the reservation. More policemen, jails, judges, and clerks would be necessary, and states feared local authorities would be forced to provide them.

The main objection to the bill, made by Indian tribes, was that states would get blanket civil and criminal jurisdiction over the tribes without regard to Indian preferences on the question.

ENACTMENT AND EFFECT OF PL 280

Overview

PL 280, was signed by President Eisenhower and became effective on August 16, 1953, on the heels of House Concurrent Resolution 108, which was Congress's formal declaration of the termination era. Under PL 280, states were classed two separate ways.

The first group of states are commonly referred to as the mandatory PL 280 states. California, Minnesota, Nebraska, Oregon, Wisconsin, and later Alaska were given civil and criminal jurisdiction, with some exceptions, over Indian lands within their boundaries. Additionally, PL 280 not withstanding, the federal Major Crimes Act of 1885 still gave jurisdiction over serious crimes in Indian country to the federal courts.

The second group of states are commonly referred to as optional PL 280 states. These states could opt to accept jurisdiction over Indian lands later. A number of states, such as Montana, North Dakota, South Dakota, and Washington, had been required to constitutionally relinquish any state power over Indian country as a condition of admission to the Union. PL 280 would allow these states to accept authority over Indians if they amended their constitutions and state statutes accordingly. Non of these states have done so.

Tribal Consent to State Jurisdiction

Under the Act as originally passed, it was not necessary for the affected tribes to consent before the state assumed control over Indian lands. Indeed, in the opinion of some, considering how weighty and important the topic was, the bill enacting PL 280 was rushed through Congress at remarkable speed. This may have been caused by Congress's failure to fully consult Indian tribes on the impact of the proposed law.

A long and unsavory history of tribe-state relations led to tribal concern over the law. Such concern was allayed somewhat in 1968, when Congress passed the Indian Civil Rights Act (ICRA). The ICRA required tribal consent before any state could assume any measure of either civil or criminal jurisdiction over Indian lands. The ICRA also provided that state jurisdiction could be acquired one tribe at a time and that such power could be limited to certain subjects and not others. For example, under ICRA, states might assume jurisdiction over air and water pollution but not over crimes on highways running through Indian country. The reality is that since the 1968 amendments made tribal consent mandatory, only one state, Utah, has assumed state control over Indian reservations. This merely underscores the fact that tribes and states continue to mistrust one another. Realization by the states that they must assume financial responsibility for serving the increased land area is undoubtedly another factor inhibiting them from further assuming jurisdiction in Indian country.

Limitations of State Jurisdiction

It is important to recognize that this Act did not affect the tax-exempt status of Indian lands in trust status or other Indian property in restricted status. Additionally, the Act as originally passed did not provide any method for a state to return civil and criminal authority over Indian country to the federal government. The Act contained several exceptions to state power over Indians, such as the authority to tax. Understandably, given the uncertainty in the interpretation of the Act, Indian tribes challenged its scope, beginning with *Bryan v. Itasca County*, 426 U.S. 373 (1976). The law also prevented states from doing anything that would affect trust property or diminish the rights granted a tribe under any federal treaty or statute or by any agreement between a tribe and the federal government, essentially preserving the status quo in these areas. For example, tribal hunting and fishing rights were left intact under PL 280. In any given situation, to properly determine whether the Act applies requires an analysis of relevant treaties, statutes, or agreements.

State criminal jurisdiction under the Act is also somewhat limited. Under the Act's terms, offenses committed by or against Indians are under state authority "to the same extent as the state's jurisdiction outside Indian country." For example, a person assaulting a Seneca Indian in a restaurant on a reservation would be punished under state law, regardless of the race of either the victim or the attacker. However, specific exemptions from the Act, such as the Major Crimes Act of 1885 and the Indian Country Crimes Act of 1948, limit the state's criminal jurisdiction. To summarize, PL 280 leaves federal Indian country crime law in effect. Such federal laws often exclude the state from exercising any criminal authority on an Indian reservation.

Tribal Court Jurisdiction under PL 280

PL 280 did not specifically extinguish the authority of Indian tribal courts over their reservations. Those tribal courts probably may exercise concurrent jurisdiction with state courts to the same extent that the tribal courts did with the federal courts prior to the Act.

Generally speaking, tribal courts have always had extensive civil authority over activities occurring on the reservation, especially as they concern tribal members. The civil law provisions of PL 280 intended that state courts recognize tribal law where it is not inconsistent with state law.

However, tribal criminal jurisdiction has always been somewhat limited by the federal Indian country crime laws and especially the ICRA. More recent changes in the law and court decisions, starting with *Oliphant v. Suquamish Indian Tribe,* 435 U.S. 191 (1978), limit tribal court criminal authority to Indians and restrict the sentences handed down by tribal courts to a maximum penalty of one year imprisonment and a $5,000 fine. The intent of the criminal law provisions of PL 280 was to substitute state for federal jurisdiction under the Indian Country Crimes Act and the Major Crimes Act.

Returning State Power to the United States

As noted earlier, the original enactment of PL 280 contained no provisions for any state to return jurisdiction over Indian country to the federal government. During House and Senate debate on the Act, both in committee and on the floor, this question was almost ignored. In response to state concerns over the financial burden of assuming jurisdiction over Indian lands and Indian dissatisfaction with the law, Congress in 1968 provided that all pre-1968 acquisitions of state jurisdiction may be returned to the federal government. What about those states (presently only Utah) who assumed power over Indian matters after 1968? The law did not answer that question.

The secretary of the interior was authorized to accept, on behalf of the government, the return of such power to the United States. No particular form of the return of power (or "retrocession of jurisdiction," in legal terminology) is required under PL 280. The secretary can accept a partial return of power; for example, a state might want to return the power to license cars but not the power to regulate air or water pollution. This selective return of power has been accomplished in several cases. The state and federal governments may then work out a manageable plan to allocate jurisdiction between both political entities. Under the Act as currently written, only the states, and not the tribes, have the authority to initiate a return of civil or criminal jurisdiction to the U.S. government.

The Future

Given the current state of the law generally, especially with more emphasis being placed on Indian self-determination and with tribal consent being required, it is unlikely that any more states will assume either civil or criminal control over Indian lands.

With the increase of Indian gaming and other tools of economic self-determination, it is highly improbable that any tribe will now surrender such a vital piece of its identity and of its very being. Tribes are unlikely to relinquish to any state or the federal government the power to "speak the law" (the literal meaning of the word "jurisdiction"), except perhaps incident to state-tribe gaming compacts.

See also **Concurrent Jurisdiction; Fee Patent; Gaming Compact; Indian Civil Rights Act of 1968; Indian Country Crimes Act of 1948; Jurisdiction; Major Crimes Act of 1885; Self-Determination; Termination; Treaty; Trust Lands**

PUBLIC LAW 638 Organizations may contract with the federal government to provide services to Indian tribes and their members under so-called 638 contracts, named after the number of the Act (Indian Self-Determination and Education Assistance Act of 1975) authorizing such contracts: Public Law 96-638. Under the Indian Self-Determination and Education Assistance Act of 1975 (ISDEAA), Congress furthered the cause of Indian self-determination by encouraging tribes to assume management responsibility for federal services provided to Indian people. Until the passage of this Act, the Bureau of Indian Affairs (BIA) and other federal agencies extensively regulated nearly all aspects of the daily life of tribal members living on an Indian reservation. This law permits tribal governments or organizations chartered by them—such as health clinics, housing agencies, school boards, or police commissions—to provide programs that were once directly administered by the federal government. Ordinarily, any contracting organization other than a federally recognized tribe itself must meet certain requirements to be eligible. Generally, such a group must be directly chartered by a tribe and must involve Indians in its management. Some types of groups, such as school boards, must also provide for the democratic election of the group's directors.

Among the most common examples of 638 contractors are local reservation schools. Some of the larger Indian reservations may have a complete public school system in each reservation community. Usually, each school has a school board composed of members elected by the community the school serves. The school hires its own staff and generally runs its own programs, subject to federal requirements. Law enforcement organizations are another example of 638 contractors. In many instances, the tribe, through a chief of police, directly assumes responsibility for reservation law enforcement. In other cases, the tribe establishes a police or law enforcement commission composed of either appointed or elected members to oversee the tribal police. Until 638 contracts were authorized by Congress, the BIA had direct control of the police departments of each tribe and the ultimate authority to hire and fire these federal employees.

Although 638 contracts give the contractors some latitude on how programs are run, the federal government still retains considerable authority over all their activities. Generally, employees of 638 contractors are not considered federal employees and the usual benefits and disciplinary procedures are dealt with in these contracts, as opposed to federal law. Federal law spells out the rights and fringe benefits of federal employees in great detail.

See also **Indian Self-Determination and Education Assistance Act of 1975**

PUEBLO The term "pueblo" is synonymous with the phrase "Indian reservation." The pueblos are found primarily in New Mexico. They possess all of the attributes of sovereignty that Indian tribes elsewhere in the United States have, including the right to determine their own membership, make their own laws, and establish their own court systems.

Many pueblos have not accepted the Indian Reorganization Act of 1934 (also known as the Wheeler-Howard Act), which required participating tribes to adopt tribal constitutions and by-laws patterned after those of the federal and state governments. The pueblos have thus kept many of the traditional aspects of their societal structure and government. Otherwise, however, the pueblos of New Mexico are eligible for the same federal services and programs as are other Native American communities. Most of the federal cases, laws, and regulations that apply to American Indians apply to the pueblos as well.

See also **Indian Reorganization Act of 1934; Reservation**

R

RANCHERIA Indian reservations in the State of California are called by the term "rancheria," derived from Spanish. Many of the Indian reservations established in that state are similar to those in other parts of the United States. The major difference between rancherias and reservations elsewhere is their size. Some western reservations may cover more than 100,000 acres, but most of the California rancherias are tiny, some as small as several acres.

REGIONAL CORPORATION Regional corporations are profit-making entities created by the Alaska Native Claims Settlement Act (ANCSA) of 1971. These businesses are organized under the corporation laws of the State of Alaska. All duly enrolled Native Alaskans may be members (shareholders) of one of 13 regional corporations. Many such shareholders have had no experience with such non-Indian forms of business, so there is a potential for unscrupulous persons to take advantage of such shareholders. These corporations are not governmental entities and they have no inherent tribal sovereignty. They do not maintain tribal courts, police forces, or other similar features of governmental bodies. Twelve of the regional corporations, along with approximately 200 village corporations, were organized to receive and manage the nearly 44 million acres of land and almost $1 billion that were given to Alaskan Natives under the ANCSA. Each of the 12 regional corporations has a geographically defined area. Members of Native Alaskan tribes who do not live in the State of Alaska are shareholders in a thirteenth regional corporation that received money but no land under the terms of the Act.

The original terms of ANCSA placed significant restrictions on transferring shares of stock in the regional corporations to other business entities or individuals. These restrictions were similar to those placed on the transfer of Indian trust land under the General Allotment (Dawes) Act of 1887. Congress later changed the ANCSA to give the regional corporations the authority to amend their governing documents—that is, their articles of incorporation—to decide to whom and under what terms stock originally issued to Native Alaskans may be transferred. The changes to the ANCSA also create the possibility that over time, nonnative Alaskans could acquire such stock.

State law imposes a duty upon these corporations, as on all other similar entities, to manage its resources (that is, land and money) in the best interests of its owners, the shareholders. Conflict might arise between the goals of maximizing the profits to be made from exploiting the land and maintaining a traditional Native Alaskan lifestyle. Such conflicts will, one hopes, be resolved by the shareholders.

See also **Alaska Native Claims Settlement Act of 1971; Corporation; Village Corporation**

REGIONAL EDUCATIONAL ATTENDANCE AREAS

In 1975, the State of Alaska attempted to provide educational opportunities to rural Alaska residents similar to those enjoyed by people in the urban areas of the state. The state created 21 regional educational attendance areas (REAAs), which deliver elementary and secondary educational services to the most rural residents of the state, often Native Alaskans. One REAA may be responsible for providing services to a number of Alaskan villages. The REAAs are governed by a regional school board, whose members reside in the region in which they serve. Until 1975, unlike most states, Alaska operated a highly centralized school system that was established and maintained by the state legislature and not by local units of government such as boroughs, counties, or cities. The REAAs have the effect of decentralizing the operation of schools by enabling the regional school boards to make most of the decisions. Despite these changes, however, the federal government still supports native education through such laws as the Johnson-O'Malley Act of 1934 and the Indian Self-Determination and Education Assistance Act of 1975.

REIFEL, BENJAMIN (1906–1990)

Benjamin Reifel, a U.S. congressman from 1961 to 1971 and an enrolled member of the Rosebud Sioux Tribe in South Dakota, represented the First Congressional District of South Dakota in the U.S. House of Representatives. He was one of very few American Indians in the history of the United States to serve in Congress. A graduate of both South Dakota State University and Harvard University, Dr. Reifel had a long career with the Bureau of Indian Affairs (BIA), where he served in many capacities. While in Congress, he took an active interest in Indian affairs, serving on committees that had oversight over the Department of the Interior, the BIA's parent agency.

REINDEER INDUSTRY ACT OF 1937 The federal Reindeer Industry Act of 1937, 25 U.S.C. § 500 *et seq.*, was enacted to help ensure the survival of Native Alaskans. Congress passed the Act in response to the intense rivalry and bad feelings between native and nonnative reindeer herders. The Act required the government to buy up reindeer owned by nonnatives, distribute them to Native Alaskans, and assist Native Alaskan organizations in the management of their reindeer herds. It also provides for a revolving loan fund for Native Alaskan individuals and organizations to finance the reindeer business. This law, which is still valid, is important as an early indication of Congress's intent to recognize the subsistence rights of Native Alaskans. It set a pattern of federal protection for Native Alaskan subsistence rights, still an important issue today.

To assist the economic development of Native Alaskans in once again building up their local reindeer herds, the Act purported to forbid the transfer of any reindeer to nonnatives. At least one court decision, in 1977, has stated, however, that this provision of the law could violate the U.S. Constitution.

See also **Subsistence**

RELOCATION PROGRAM The Relocation Program was established by the federal government during the termination era of the 1950s to move Indian people off the reservations and into the mainstream of American life. It is no longer in effect. This policy was designed to take people away from their customs and traditions and integrate them into the life of such large cities as Chicago, Denver, and Los Angeles.

The Bureau of Indian Affairs was responsible for administering this plan. During its life, thousands of people left the reservations, many never to return. In exchange for agreeing to move, a family or an individual tribal member received some subsistence payments and expenses for moving and setting up a home in the new city. The bureau also provided some job-placement assistance.

See also **Termination**

RESERVATION Land set aside for the use, possession, and benefit of an Indian tribe and its members by the president or Congress is called a reservation. Ordinarily, such land is considered to be

Indian country, and the tribe for whose benefit the land was set aside is allowed to exercise some measure of self-government; that is, it may establish courts to resolve civil disputes and to try and punish violators of tribal laws. Of course, some Indian tribes have occupied their ancestral lands since before the founding of the United States. Typically, land came to acquire the status of an Indian reservation through aboriginal title, treaty, federal statute, or agreements or by executive order of the president. Generally, the sovereign status of an Indian tribe is not affected by the origin of the reservation. However, the manner in which a reservation was established may be important when considering questions of compensation for land taken by the government or when determining what water, hunting, or fishing rights exist with respect to a particular parcel of Indian land.

RESERVED RIGHTS DOCTRINE The Reserved Rights Doctrine is a fundamental principle of Indian law created by the courts. It holds that certain rights of self-government, as well as property rights that are not the result of negotiation and that have not been taken away by Congress, are retained by (or reserved to) the tribes. This rule's origins date to the founding of the United States in the late 1700s. At that time, Indian tribes were sovereign nations, with complete powers of self-government and control over their own lands. When the federal government made treaties with these nations, only those rights and benefits negotiated were changed. The tribes retained all other rights and benefits not contained in the treaties.

There are generally two ways in which Indian tribes lose property rights or powers of self-government. The first is when a tribe, by treaty or some other agreement with the federal government, gives up, or cedes, some of those rights to the government. Many treaties and executive agreements called for the tribes to give up some of their lands in return for government-provided benefits such as education, food, and health care. Such rights may also be lost when the U.S. Congress exercises its plenary powers over Indian affairs and expressly either limits or extinguishes those rights. Historically, Congress, under pressure from white settlers, often extinguished tribal ownership of certain lands. If Congress clearly and explicitly does this, then the tribes might no longer have any jurisdiction or hunting or water rights in those lands.

This principle is closely related to and a part of the Canons of Construction in Indian law, which hold that in cases of uncertainty or ambiguity, treaties, laws, and so on should be interpreted in favor of the tribes. The doctrine is of great importance today in determining Indian hunting, fishing, and water rights. Many disputes exist, for example, between Indian and non-Indian landowners over how much water can be taken from streams passing though Indian country. The courts often must read early treaties and federal laws to determine whether or not the tribes gave up those rights when Congress and the president made agreements with the tribes or unilaterally erased Indian claims to land. Generally, unless Congress and the president expressly meant to limit water or other rights, the tribes still retain them.

See also **Canons of Construction; Inherent Sovereignty; *Winters* Doctrine**

RICE V. CAYETANO (2000)

The U.S. Supreme Court case *Rice v. Cayetano*, 98-818; 528 U.S. (2000), decided what voters were eligible to participate in elections to select trustees of the Office of Hawaiian Affairs (OHA). Since its creation in 1978, the OHA has allowed people to vote for OHA trustees only if they could claim descent from a person living in what is now the state of Hawaii in 1778 or earlier. The OHA, a Hawaiian state agency, is charged with administering approximately 1.2 million acres of land originally ceded to the United States and later returned to the state upon its admission to the Union. This office is to spend monies derived from the sale or lease of these lands largely for the benefit of two classes of citizens: "Native Hawaiians," who are one-half part, by blood, of the races inhabiting Hawaii before 1778, and "Hawaiians," a larger group who are descendants of people inhabiting the Hawaiian Islands in 1778. The money is to be spent for education, health care, and housing, among other purposes. The OHA is governed by its board of trustees, and the trustees must themselves be Native Hawaiians or Hawaiians.

Harold Rice, the plaintiff in this case, did not fit either category required for voting in the OHA election. (For the remainder of this entry, the term "Native Hawaiian" will include both classes of eligible OHA voters.) Rice contended that this voting restriction was racially based, and that as such it violated the U.S. Constitution. Both the district court (which was the trial court) and the circuit court of appeals found that because the United States maintained a trust relationship with Native Hawaiians, somewhat analogous to that between the United States and American Indians, the Hawaiian ancestry requirement for voting in OHA elections was reasonably related to the maintenance and strengthening of the U.S.–Native Hawaiian relationship. The lower courts reasoned that because the OHA manages trust assets—that is, land for a special group, the Native Hawaiians—it is logical and reasonable to restrict voting for trustees to the group of people whom the OHA was designed to serve and benefit.

The Supreme Court, however, struck down this voting restriction under the Fifteenth Amendment to the U.S. Constitution, which forbids discrimination in voter eligibility based upon race, color, or national origin. (This amendment has its origin in the post–Civil War Reconstruction Era.) Seven of the nine justices agreed that restricting the right to vote in this manner violated the Fifteenth Amendment to the U.S. Constitution and that there was no special or political relationship between Native Hawaiians and either the state or federal government. The Court found that *Morton v. Mancari,* 417 U.S. 535 (1974), which allowed for Indian hiring preference at the Bureau of Indian Affairs, did not apply to *Rice.* In *Mancari,* the Supreme Court reasoned that such discrimination is logically related to the lawful government objective of furthering Indian self-government, where Indian employees supervise federal programs for the benefit of Indian tribes and individuals.

Two justices of the Supreme Court, Justice John Paul Stevens and Justice Ruth Bader Ginsburg, dissented in part, agreeing with the lower courts that in fact a special relationship *does* exist between Native Hawaiians and the state and federal governments. In support of their contention they noted these, among other facts: (1) Congress mandated that the land that the OHA administers be used for specified purposes, mainly for the benefit of Native Hawaiians. (2) In the last 20 years, Congress has included Native Hawaiians in a number of laws concerning the administration of Indian affairs at the federal and state levels. (3) Congress is aware of the history of Hawaii and since annexation has enacted numerous laws attempting to preserve the culture, health, and general well-being of the native peoples there. The dissenting justices believed that these factors contributed to a finding that Congress does, in fact, maintain a trust relationship with Native Hawaiians.

Many Hawaiian citizens believed that Indian law doctrines have a place in Hawaiian law. This case, however, signals the unwillingness of the Supreme Court to extend Indian law principles, protections, or benefits to any group of people that Congress does not explicitly recognize as an "Indian tribe." In other words, the Court did not find that a trust relationship exists between Native Hawaiians and the federal or state governments. It is likely, then, that if Native Hawaiians are to enjoy any benefits of such a relationship, they will have to secure the enactment of appropriate legislation from Congress.

See also ***Morton v. Mancari*; Office of Hawaiian Affairs**

RIGHTS-OF-WAY

The legal concept of rights-of-way allows certain private real property to be used for public purposes, such as for roads, electric or telephone lines, or underground utility cables. The term "right-of-way" is synonymous with "easement," and the phrase is most commonly used when discussing roads, highways, or the right of one person to pass over the property of another. In many cases, the owners' use of the land taken or occupied for public purposes is undiminished. For example, a farmer may find that buried electric or telephone cables do not interfere with farming operations. Conversely, for example, an interstate highway or other major road will probably cause serious inconvenience to a farmer or rancher whose property is now cut in two. Rights-of-way are as common in Indian country as elsewhere in the United States.

See also **Easement; Eminent Domain**

RIPARIAN RIGHTS Riparian rights refer to the water rights of landowners whose property contains a stream or river. The term "riparian" generally means belonging to or relating to the bank of a stream of water. All owners of land upon which water flows or stands, on the ground or underground, share the water in times of scarcity. Generally speaking, each owner of land through which a natural stream passes has the right to use that stream or watercourse for all lawful purposes. This doctrine is part of the law carried over from England (that is, common law) when the United States became a separate country. The eastern states, which are generally wetter than the western states, follow this rule.

Four basic principles characterize these rights: (1) The title to land adjacent to a stream carries with it the right to use the water for all "reasonable" purposes. (2) No user may alter the water flow or quality in a way that may adversely affect his riparian neighbors. (3) There is no specific quantification of the precise amount of water one riparian user may withdraw from the stream, provided that the usage is "reasonable." (4) The riparian right is not lost through nonuse of the water, because riparian rights are a part of the land itself.

Each state may apply its own laws to regulate water usage of streams that flow through those states. This rule is one of the two rules governing water usage in the United States. The other, the Prior Appropriations Doctrine, is used in the western United States.

See also **Indian Water Rights; Prior Appropriation Doctrine**

S

***Santa Clara Pueblo v. Martinez* (1978)** A lifelong female member and resident of the Santa Clara Pueblo in New Mexico, Julia Martinez, married a nonmember Indian and sought to have her children of the marriage enrolled there. When her application was denied, she brought a class-action suit against the pueblo in the federal district court. The children, like their parents, lived all their lives at the Santa Clara Pueblo. Several years before the children were born, the pueblo had passed a tribal enrollment law granting pueblo membership to offspring of male pueblo members but denying it to the children of female members. In this case, the woman claimed that the Indian Civil Rights Act (ICRA) of 1968 prevents the tribe from enforcing laws that allegedly illegally discriminate on account of the sex of the parent in determining tribal membership.

The U.S. Supreme Court in this landmark case held that Congress, in enacting the ICRA, did not intend to intrude into the sovereignty of tribal governments and allow civil lawsuits against them in such matters. In other words, the Court decided that the doctrine of sovereign immunity prevents people from suing tribes over such matters as enrollment of members. The Court followed a long line of its previous decisions in finding that Indian tribes are somewhat independent political communities, which retain their original natural rights in matters of local self government.

The Court had to balance the right of the tribes to manage their own internal affairs with the constitutional rights of individual members. The Court realized that nothing is so essential to the cultural identity of an Indian tribe as the question of who is a member. The Court went on to apply the Canons of Construction to find that Congress did not, in enacting the ICRA, waive the right of people or corporations to sue tribes. The Court found that sovereign immunity is an inherent part of self-government and that only Congress can expressly waive it for the tribes, subjecting them to suit in courts that Congress would designate. Nothing in the ICRA, according to the *Santa Clara Pueblo* decision, indicated that Congress meant to end such tribal immunity from civil lawsuits.

See also **Enrollment Process; Sovereign Immunity; Tribal Membership**

SECRETARIAL ELECTION A tribe must have the approval of the secretary of the U.S. Department of the Interior before it may vote on certain major governmental actions, such as amending its constitution. Such elections are called secretarial elections.

When a tribe determines that such an action is necessary, it notifies the Department of the Interior, which then calls for the preparation of a roll of eligible tribal voters. Most tribes have a considerable number of their members living off the reservation, some of them hundreds of miles away. Depending on the particular tribe, the tribal members may be required to actually reside on the reservation to be eligible to vote. After the election roll is prepared and certified, the tribe, under the auspices of the Department of the Interior, then conducts the election and forwards the results to its Bureau of Indian Affairs area office or to Washington, D.C. The secretary of the interior is likely to ratify and follow the results of the election.

If the secretary finds that the proposed tribal election contravenes the tribe's governing document or federal laws or regulations, then he or she would refuse to call for the election. As with most actions of the federal government, the tribe would then have the right to appeal such a denial to the federal courts.

SECRETARY OF THE INTERIOR The secretary of the interior is the top official of the U.S. Department of the Interior and is also a member of the president's cabinet. He or she is appointed by the president, but the appointment is subject to confirmation, that is, approval, by the Senate. The secretary serves only as long as he or she has the confidence of the president. Unlike the jobs of the vast majority of federal employees, the secretary's position is not part of the federal civil service.

This official has tremendous authority and influence over Indian matters. The decisions that he or she must make include holding secretarial elections, extending federal recognition to new tribes, approving federal contracts, approving the transfer of lands in and out of trust status, and managing individual Indian money accounts and other monies and property held for the benefit of Indian tribes.

Most of these responsibilities are actually delegated to lower officials of the Department of the Interior. These lower-ranking officials make investigations and recommend decisions to the secretary. In all but the most serious or controversial matters, the secretary is most likely to follow the recommendation of his officials. Pursuant to federal law, some of these decisions can actually be made by lesser administrators, such as the appropriate area director.

Not all holders of this office have had experience in Indian affairs. The secretary also must deal with many other areas, such as the environment, forest and wildlife management, and mining and land reclamation matters.

See also **Area Director; Department of the Interior; Secretarial Election**

SECTION 2415 CLAIMS

Section 2415 claims are special claims by Indian tribes against a state for trespass on lands in which tribes held aboriginal title. In 1966, Congress enacted a special statute of limitations statute, 26 U.S.C. §§ 2415–2416, that opened the federal courts to certain lawsuits on behalf of Indian tribes or tribal members. Section 2415 gave tribes and individual tribal members additional time to file legal claims for trespass on their ancestral lands. In many types of lawsuits, a plaintiff only has a certain period of time in which to file a lawsuit. This law extended the period in which to file land trespass claims and allowed for monetary damages occasioned by such trespass.

Many of these claims originated in the eastern states, where state involvement in Indian affairs preceded the formation of the U.S. government. The Non-Intercourse Acts, 25 U.S.C. § 177, which Congress enacted early in the history of the United States, require federal approval for any transfer of lands held by an Indian tribe. Some states—such as Maine, Massachusetts, and New York—had, by treaty or agreement, taken Indian lands in violation of the Non-Intercourse Acts. Congress recognized the problems caused to non-Indian economic interests by these lawsuits for trespass arising from illegal state acquisitions of Indian land. These lawsuits put into question the actual ownership of large tracts of land. As a result, non-Indians whose ownership of the lands was questioned were reluctant to develop the land as long as the ownership was unsettled. In response to the problem, Congress passed laws such as the Rhode Island and Maine Claims Settlement Acts of 1980, 25 U.S.C. §§ 1701–1735, which extinguished Indian aboriginal title to land in exchange for a monetary payment and other federal assistance to the affected tribes.

See also **Statute of Limitations**

SELF-DETERMINATION The phrase "self-determination" denotes the current official federal policy of encouraging Indian tribes to manage their own affairs, including the delivery of federal services to Indian people by their own agencies rather than by agencies of the U.S. government. The shift toward this policy came on the heels of the termination era, in which the federal government actively attempted to repudiate its trust responsibilities toward Native Americans. During that period, which started just after World War II and lasted into the late 1960s, the government actually terminated its formal government-to-government relationship with a number of Indian tribes.

At the beginning of the Nixon administration, the government reversed course and conceded, through the enactment of legislation, that its termination policy had been a failure. This about face was partly driven by public opinion: The extreme measures of the termination era brought diverse Indian groups together to bring public attention to their plight. Also, state governments began to realize that they would have to bear the costs of providing law enforcement, social, and other services to people and lands previously dealt with by the United States. The states then began to reconsider their support of the policy of ending the trust relationship between the federal government and the Indian tribes.

On the eve of self-determination in the late 1960s, the Bureau of Indian Affairs, the Indian Health Service, and assorted other agencies exercised nearly complete domination over the Indian people who lived on reservations. Decisions on housing, health care, food, and education were largely controlled by the government. No other ethnically distinct group in the United States was subject to the kind of oversight by the federal government that American Indians and Native Alaskans were.

Numerous congressional enactments, many of which are discussed in this book, reversed the tide and expanded the autonomy of tribal governments. Among them are the Indian Financing Act of 1974, which sets up a revolving loan fund to finance tribal enterprises; the Indian Self Determination and Educational Assistance Act of 1975, which allows tribes to manage and operate federal programs serving Indian people; and the Indian Child Welfare Act of 1978, which gives tribes great authority over the adoption and foster placement of Indian children. More recently, Congress enacted the Indian Gaming Regulatory Act of 1988, which allows tribes to promote and regulate gambling enterprises, and the Native American Housing Assistance and Self-Determination Act of 1996, which gives tribes more latitude in managing federal programs to provide affordable housing for Native Americans in Indian country. How effective these laws are in promoting self-determination for Indian nations is for the reader to decide.

See also **Termination**

SEMINOLE NATION V. UNITED STATES (1942)

Seminole Nation v. United States, 316 U.S. 286 (1942) is a modern case that reaffirms the importance of the federal government's duty to Indian tribes to manage Indian property in their best interests. This U.S. Supreme Court decision concerned monies that the Department of the Interior had paid to an Indian tribe in the nineteenth century, pursuant to a treaty. The government paid the funds to the tribal council instead of directly to tribal members, which was in direct conflict with the provisions of the treaty. The tribal council was apparently corrupt, and the money went into the pockets of council members. More than 50 years later, the tribe sued the U.S. government for improperly disbursing those funds. The tribe claimed that the government was aware of the corruption then going on in the tribal government when it paid the funds out. The U.S. Court of Claims dismissed the lawsuit.

On appeal, the U.S. Supreme Court in *Seminole* held that even though the government had already paid out the money it owed under the treaty, the government is held to a high standard in making sure that tribal property is managed in the best interests of both a tribe in general and tribal members. This trust relationship requires the United States to exercise great care in its dealings with the Indian people. The Court found that a trial must be held to determine whether or not the government actually knew or should have known of the dishonesty of the tribal council when the funds were paid to them for the benefit of their members.

This case is still very important and relevant today. The Department of the Interior, the agency involved in the *Seminole* case, is the department accused today of breaching its trust obligation by allegedly mishandling millions of dollars of funds it holds for the benefit of both Indian tribes and their members. This case helped set a modern standard by which the federal government administers Indian property.

See also **Trust Responsibilities**

SERVICE OF PROCESS

Before a person can be held accountable for the results of a lawsuit or be made to testify or otherwise participate in legal proceedings, he or she must be given advance notice. The legal process of notification is service of process. This is the process by which a defendant is notified that someone (called the plaintiff, complainant, or petitioner) has started a lawsuit against him or her. It is also the process used to summon a witness to testify in a criminal or civil lawsuit.

This notice of a lawsuit (summons) or requirement to appear and testify (subpoena) is served either personally or by mail on the person to be notified. Usually a sheriff or other law enforcement official serves these papers. However, some states or tribes allow any adult registered voter who is not part of the legal proceedings to deliver the papers. Each state or tribe determines its own procedure. Failure to properly serve such papers may affect the outcome of the legal action. Virtually all Indian tribes with their own court systems have established rules for the service of legal documents. Often it is necessary to serve persons outside the state or tribe where the legal action started. Sometimes, persons or legal entities such as corporations may be served by publication of the summons or other legal document in some newspaper where they would be likely to get notice of the lawsuit.

SNYDER ACT OF 1921 The Snyder Act of 1921, 25 U.S.C. § 13, authorized the Bureau of Indian Affairs (BIA) to expend its appropriated funds for the care and benefit of Indian people on a continuing basis. Prior to passage of the Snyder Act, Congress made appropriations for Indians on a piecemeal basis. Bills to allocate money for Indian affairs were often defeated in Congress. The Act streamlined the passage of appropriations bills for issues concerning Indians. The Act, for the first time, codified broad authorization for the BIA to spend funds for a wide variety of activities, such as education, job training, and agricultural issues. The Act was another tacit recognition by Congress of its responsibilities for and unique relationship with Native Americans. This law constitutes the general authority for the BIA to spend federal funds for activities to benefit Indian people.

SOVEREIGN IMMUNITY The principle of sovereign immunity is a legal doctrine that in certain circumstances prevents a person from suing the sovereign without its consent in a civil (not criminal) lawsuit for a wrong he or she has suffered, regardless of whether or not the legal claim is just and meritorious. For instance, a person who is owed money under a contract with a state or tribe may not be able to collect it by suing the tribal government.

Usually, this principle applies to allegedly wrongful acts by a government such as firing a tribal employee or using excessive police force in arresting a criminal suspect. The doctrine originated in England on the theory that the Crown (that is, the royal government) was supreme and just and therefore could do no wrong. As a result, citizens could not sue it for damages they suffered at the hands of the king or queen.

There is a risk to a government in adhering to such immunity in all cases. If it acts irresponsibly and refuses to honor its contracts or properly train its employees, others will not do business with it. For example, it may not find suppliers willing to sell goods to it if there is a reasonable probability that the supplier will not get paid. If, for instance, a tribe must pay a higher price for the goods and services it needs because the private supplier must take a greater risk of nonpayment, this has the effect of retarding economic development in the region where the tribal government has the authority to subject people to its laws and regulations.

Because of the potential harm from adhering too strongly to this doctrine, it has largely been eroded, at all levels of government in the United States, by the passage of special statutes. Through these laws, the government automatically gives its permission to be sued for certain types of cases—for example, a negligence case in which a government automobile runs into a pedestrian. Many states have also passed similar legislation. Each tribal government may decide for itself whether it chooses to waive sovereign immunity and allow itself to be sued. Some tribes still refuse to waive immunity at all.

See also **Federal Tort Claims Act of 1946; Jurisdiction; Waiver of Sovereign Immunity**

Squire v. Capoeman (1956)

Squire v. Capoeman, 356 U.S. 1 (1956) is the leading U.S. Supreme Court case dealing with the federal taxation of income derived from activities on land allotted to individual tribal members under the General Allotment Act of 1887 (the Dawes Act). Many allotments are still in existence to this day, even though the Indian Reorganization Act of 1934 ended the national allotment process.

The Court began with the proposition that as a general rule, Indians involved in commercial activities outside a reservation are to be treated the same as all other people. In other words, the sale or purchase of goods and the earning of income off a reservation is subject to federal taxation. In deciding the case, the *Squire* Court reasoned that Congress, in allotting Indian lands to individuals free of taxes, intended to give Indians a chance to adjust to mainstream American life. Therefore, the Court exempted income derived directly from the land itself, such as the harvesting of crops or the sale of timber. This was a broad reading of the law. However, subsequent lower court and Internal Revenue Service decisions have been less generous to allottees. Examples of income derived from allotments that has been held taxable include income earned from a motel on the land, interest on income derived from the sale of crops, and income derived from the lease of grazing rights on allotments.

The case is significant because in it the Court seemed to reverse the principle that federal statutes are to be construed liberally in favor of Indians. Under this principle, which pervades the field of Indian law, if a law purporting to create an exemption for Indians from a federal tax is ambiguous, the courts would normally find that Indians are entitled to the tax relief. However, the *Squire* Court found that in order for an Indian tribe or individual tribal member to be entitled to a tax exemption, Congress must have clearly expressed in the law its intention to grant that exemption. Normally, under the Canons of Construction, when Congress intends to eliminate or reduce the rights or privileges of Indians, it must clearly state that intention in the law. When it comes to Indian rights and federal tax law, the exact opposite is true: to *grant* a tax exemption (a right or privilege) to Indians, Congress must explicitly say that it intends to grant the exception.

See also **Canons of Construction; Indian Taxation**

STATUTE OF LIMITATIONS State or national governments pass statutes of limitation to encourage the prompt resolution of legal disputes, whether civil or criminal. These laws require a person or legal entity that may have any type of legal claim to file the lawsuit and serve the defendant with notice of the lawsuit within a certain time period. That time is usually computed from when a plaintiff knew or should have known he or she had a legal claim, to the time the lawsuit was initiated by serving the defendant with notice of it (this notice is usually called a summons). How long a person has to file a case depends upon the type of case. Different classes of disputes have different time limits. For example, claims arising out of a personal injury may have a shorter time limit than those involving contracts or trespasses to land.

These laws recognize the problems judges and juries have when called upon to decide old disputes. Over time, witnesses become impossible to find, or their memories fade. Physical evidence, such as documents or anything else, may become lost or disintegrate over time. Regardless of the merits of a case, if it is not started within the specified time limit, the courts no longer have any authority to hear it. Recognizing the problems Indian tribes or their members have had in gaining access to the legal system, either because of unfamiliarity with it or because of a lack of money with which to hire attorneys, Congress has passed many special statutes authorizing federal courts to hear older claims.

***STRATE V. A-1 CONTRACTORS* (1997)** The U.S. Supreme Court case *Strate v. A-1 Contractors*, 520 U.S. 438 (1997), defines the extent to which tribal courts may hear certain types of lawsuits involving non-Indians over conduct occurring on an Indian reservation. In *Strate*, a non-Indian driving a car on a state highway that crosses tribal trust land collided with a vehicle driven by an employee of a contractor doing some work for the tribe. Both the contractor and the employee were non-Indian.

The Court ultimately decided that the tribal court had no subject matter or personal jurisdiction over the defendant employee or over this type of case. It applied the rule of civil jurisdiction over non-Indians that was first announced in the case of *Montana v. United States*, 450 U.S. 544 (1981). The *Montana* rule barred tribal civil jurisdiction over non-Indians for activities arising on non-Indian owned lands on a reservation, with two exceptions. The *Strate* Court decided that neither exception to the *Montana* rule applied. *Strate* held that even though the highway right-of-way was on Indian trust land, nonetheless, for civil jurisdiction purposes, it is the equivalent of privately owned land. A highway right-of-way is simply a license for the public to cross land owned by some particular person or entity. The *Strate* Court also found that the defendant's company did business with a tribal entity. Nonetheless, the fact that the defendant employee was involved in a car accident was not enough to bring this case within the first *Montana* exception of a party voluntarily entering into a relationship of some type with the tribe.

After making these determinations, the Court admitted that careless driving on highways crossing an Indian reservation may jeopardize the safety or health of tribal members but held that this was not enough to invoke the second *Montana* exception, which would allow a tribal court to hear the case. That exception allows tribal courts civil jurisdiction if tribal regulation of such matters would be necessary to protect "the health, welfare, or political integrity of tribal members or the tribe."

The *Strate* Court stated that to allow tribal court authority to hear highway accident cases involving non-Indians would "severely shrink the *[Montana]* rule." This case is as an example of the Supreme Court's occasional seeming reluctance to acknowledge the ability of tribal courts to handle such disputes. It appears from this case that before a tribe's courts may hear non-Indian civil disputes arising on non-Indian lands, it must bring in substantial evidence to prove that particular conduct (such as involvement in accident cases) by non-Indians would have a substantial impact on the welfare of the tribe.

See also ***Montana v. United States***

SUBSISTENCE The term "subsistence" refers to the ability of native peoples to support themselves by living off the land, using its resources to feed, clothe, and house themselves. Subsistence has always had great cultural significance to America's first citizens. However, in Alaska subsistence rights are crucial to the survival of Native

Alaskans, for many of them still live off the land, being remote from the cash economy of non-Indian cities and towns. Many Native Alaskan villages can still be reached only by foot or sled. An increase in the nonnative population of Alaska has strained the state's fish and wildlife resources. Commercial and recreational utilization of natural resources often conflicts with native subsistence rights.

In the continental United States, hunting and fishing rights have often been protected by treaties and other specific federal laws that have normally been applied to Indian reservations. The states have a long history of hostility to the rights of native peoples. The subsistence issue is no exception. Because the Alaska Native Claims Settlement Act of 1971 abolished all but one reservation in Alaska, natives must rely on specific federal enactments to protect their subsistence rights. Apart from a few treaties with foreign nations and other agreements, the major federal law that governs Native Alaskan subsistence rights is the Alaska National Interest Lands Conservation Act of 1980, 16 U.S.C. § 3111 *et seq.* Under general principles of Indian law, a U.S. federal government trust responsibility to protect Native Alaskan subsistence rights has emerged with the passage of these laws and treaties.

Three subsistence issues are constantly being debated among all interested parties: (1) Who should regulate hunting and fishing rights? (2) What persons should be given priority rights to take fish and wildlife? (3) To what extent, if at all, should undeveloped lands in Alaska be exploited for their natural resources? These questions are being answered in Congress, in the Alaska state legislature, and in the courts.

See also **Alaska National Interest Lands Conservation Act of 1980**

SUPERINTENDENT Typically, the larger Indian reservations have a fully staffed Bureau of Indian Affairs (BIA) office to provide assistance to the tribe. The local representative of the BIA at an Indian reservation, and the person in charge of the local BIA office, is the superintendent. His or her immediate supervisor is an area director of the BIA, who is responsible for a specific geographic region, often encompassing several states. The local superintendent is usually a member of the federal civil service, often working up through the ranks in the BIA. The superintendent, like most other BIA employees, can only be fired for cause. Indian hiring and promotional preference laws apply to superintendent positions. Many superintendents are members of a federally recognized tribe.

See also **Bureau of Indian Affairs**

SUPREMACY CLAUSE Article VI, Clause 2, of the United States Constitution, the Supremacy Clause, when read with the Treaty and Indian Commerce Clauses, gives the president and Congress supreme power over Indian affairs in the United States. Under this interpretation by the courts, Congress is given tremendous authority over Indian affairs in defining the tribes' relationship to the federal government. This doctrine was first enunciated by the U.S. Supreme Court in the early days of the Republic.

This clause specifically reads:

> This Constitution and the laws of the United States which shall be made in pursuance thereof; and all Treaties made or which shall be made, under the Authority of the United States, shall be the supreme Law of the Land; and the Judges in every State shall be bound thereby, any Thing in the Constitution or Laws of any State to the Contrary notwithstanding.

Modern Indian law cases in the Supreme Court describe state laws as being "preempted" by federal laws or treaties.

See also **Indian Commerce Clause; Preemption; Treaty Clause**

T

Talton v. Mayes (1896) In its important *Talton v. Mayes*, 163 U.S. 376 (1896) decision, the U.S. Supreme Court held that the Cherokee Nation, located in what was then Oklahoma Territory as a sovereign nation, had a basis of power outside of the U.S. Constitution. *Talton* concerned the murder of one tribal member by another on the Cherokee reservation. A tribal grand jury of five members indicted the appellant (that is, the one making the appeal), who argued that the tribal grand jury was illegal under the Fifth Amendment to the U.S. Constitution.

The *Talton* Court, after reviewing history, laws, its prior decisions, and treaties and agreements made with the Cherokee, concluded that the Constitution, and specifically the Fifth Amendment right to grand jury indictment in felony cases in federal court, did not apply to the Cherokee Nation. This case, although recognizing Congress's plenary powers over Indian tribes, nonetheless refused to apply the Bill of Rights to Indian country. In 1968, however, Congress did just that with the passage of the Indian Civil Rights Act. This Act extended portions of the Bill of Rights to Indian country. This case is part of a continuing body of Indian law that recognizes the separate and independent basis of power that Indian tribes retain, distinct and apart from the federal Constitution.

Taylor Grazing Act of 1934 The federal Taylor Grazing Act of 1934, 43 U.S.C. §§ 315–316o, seeks to promote the highest use (that is, producing the most revenue) of federal public lands not already used for some specific purpose such as forests or parks. The Act covers more than 100 million acres of public lands in many of the western states, including some lands in which Indian tribes and their members claim ownership interests. The Act provides for a system for issuing permits to allow livestock owners to graze their cattle on these lands. It was designed to generate income from the use of these lands and to prevent overgrazing. The government may, without tribal consent, issue grazing permits for Indian lands held in trust for tribes or their members. However, the Act does not by itself extinguish aboriginal or Indian title to such lands. Moreover, a portion of the fees that the government receives from the issuance of permits for grazing on Indian lands is given to the tribe or tribal member holding an interest in the land.

TERMINATION From the late 1940s though the early 1960s, which has come to be known as the termination era, federal Indian policy once again favored assimilating, or mainstreaming, Native Americans into the American way of life. Many policy makers thought that it was high time to get out of the "Indian business." The termination era was but part of a movement by Congress to downsize the entire federal government after fighting two major wars in the preceding dozen years or so. The federal government minimized its trust responsibilities by encouraging individual Indians to move off the reservation into large American cities. The purpose was to have Indians lose their customs and traditions.

A second component of the termination era, which actually began in 1953 with passage of House Concurrent Resolution 108, was to end the federal trust, or government-to-government relationship between the U.S. government and a particular tribe and its members. This was actually carried out against a number of federally recognized tribes, among them the Menominee of Wisconsin, the Klamath of Oregon, and the Peoria and Ottawa of Oklahoma. A dozen or more tribes had their relationship with the United States severed.

The legal effect of termination was to revoke the federal recognition of the terminated tribes and to strip their lands of trust status. The tribal members would always be Indians, but the federal government would no longer grant them recognition. Members of the affected tribes no longer had access to special federal programs for education, health, or subsistence. Their lands were treated just as any other land was in the state and county where they were located. For all practical purposes, the affected Indians were to be treated just as non-Indians were by the federal, state, and local governments. Other tribes, however, were free to continue to recognize them as Indian.

This meant that under termination, (1) Indian lands were appraised and sold to the highest bidder—just as would be the case at a private land sale; (2) the state took complete civil and criminal jurisdiction over the former tribal lands; (3) the lands became fully subject to state and local real estate taxes; and (4) tribal sovereignty no longer existed. The tribes simply ceased to exist as governmental entities. However, under some court decisions, tribal water, hunting, and fishing rights guaranteed to tribes under treaties were still in effect, not withstanding the new status of the land. Many tribal members simply received a cash payment for their interest in tribal lands. Tribal members usually used this sum for survival rather than for future investment. As a result, some members were left in a worsened economic situation after termination. The goal of making Indians self-sufficient and mainstreaming them into American culture did not work in many cases. In other situations, affected members left the area, never to return.

Realizing that this policy had failed for most affected tribes, Congress eventually rerecognized several tribes, which had the effect of granting them their former tribal status. Among such rerecognized tribes are the Klamath and the Menominee. With the passage of the Tribally Controlled Schools Act of 1988, Congress expressly repudiated House Concurrent Resolution 108, thus formally bringing the termination era to a close.

See also **House Concurrent Resolution 108; Relocation Program**

***THREE AFFILIATED TRIBES V. WOLD ENGINEERING* (1984)** In *Three Affiliated Tribes v. Wold Engineering*, 467 U.S. 138 (1984), the U.S. Supreme Court ruled that tribal sovereignty is not necessarily impeded when state courts decide a civil case concerning activities on the reservation and involving non-Indians. In this case, the tribes themselves—the Three Affiliated Tribes of the Fort Berthold Reservation—sued Wold Engineering, the defendant in state court, over a contract dispute over work Wold had done for the tribe on the reservation. Pursuant to Public Law 280 (PL 280), the state had assumed jurisdiction over civil cases arising on the reservation. However, as a condition of access to state courts, the state required that the tribe give up all tribal authority to decide any civil disputes arising in Indian country. The U.S. Supreme Court applied the preemption and infringement tests to find that although the state courts could decide this type of case, PL 280 did not allow states to require that tribes surrender concurrent jurisdiction to allow their own courts to decided these same types of cases. This case, however, is unusual in that when it was filed in the state courts, the tribal governing body did not give its own courts subject matter jurisdiction over this particular type of case, that is, torts (negligence) and contract disputes. This fact was an important reason (along with authority under PL 280) why the U.S. Supreme Court found that state courts had civil jurisdiction in this case. The tribe, not being able to sue in its own courts, could only turn to state courts in such a case. After the Court sent the case back to the North Dakota Supreme Court to consider the conditions under which a state would allow Indians access to its courts, *Wold* came back to the U.S. Supreme Court a second time in *Three Affiliated Tribes of the Fort Berthold Reservation v. Wold Engineering, PC*, 476 U.S. 877 (1986) (*Wold II*).

This second Court decision held that PL 280 does not allow a state to make access to state courts conditional on a tribe's giving up its sovereign immunity and concurrent jurisdiction over civil cases arising in Indian country. The U.S. Supreme Court found that to do so would effectively bar tribes themselves from access to state courts. A tribe would have no way to hold accountable those who may have wronged it. Even if a tribe could sue in its own courts and win, the Full Faith and Credit Clause of the U.S. Constitution does not require the courts of any state to recognize a tribal court judgment. In other words, a tribe that wins a money judgment or other relief against a defendant in its own courts could not require a state court anywhere to enforce that judgment, although states may voluntarily choose to recognize tribal court orders under principles of comity. Under the North Dakota scheme for granting tribes access to state courts, the tribe had two choices: It could either give up its sovereign immunity and right to have its own courts handle these types of cases, and thereby gain access to state courts, or it could retain its powers of self-government, but without the ability sue in state courts to hold defendants accountable for civil wrongs—such as breach of contract or negligence—committed against a tribe.

See also **Concurrent Jurisdiction; Infringement Test; Preemption Test; Public Law 280: Indian Self-Sovereignty**

TRADE AND INTERCOURSE ACTS

The Trade and Intercourse Acts, a series of federal laws first enacted in 1790, regulate non-Indian conduct in Indian country and trade and land transactions with Indians and their tribal governments. The laws, codified at 25 U.S.C. § 177 and elsewhere in Title 25, require the consent of the federal government before any land owned or occupied by an Indian tribe may be sold, leased, or otherwise transferred to anyone else. The title to any land purchased from an Indian tribe without federal consent was to be considered null and void.

In the late 1700s, many Indian tribes were still military powers, and the young U.S. government needed a way to stabilize its relationship with those nations. To help provide for orderly settlement of the West and to prevent non-Indian trespass and violence against Indians, Congress enacted Indian Non-Intercourse laws to regulate both non-Indian trade with and land purchases from Indian tribes. Also, because some eastern states had a history of making private land deals with the Indian tribes, these federal laws attempted to nationalize Indian policy.

The current restrictions on the sale or transfer of Indian lands from tribal members or from the tribes themselves derive from these early laws. Several cases involving Indian tribes in eastern states have considered the validity of this law in the present day. To answer some of those concerns, Congress enacted laws in 1980 to provide Indians in a number of states with a monetary and land settlement in exchange for the tribes' giving up their claims to violations of the Non-Intercourse Acts.

See also **Section 2415 Claims**

TRADITIONAL GOVERNMENTS The methods used by Indian tribes to provide for the common good or welfare of the people before significant contact with non-Indians are referred to by the term "traditional governments." Although there were (and are) significant differences among the tribes as to styles of governance, some common traits can be seen. Some features of tribal self-governance before contact with non-Indians are still in evidence today.

One common characteristic of the early governing styles was its decentralized nature. Few tribes had one single leader who governed all members of a tribe, band, or nation. Typically, each village or extended family unit had a group of elders who would settle disputes among village or family members.

The leaders, either at the local or the band/national level, did not so much command as persuade. The leaders at all levels were chosen on the basis of respect, either for their deeds as warriors or hunters, or generally for their intelligence, understanding, and wisdom. Some Indian tribes also chose women to serve as their leaders.

The leaders did not so much form public opinion as follow or reflect the opinions and thoughts of their people. The leaders needed the support of the community. When there were disputes to be settled, such as those between several families, the elders or leaders might discuss and debate the matter for hours before reaching a consensus as to how the dispute should be resolved. If one tribesman committed a crime against another, the leaders might deliberate for some time before deciding how to punish the offender. Unanimity was important, if it could be reached. Achieving unanimity, of course, meant a great deal of compromise. To ensure the safety of the tribe against its enemies, it was always important to have the cooperation of all segments of tribal society.

A major difference between non-Indian and traditional forms of government was (and to some extent, still is) the traditional system's emphasis on compromise rather than the winner-take-all attitude of the U.S. system of justice. Traditional governments almost always encouraged the parties to settle a dispute informally before taking it to the tribal leaders.

Even when the leaders of the entire tribe met to work out a solution, they attempted to solve the problem in a way satisfactory to all, much as a mediator would. To this day, many Indian tribal courts use this mediation or arbitration approach, encouraging the litigants to settle the dispute out of court if possible. Even after a case goes to trial, the judge may be less of a referee in the U.S. style and more of an impartial mediator, assisting the parties in reaching a solution to the lawsuit that they can all accept.

The structure of traditional tribes varied from group to group. One of the most complex was the Iroquois Confederacy, a group of six distinct tribes that banded together to provide for a common defense and other needs shared by all of the tribes. Each tribe sent a number of its leaders to a main council that settled disputes between two or more tribes. Matters affecting only one of the tribes were settled at the individual tribal level. The leadership of the confederacy rotated from time to time. Each tribe's population determined the number of leaders it sent to the council. Some features of the government established by the U.S. Constitution are patterned after the Iroquois Confederacy. Other tribes may have a much simpler method of settling differences by simply referring them for a decision to one or more men or women of the tribe respected for their wisdom.

TREATY A treaty is a formal agreement made between two or more governments for some benefit to each party to the agreement. Such agreements or compacts typically concern mutual defense against common enemies, or economic matters to encourage or discourage foreign trade. Modern examples include the North Atlantic Treaty Organization (NATO), which provides for the common defense of member nations, and the General Agreement on Tariffs and Trade (GATT), which deals with economic relations among the member nations.

The U.S. government, from the earliest colonial days to 1871, treated with the Native American tribes. The War Department and later the Interior Department needed, for national security purposes, to ensure peaceful relationships between the United States and the various tribes. War with the Indian nations was always a possibility. From the earliest days of the Republic, the executive branch took the initiative in treaty talks with Indian nations, first through the secretary of war and later, when responsibility for Indian affairs was transferred to the Interior Department, through the secretary of the interior.

The actual negotiations were conducted either by agents of the Bureau of Indian Affairs, by special commissions appointed by the president, or by his designated persons. The Indian agents or treaty commissioners would often go to the homelands of the tribe to negotiate and prepare a tentative treaty, which was then forwarded to the president for his review. If he was satisfied with it, he would submit it to the Senate for ratification, or approval. The U.S. Constitution provides that the president is primarily responsible for foreign affairs, and he has the responsibility for proposing treaties. A treaty is not valid until ratified by the Senate, but the Senate does not always do so.

Once the treaties were ratified by the Senate, they had the force of law. This means that treaties had the same legal effect as federal statutes enacted by Congress and signed by the president. Violations of treaties, therefore, were also violations of federal law. In effect as well as name, treaties became the supreme law of the land. The Indian tribe that signed the treaty was, of course, also obligated to live up to its terms as well. Whether or not Congress appropriated funds to carry out the treaties, such as providing Indian tribes with medical care and sustenance and generally leaving them alone, was another matter.

As time passed, the power of Indian tribes to threaten the security of the United States decreased, and there was less need for the government to assure its own stability by treating with the various Indian tribes. In addition, the House of Representatives continued to resent its exclusion from the treaty-making process. Only the Senate ratified treaties. The House, of course, had to appropriate funds to carry out their purposes. In 1871, the treaty-making process (as it concerned Indian tribes) fell victim to politics. In that year, Congress passed a law providing that Indian tribes are not considered to be sovereign nations with whom the government could make treaties. However, Congress also declared in that law that existing treaties were still valid.

This loss of status had great consequences for Indian nations. The federal government no longer had to enter into agreements with the tribes; that is, it no longer had to trade land for federal protection and educational, health, and vocational benefits and sustenance for tribal members. Congress could now simply pass laws to take Indian lands away from the tribes, in effect canceling, or abrogating, the treaty, declaring it invalid.

Once the treaty-making process was abandoned, the president, through the Department of the Interior, would make "executive agreements" to resolve disputes or strike bargains with the various tribes. Such agreements do not need the approval of the Senate. Just as with treaties, of course, Congress must appropriate funds to carry out such agreements.

However, many treaties are still valid today. Certain rights guaranteed to tribes in years past through treaties that have been abrogated by the U.S. government may still be in effect. For example, hunting, fishing, and water rights guaranteed to tribes by treaties long-since canceled still apply to lands that have since passed out of Indian hands. The national government's obligation to furnish Indians with some of the benefits mentioned above may be based upon treaties. Today, state and federal courts often look to those treaties to try and determine the rights of Indians and non-Indians when disputes over rights come before them.

See also **Canons of Construction; *Lone Wolf v. Hitchcock;* Treaty Clause**

TREATY CLAUSE The part of the U.S. Constitution that gives the president the authority to make treaties is the Treaty Clause, found at Article II, Section 2, Clause 2. Although the Constitution does not specifically mention Indian tribes, the federal government from earliest times regularly made treaties with Indian tribes in order to provide for the peace and security of the people. The tribes were considered, to some extent, to be the equivalent of foreign nations with separate political status. Under the Treaty Clause, the president proposes treaties, and the Senate, by a two-thirds vote of senators present, must approve the treaty before it may be put into effect.

Under other provisions of the Constitution, a valid treaty has the status of federal law. States are bound to obey treaties. A violation of a treaty is considered a violation of federal law.

See also **Treaty**

TRIBAL COUNCIL The part of tribal government that corresponds to the legislative branch of government at the federal, state, or local levels is the tribal council. The composition of such councils is as varied as it is in other jurisdictions around the world. One feature common to many tribal councils is that their members are popularly elected from specific geographic districts, rather than at-large as in some counties and cities. Unlike in the U.S. system of government, however, some tribes allow their councils to overrule or modify certain decisions of the tribal courts. Not all tribes find it desirable to maintain the checks and balances system found in the U.S. Constitution.

In many tribes, the position is a part-time one. Many councils were organized under the Indian Reorganization Act of 1934. Some of them predate the founding of the United States. Their duties are generally to pass laws for the operation of the tribal government, to investigate various areas of interest to them and their constituents, and to set the overall policy of the tribe in matters subject to their control.

See also **Indian Reorganization Act of 1934**

TRIBAL LANDS The term "tribal lands" denotes land owned either by an Indian tribe or by Indian individuals. As generally understood, this expression also means that such lands are held "in trust," either for the tribe or for individual tribal members. Native Americans can, of course, also own land in nontrust status, which is taxed by states and local governments and regulated just as is real estate owned by non-Indians.

See also **Trust Lands**

TRIBAL MEMBERSHIP The legal and cultural relationship a person has with a particular Indian tribe, especially one that is federally recognized, is his or her tribal membership. Federal law and tribal ordinances both define the criteria for tribal membership and define the rights and responsibilities of that relationship. The advantages of tribal membership include the right to vote in tribal elections, to hold office in the tribal government, and to participate in tribal and federal educational, housing, and other programs.

Criteria for membership typically include a specified percentage of Indian blood, commonly called the "blood quantum." Residency on the particular reservation for a period of time may be required. Perhaps the most important criterion is the ability to prove to the appropriate tribal officials that one's ancestors and relatives are tribal members. A tribe may have an enrollment committee or set of officials whose primary task is to investigate applications for tribal membership. Once the investigation is complete, the committee or officials make a recommendation to the governing body of the tribe, which then must approve or deny the application. If the application is approved, the Bureau of Indian Affairs (BIA) is notified. In determining the applicant's eligibility for participation in federal programs directed toward Indians, the BIA or other federal agency (depending on the particular federal program involved) may or may not accept the tribal decision of Indian membership.

A person may claim to be "Indian" without benefit of tribal membership. Unless such a claim is made for some fraudulent purpose—such as obtaining tribal, federal, or state benefits—it is not usually in and of itself unlawful. A tribe might perhaps consider such a claim to be grounds for excluding that person from living on its reservation.

See also **Blood Quantum; Enrollment Process;** ***Santa Clara Pueblo v. Martinez***

TRIBAL ORDINANCE OR RESOLUTION Tribal ordinances or resolutions are laws or formal expressions of policies made by the governing body of an Indian tribe. Like city or county governments, the governing body of an Indian tribe (typically called a council or commission) has the right to enact laws or regulations for the conduct of its members.

Ordinances are generally formal enactments of laws or rules applicable to all persons within the tribe's jurisdiction. They carry the force of law, that is, tribal members may be punished by the tribe for violating such ordinances. Penalties for violations may include fines, incarceration, or other sanctions such as exclusion from a tribal program.

The major difference between tribal ordinances and those of non-Indian cities and counties is that by decision of the U.S. Supreme Court in *Duro v. Reina*, 495 U.S. 676 (1990), a tribe may only punish its own members for violating its ordinances (later amended by the 1968 Indian Civil Rights Act, 25 U.S.C. § 1301[4], to include nonmember Indians). Tribal governments, though they are political entities, have no authority or jurisdiction to punish any non-Indian for violation of ordinances that carry a criminal penalty such as a fine or imprisonment in a tribal jail.

However, any tribal ordinance that provides for civil sanctions, such as the forfeiture of certain legal rights, are fully applicable to all residents of Indian reservations, whether they are members of that particular tribe, members of another Indian tribe, or non-Indians. The legal rights that may be taken away for violating an ordinance include the right to participate in tribal programs or the right to possess or use certain types of real or personal property. For instance, tribes may regulate the use of land within a reservation. A landowner who fails to abide by tribal ordinances on land use may be subject to an injunction forbidding the illegal use of the land. Failing to abide by the injunction may subject the landowner to contempt proceedings in tribal court, perhaps resulting in fines or forfeiture of personal property.

Resolutions are expressions of policy or decisions on particular issues rather than laws of general application to all residents. One example of a resolution would be a request by the council that the Bureau of Indian Affairs (BIA) or the state government take a certain position on an issue. Or, for example, a resolution might approve a person's application for tribal membership or ratify or confirm the tribal chairman's appointment of persons for certain government positions.

The process for enacting ordinances or resolutions is similar to that of cities and counties, although the specific procedure may vary from one tribe to another. The proposed ordinance or resolution is placed on the agenda for the governing body's meeting, and the agenda is published or otherwise made available to the public in advance of the meeting. After the council hears public input and discusses the proposed ordinance or resolution, it takes a vote on the measure. If the council votes to approve the measure, then the tribal chairman either signs it or vetoes it. If the measure is signed, it becomes effective after publication in the official newspaper of the tribe.

The "official newspaper" is simply a newspaper designated by the tribe as one in which all legal notices from the tribe to the people are published. This is a method by which a tribal government makes the public aware of newly issued laws or regulations. The purpose of publishing ordinances or resolutions in a newspaper is to allow enough tribal members (or city or county residents, as the case may be) the chance to get other tribal members to agree to refer the enacted ordinance or resolution to a vote of the membership. This might be done to allow the public to make the final decision, in a special election, as to whether a particular ordinance or resolution shall become law.

Once the resolution or ordinance becomes effective, an official copy is sent to the local office (agency) of the BIA. In many instances, the operation of certain federal programs depends on official action by the tribal government. For instance, eligibility to participate in federal Indian educational programs depends on whether a participant is enrolled as a tribal member. The BIA depends on the tribe to make that determination, which is often expressed as a tribal resolution.

TRIBE A tribe is a group of ethnically related people who share a common culture, spirituality, language, and set of customs. The group may or may not be officially recognized, or considered to be an Indian tribe, by the U.S. government. The process for gaining such recognition is lengthy, arduous, and expensive. Not all groups who consider themselves to be Indian tribes are officially acknowledged as such by the United States.

See also **Federally Recognized Tribe**

TRILOGY CASES Also know as the Marshall Trilogy, the Trilogy Cases are three early Supreme Court cases that established how the young United States would treat American Indians from a legal perspective. These decisions, *Johnson and Graham's Lessee v. William McIntosh,* 21 U.S. (8 Wheat.) 543 (1823); *Cherokee Nation v. Georgia,* 30 U.S. (5 Pet.) 1 (1831); and *Worcester v. Georgia,* 31 U.S. (6 Pet.) 515 (1832), were all decided between 1823 and 1832. They concern the ownership of lands occupied by the first Americans and the legal authority that the Indian tribes have over their lands. These opinions are still relevant today in Indian law, for they still guide U.S. courts as they continue to resolve disputes that arise in Indian country. Each of the cases is individually discussed in this book.

TRUST LAND LEASES Many parcels of trust land are owned by people who neither live on the land nor earn their livelihood from it (for example, in such activities as farming, mining, or ranching). Trust land, just like deeded real estate, is often leased out to farmers, ranchers, or others who can make profitable use of it. The Bureau of Indian Affairs (BIA) arranges for and must approve any leases of such land. Because of the fractionalized (that is, heavily split) ownership of many trust lands, the income an owner receives is often minimal at best. A landowner may receive as little as a few cents per year. These small amounts of money are held by the BIA for the landowner in individual Indian money accounts, to be paid to the owner as soon as the income rises to an amount specified in federal regulations. The cost of issuing small checks to landowners is quite high.

See also **Individual Indian Money Account; Trust Lands**

TRUST LANDS Trust lands are a special status of real estate in which the land is, strictly speaking, owned by the U.S. government rather than by private individuals. Prior to 1887, the federal government had no coordinated policy concerning this type of land. At that time, Congress passed laws regulating Indian lands. The term "trust lands" generically refers to the special status of that realty (that is, real estate) that is found only within or near Indian reservations in the United States.

Early federal statutes and treaties creating trust lands provided that they would not remain trust lands indefinitely. Under the most common scheme, once a parcel was assigned to an individual tribal member, the government would hold it in trust status for a period of 25 years, which was meant to give the member a chance to learn how to farm or otherwise manage the land by non-Indian standards. After the period had expired, the trust status was removed, and the land became deeded and was recorded with the local county official who maintains land records. Once in deeded status, the land shared none of the special characteristics discussed below. Because of a number of problems, among them the alarming erosion of the Indian land base, Congress stopped most of these transfers in 1934 with the passage of the Indian Reorganization Act. Currently, no trust lands may be transferred to deeded status without a request by the tribe or tribal member and the specific consent of the federal government.

There are actually two categories of trust lands. The first is the realty held in trust by the United States for the benefit of an Indian tribe. Such land might be where a tribe maintains, for example, a gambling casino, timber reserve, or ranch for the benefit of all tribal members in common. The second type is the land held in trust for the benefit of individual tribal members. This type of parcel, for example, may be where a tribal member has a family home, along with acreage for livestock, crops, or gardening. The characteristics of trust lands discussed in this article generally apply to both types.

Trust lands are not subject to state or local taxation. A city, county, or school district, for instance, cannot impose a property tax on trust lands located within its boundaries. Indian people earning money from activities located on such lands are, generally speaking, exempt from state income taxes as well. This tax-exempt attribute of the land has generated a tremendous amount of litigation between tribes and individual Indians on one side and state and local governments on the other side, the latter wanting additional tax revenue. Even though local and state governments are not allowed to tax trust lands, they must, in many cases, still provide services to all persons residing on such lands. Such services may include welfare, child support, fire protection, ambulance services, and law enforcement services. This depends on what jurisdiction Congress has allowed or required states to assume over such lands.

Congress, realizing the burden that untaxed land places on the budgets of local governments that must nonetheless provide services thereupon, has passed legislation paying local government monies to replace the lost taxation. (Similar federal appropriations are also made to local governments for other federal property, such as military bases, national forests, and national monuments, which also are not subject to local taxation.)

All Native Americans who meet age and residency requirements may vote and hold office in all levels of government. Thus, they may influence a local government's policy toward trust lands within its borders. Yet many tribal members, for many reasons, choose to remain outside of the political process of local and state governments.

Another characteristic of trust lands is that persons or other legal entities such as corporations may not place mortgages or other encumbrances or liens against the land. If a tribal member wants to borrow money to build a house on the land, a lender will probably not make a loan unless that person has other collateral or security to put up to help ensure repayment of the loan. A borrower who wants to build a house usually gives the lender a mortgage against the property, but that is not possible with trust land. This is one reason why the trust status of a parcel may not always be desirable, despite the exemption from property taxes. There exists a procedure in federal law to transfer such land from trust status to deeded status.

A third characteristic of trust land is that it may not be sold or transferred ("alienated," in legal terminology), either by a tribe or by a tribal member, without the approval of the U.S. government. Congress has delegated the power to deal with land transfers to the Bureau of Indian Affairs (BIA), and a tribe or tribal member who wants to sell or mortgage the land must make application with the BIA to do so. Indian tribes themselves on occasion may have reason to want to transfer or sell parcels of their lands. Such reasons may include exchanging lands with the owners of deeded, that is, nontrust, lands in order to have a single large parcel of land for development for housing, grazing, mining, or crops. The tribe might negotiate with a neighboring landowner to sell him or her tribal land in exchange for land closer to the land the tribe wants to develop.

A final characteristic of trust lands has to do with state jurisdiction over such lands. Generally, unless Congress specifically states otherwise, such parcels are not subject to state criminal or civil jurisdiction. For example, if a person, whether Indian or not, is arrested by a state trooper for a traffic offense, the status of the land may affect the legality of the arrest and whether the state can prosecute the person for the offense. In addition, states, counties, and cities may not be able to impose zoning or environmental regulations over trust lands. When such lands are mingled with deeded lands, much confusion results for all law enforcement officials and other governmental agencies.

See also **Aboriginal Possession or Title; Checkerboard Lands; Deeded Lands; General Allotment Act of 1887; Indian Reorganization Act of 1934; Jurisdiction; Reservation**

TRUST RESPONSIBILITIES The U.S. government has special trust responsibilities toward Indian tribes and individuals. This Indian law policy originated with the U.S. Supreme Court in the so-called Trilogy Cases. Under general principles of the law of trusts, one person, called a trustee, has a special obligation to manage any property placed in his or her care for the best interest of the trust's beneficiary. In Indian law, the Bureau of Indian Affairs is the branch of the federal government generally responsible, as the trustee, to manage Indian property—such as money, other personal property such as equipment, and trust lands—for the benefit of tribes and tribal members. However, this trust obligation applies to all federal agencies that deal with Native Americans. This relationship can also be described as a "guardian-ward" relationship.

The trust principles have evolved over many years when the Supreme Court and lower federal courts have been called upon to resolve a myriad of legal disputes. These trust obligations define the standard of conduct for governmental officials and for Congress itself. Treaties, statutes, executive orders, and administrative regulations are interpreted by the federal courts applying these principles.

When Congress singles out Indians for special treatment, either in their favor or against, such legislation must be "tied rationally" to Congress's trust obligations toward Indians. In other words, there must be some rational relationship between Congress's action and its duties toward the Indian tribes. Although Congress still has nearly absolute, or plenary, authority to legislate in Indian affairs, its actions must be read in light of its responsibilities to protect Indians.

The trust responsibility has resulted in the development of the Canons of Construction, which are rules of interpretation that protect Indian interests whenever federal statutes, treaties, or like pronouncements of the government need clarification. Generally, whenever the federal government establishes or reserves Indian rights—for example, in water rights issues—its pronouncements are given the broadest possible interpretation. For instance, if fishing rights are an issue between the state government and an Indian tribe, there may be an early treaty or presidential executive order that deals directly or indirectly with such an issue. The courts, in clarifying what those documents mean, will if possible choose an interpretation that upholds and protects the Indian fishing rights.

Conversely, when a federal law or regulation purports to extinguish or limit some Indian right, the courts may interpret that law or rule narrowly to avoid reduction of Indian rights. For example, a question may arise as to whether a parcel of land is still in trust status. Before ruling that the land is no longer in trust status, the federal courts will look at all relevant evidence to make sure that Congress and the president specifically intended it to be withdrawn—a limitation of Indian rights. The courts generally will not find by implication that Congress or the president intended to reduce Indian rights. Congress must expressly, specifically state that it intends to cancel or limit Indian rights in a particular situation.

This Indian trust responsibility may be found to exist even if no specific federal statute or treaty deals with the situation in question. So long as Congress does not specifically intend to reduce Indian rights, the courts may use the trust doctrine to prevent a federal or state agency from limiting Indian rights. This may occur in such areas as Indian water rights. For example, if reclamation officials seek to divert water from a stream and the diversion may adversely affect the quality or quantity of waters located within an Indian reservation, federal courts might not allow the water to be diverted, even though no legislation specifically addresses this issue. As with all other judicial doctrines, the trust responsibility is subject to change and refinement over the course of time. The nature and extent of the federal government's trust responsibility may vary as new legal disputes come before the federal courts.

See also **Canons of Construction; Trilogy Cases; Trust Lands**

U

United States Commission on Civil Rights

The U.S. Commission on Civil Rights is an agency of the U.S. government established by Congress in 1957 to investigate and study civil rights issues. Currently, the commission has eight members, half appointed by the president and half appointed by Congress. No more than half of the members may be of the same political party. Among other duties, the commission maintains a national clearinghouse on information pertaining to civil rights and investigates complaints of official discrimination against persons on account of race, national origin, color, sex, and the like.

The commission has the right to hold public hearings on civil rights issues and to make recommendations to Congress and the public based on its findings. Like many federal boards and commissions, it has the power to subpoena, that is, to compel persons to appear at its hearings and give testimony under oath, and also to produce relevant records in matters dealing with civil rights. From time to time, the commission has held hearings in Indian country to examine Indian civil rights issues.

United States Supreme Court

The U.S. Supreme Court is the highest court of the United States. The vast majority of its cases are appeals from the lower courts of the United States and from the highest courts of each of the 50 states. The president appoints the chief justice and the eight associate justices. All members, once confirmed by the Senate, serve until they choose to retire or until they die. Only Congress may remove a justice from office. In Indian law, the Court is of special importance. By legal custom and tradition, the Supreme Court is the final arbiter or interpreter of the U.S. Constitution, and its decisions are final. The Supreme Court also shapes and defines the relationship among the federal and state governments and the nation's Indian tribes. Although Congress has great power to limit or eliminate Indian tribes' powers of self-government, the Supreme Court may set limits on the Congress's powers to do so. Over the history of the United States, the Court has handed down many decisions that define, for example, the extent to which tribes may regulate the activities of non-Indians living in Indian country. The Court has a mixed record in according respect to Indian tribes as sovereign entities, with powers of self rule.

UNITED STATES V. ANTELOPE (1977)

In *United States v. Antelope,* 430 U.S. 641 (1977), the U.S. Supreme Court held that for crimes committed on a reservation, it was constitutionally permissible to treat Indian and non-Indian defendants differently. In the case that led to *Antelope,* the defendants, both Indian, broke into a non-Indian's home located on their own reservation. They were tried and convicted for murder and other crimes under the authority of the Major Crimes Act of 1885. That law, one of the earliest to deal directly with criminal jurisdiction in Indian country, gives the federal courts the power to try such cases. (The Act is still in effect.)

Antelope and his codefendant contended that because of their race, they were treated differently than non-Indian defendants would have been. Normally, under the Fifth Amendment and the Fourteenth Amendment to the U.S. Constitution, all governments are prohibited from discriminating against persons solely on account of their race. (One of the very rare exceptions to this limitation deals with Indian-preference laws in employment at the Bureau of Indian Affairs.) Criminal defenses and some procedural matters are handled differently in state courts than in the federal system. For example, the federal government needs less evidence to prove first-degree murder than would the prosecutor in state courts. Under federal law, had the defendants been non-Indian, their case would have been tried in the state courts.

The Supreme Court, nonetheless, rejected Antelope's claim, which on its face *does* treat defendants differently on account of race. The *Antelope* Court decided that the passage and operation of the Major Crimes Act was based not on race but, rather, on the long-standing political relationship between the federal government and the Indian tribes. Congress has extensive authority to regulate all types of activity in Indian country. Alone among ethnically distinct groups in the United States today, Indian tribes have a government-to-government relationship with the federal government, as evidenced by the more than 300 treaties and agreements made between these sovereigns. The Court also decided the case partly on the basis that the Indian defendants in this case had the same constitutionally mandated procedural protections—that is, the right to counsel, the right to a jury trial, the right to subpoena witnesses, and so on—in the federal courts that all other defendants do.

See also **Due Process; Major Crimes Act of 1885**

UNITED STATES v. KAGAMA (1886)

In *United States v. Kagama,* 118 U.S. 375 (1886), the U.S. Supreme Court enunciated the Plenary Powers Doctrine of Indian law.

One year prior to this decision, Congress had enacted the Major Crimes Act of 1885, which at the time gave U.S. federal courts jurisdiction to punish criminal acts committed by Indians against other Indians in Indian country. In *Kagama,* two Indians, who had been indicted (charged) with the crime of murdering another on a reservation in California, challenged the constitutionality of the Act, claiming it was outside Congress's law-making authority over Indian tribes.

The Court decided that Congress did indeed have the authority to regulate such conduct, but its decision did not rely on the Indian Commerce Clause (the clause of the Constitution that gives Congress the power to regulate Indian affairs). Rather, the Court relied on a much broader principle: that Indian tribes, as "domestic dependent nations," are in a guardian-ward relationship with the U.S. government. Therefore, according to the Court, the government has some responsibility to provide for the well-being of the tribes.

Thus the Plenary Powers Doctrine came into being. It gives Congress nearly total authority to regulate every aspect of life for Indian people, even in matters that do not deal with commerce or economic matters. However, although this doctrine is still quite effective today, the Constitution does place some limits on Congress's authority to manage Indian affairs.

See also **Indian Commerce Clause; Plenary Powers Doctrine**

UNITED STATES v. MCBRATNEY (1881)

In *United States v. McBratney,* 104 U.S. 621 (1881), the U.S. Supreme Court granted states general criminal jurisdiction over crimes in Indian country when both the wrongdoer and victim are non-Indian. Even though regulation of criminal behavior in Indian country is an essential part of tribal self- rule, the Court ruled that the state had exclusive jurisdiction over the crime, notwithstanding the fact that Congress had never expressly forbidden tribes to deal with these matters.

This reasoning and ruling is an unusual departure from the doctrine of inherent sovereignty. Normally, Indian tribes possess all powers of self-government except those specifically limited or abolished by Congress.

In this case, however, the Court found that the "equal-footing" principle mandated that only the state is allowed to try such cases, even though Congress never expressly permitted this. This principle holds that all newly admitted states have the same rights, privileges, and relationship with the national government as did the original 13 states. This "equal-footing" principle took precedence over the right of the tribes to govern activities arising within their borders. This case is also known as the *McBratney* exception, and it is still in effect today.

McBratney was the first in a series of cases in which the Supreme Court was willing to permit state authority in Indian country without specific congressional approval. This represents a significant erosion of the long-standing principle of tribal sovereignty, first enunciated in the Trilogy Cases decades earlier. *McBratney* demonstrates the fact that tribal self-rule is only what Congress or the courts say it is. The *McBratney* decision, followed to the present, opened the way for states to assert their authority in Indian country even when Congress has failed to address the issue.

See also **Criminal Jurisdiction; Inherent Sovereignty**

UNITED STATES V. SIOUX NATION OF INDIANS (1980)

In *United States v. Sioux Nation of Indians,* 448 U.S. 371 (1980), the U.S. Supreme Court demonstrated that there are limits to the Plenary Powers Doctrine, whereby the federal government may regulate the use and disposition of Indian lands. This decision is also known as the Black Hills Case. In the 1860s, the United States entered into several treaties with some of the Sioux Nations. In exchange for peaceful relations with the Indian tribes, the government set aside certain lands for the exclusive use of the Indian people. Eventually, the public pressured Congress to open these treaty lands to non-Indian settlement. As a result, the government entered into an "executive agreement" with a small number of Sioux leaders by which the latter would give up their claims to these lands. This agreement, later ratified by Congress, abrogated (that is, canceled) the earlier treaties. Many tribal leaders, unaccustomed to the legalisms of non-Indians, misunderstood the meaning of this agreement.

Through decades of litigation in the federal courts of claims (specialized federal courts that deal only with claims, usually for money, that a person has against the federal government itself) and the Indian Claims Commission, the courts eventually determined that the government had taken tribal property (the former treaty lands) for public use and that the Sioux people were entitled to monetary compensation. The Supreme Court, in *United States v. Sioux Nation of Indians,* affirmed the decision of the court of claims, awarding the Sioux Nations money damages plus interest. This case demonstrates that Congress's authority to dispose of tribal property, although nearly total, is not without its limits. One of the few restrictions to this power that the Supreme Court has imposed is the requirement that Congress, under the Just Compensation Clause, must pay an Indian tribe when it takes its property for public uses, such as a national park.

See also **Indian Claims Commission; Just Compensation Clause; Plenary Powers Doctrine**

UNITED STATES V. WASHINGTON (1974)

United States v. Washington, 384 F.Supp. 312 (W.D. Wash. 1974) is an important case of the U.S. District Court in the State of Washington upholding the rights of Indians in Washington to fish on off-reservation lands. This case, also known as the Boldt Decision (named after George Boldt, the federal judge who wrote it), was ultimately approved by the U.S. Supreme Court in a related case, *Washington v. Washington State Commercial Passenger Fishing Vessel Association*, 443 U.S. 658 (1979).

In the mid-1800s, 14 tribes in what is now the State of Washington entered into treaties with the United States. All of these accords contained a provision that allowed Indians to take fish "at all of their 'usual and accustomed grounds', in common with all the citizens of the Territory [now State of Washington]." The Boldt Decision is noted for its detailed account of the history of the tribes involved in the decision and of the treaty-making process. This case is also an excellent example of the operation of one of the Canons of Construction: Indian treaties are to be construed, or interpreted, as the Indians would have understood them when they were made. According to this court decision, at that time there were no words in the local Indian dialects that would have conveyed the idea that the tribes were agreeing to have their rights to take fish limited.

At issue was the meaning of the treaty clauses giving the Indians the right to fish at their usual and accustomed places in common with other citizens of the territory. Judge Boldt also applied another of the Canons of Construction: Ambiguities in words or phrases of treaties are to be construed to favor Indian rights. In other words, if such phrases have two or more equally reasonable meanings, they are to be given the interpretation that would favor Indian rights. Based on historical research, Boldt believed that during the treaty-making process, the Indians were not told that these treaties would limit their rights to take fish. He reasoned that as the tribes depended on fishing for survival, it was highly unlikely that they would agree to anything that would threaten their survival. Accordingly, the court, in interpreting this treaty provision concerning fishing rights, awarded one-half of the harvestable fish to the local Indian populace.

Predictably, Judge Boldt's decision was highly unpopular with local non-Indian commercial and sport fishermen. Over the years, both the state and local fishing and sporting interests continually attacked his decision. Nonetheless, it has stood the test of time and remains good law as a recent expression of the Indian Reserved Fishing Rights Doctrine, which was first enunciated in the Supreme Court case of *United States v. Winans,* 198 U.S. 371 (1905), more than 70 years earlier.

***UNITED STATES V. WHEELER* (1978)** In *United States v. Wheeler,* 435 U.S. 313 (1978) the U.S. Supreme Court decided whether or not both a tribe and the federal government may punish an individual for crimes arising out of the same incident. Anthony Wheeler, an Indian, pled guilty to several minor offenses in the Navajo Tribal Court. He was subsequently indicted by a federal court for rape; the indictment arose out of the same episode that had led to the guilty plea in tribal court. Wheeler appealed the federal court action. He claimed that the Double Jeopardy Clause of the Fifth Amendment barred his prosecution in federal court because he had already pled guilty in tribal court.

The Double Jeopardy Clause bars a governmental entity from trying a person twice for the same acts. For example, if a set of facts gives rise to a burglary charge and the defendant is acquitted, a state or the federal government cannot try the same defendant a second time for the same offense.

Only different governmental entities, which derive their authority to govern from sources independent of each other, may both try a person for criminal acts arising out of the same set of facts. Local governments, that is, cities and counties, are considered to be subdivisions or agents of a state government. Territorial governments—such as those of American Samoa and Guam—were created by Congress, and they derive their authority from the U.S. government. Thus, states and local governments, or U.S. territories and the federal government, cannot try persons for crimes arising out of the same set of facts, even if each has its own criminal law covering the same act. The state and federal governments, however, derive their authority from different sources, that is, state constitutions and the U.S. Constitution, respectively. Therefore, it is not double jeopardy for both a state and the federal government, for example, to try a person for violating both state and federal drug laws.

Because Indian tribes are neither U.S. territories, states, or local governments, the Supreme Court felt compelled to decide this issue. Analyzing the source of the powers of Indian tribes, the *Wheeler* Court once again adopted the doctrine of inherent tribal sovereignty. Indian tribes, according to the Court, possess powers of self-rule that predate the founding of the United States. The *Wheeler* Court followed much of its own precedent by holding that these powers are not dependent on the

U.S. Constitution but are inherent, that is, a natural part of the Indian tribes as political entities. Tribes are not merely extensions of the federal government. However, tribes do not have the full powers of self-government that foreign nations do. Congress may extinguish or otherwise limit Indian tribal powers of self-government. Nonetheless, tribal and federal prosecutions for crimes arising out of one set of facts do not violate the Double Jeopardy Clause.

The *Wheeler* decision was handed down only several months after the Court decided the case of *Oliphant v. Suquamish Indian Tribe,* 435 U.S. 191 (1978). The Court in the latter case found that Indian tribes had only those powers delegated to them by Congress, a radical departure from the inherent sovereignty doctrine just discussed. Nevertheless, the *Wheeler* case is still relied on today by the courts.

See also **Inherent Sovereignty; *Oliphant v. Suquamish Indian Tribe***

UNITED STATES V. WINANS (1905)

In *United States v. Winans,* 198 U.S. 371 (1905), the U.S. Supreme Court recognized the importance of treaties to American Indian fishing rights. In the mid-nineteenth century, the Yakima Nation negotiated a treaty with the United States. This treaty, among other things, reserved to the Yakima Indians (1) the use and occupancy of certain described lands, (2) the exclusive right to take fish on the reservation, and (3) a right to take fish off their reservation, at all of their "usual and accustomed places," along with citizens of what is now the State of Washington. Some time after the treaty was signed, some non-Indians engaged in fishing on lands that had long passed out of tribal hands. Although this land was in fee (land that the owner may sell or otherwise transfer without the permission of the government or another person), it was located at places where the Yakima had traditionally fished for centuries. Lineas and Audubon Winans and some other non-Indian landowners refused to allow tribal members to fish at these places.

The United States subsequently brought a lawsuit on behalf of the tribe to prevent Winans and the others from obstructing tribal members from fishing. The lower courts agreed with Winans, deciding that since he and the other property owners had acquired good title to the land, they had the right to exclude whomever they chose from their property.

In its decision reversing the lower courts and upholding Indian fishing rights, the Supreme Court reasoned that treaties are not grants of rights *to* Indians but, rather, a grant of rights *from* them. In other words, the treaty process meant that in exchange for certain things from the United States, the Indians had given the government some of their authority over their lands and had reserved to themselves all other rights and privileges not given up. The Indians were granted an easement (that is, permission to cross over public or private lands) to exercise their fishing rights. The *Winans* Court further went on to decide that land that passes out of Indian hands is still burdened with treaty fishing rights in favor of Indians. The Court realized that fishing was a matter of prime importance to the Yakima Nation. It was an essential part of their livelihood. Given that fact, the Court reasoned, the tribe would not have knowingly bargained away rights upon which their survival depended. If they had, the tribe would have been left with a reservation perhaps incapable of supporting the members who lived there. The *Winans* decision confirmed the importance of the Canons of Construction, that is, that Indian fishing rights reserved to tribes by treaties will not be considered to have been extinguished unless Congress expressly states its intent to take those rights away. This is one of the fundamental principles of Indian law. This concept of Indian reserved fishing rights as announced in the *Winans* decision endures today and is of prime importance to many tribes.

UNITED TRIBES OF ALASKA The United Tribes of Alaska (UTA) is a statewide organization that advocates on behalf of tribal governments in Alaska. Whereas the Alaska Native Brotherhood and Sisterhood and the Alaska Federation of Natives concern themselves primarily with land and social issues, the UTA's purpose is to advocate for the sovereignty of Native Alaskan tribal governmental bodies. Unlike regional or village corporations, the tribes are true governing entities, in many respects like Indian tribes elsewhere. The UTA, founded in the early 1980s, is purely a political action group for the benefit of its member tribes. It does not deliver social services to Native Alaskans, and it is itself not considered by the federal or state governments to be a tribe or tribal government.

USUFRUCT In the civil law, usufruct is a license or right to use the property of another for whatever advantage it might bring to the user. The person or entity who has this right may do so, as long as he or she does not alter the property. A usufruct is merely a right to use, not change, the property. For instance, an Indian tribe may, for a fee, lease tribal grazing lands to a non-Indian rancher to feed his livestock. The rancher may run his cattle on the land, as long as he does not damage it. The rancher will never own the property. He merely has the right to use it for a time. Usufructs include easements, leases, permits, and the like.

V

VICTORIA, FRANCISCO DE (1480–1546) Francisco de Victoria, a Spanish legal scholar and Catholic priest, wrote extensively on Native Americans' legal rights to retain their lands in the face of foreign conquest. The American government in colonial times incorporated his ideas and theories into its legal treatment of Native Americans. He took the enlightened view that Native Americans possessed certain rights as a free and rational people. These rights included the right to control their own destiny and complete rights to own and use their lands as they saw fit. He did not necessarily subscribe to the then widely accepted notion that those who did not live as Europeans did were unintelligent or incapable of rational thinking and therefore not deserving to control their own property. He believed that the only reason native peoples could be deprived of their property and control over their own affairs would be if they were incapable of rational thought.

Victoria's views on Indian rights were not shared by his contemporaries, however. Most other scholars of his day believed that all non-Christian people, especially those who were not "civilized"—that is, who were not like Europeans—were subject to conquest and colonization by the superior and Christian European nations. The prevailing thought of Victoria's day gave conquering nations complete control of the lands of native inhabitants. The rationale for this was to Christianize and "civilize" the barbaric (that is, non-European-thinking) aboriginal peoples. Victoria's beliefs helped provide a rational and humane basis for the treatment of Indians in the state and federal courts of the United States.

See also **Doctrine of Discovery**

VILLAGE CORPORATION Village corporations are profit-making entities created by the Alaska Native Claims Settlement Act (ANCSA) of 1971. These businesses are organized under the corporation laws of the State of Alaska. There are some 200 village corporations in the state, each located within one of 13 regional corporations. The village corporation's primary duties are to manage the land and funds entrusted to them under the terms of ANCSA. However, they may also provide educational, welfare, health, and other benefits to their members. Village corporations have the same obligations as do the regional corporations to manage their assets for the best interests of their owners, the Native Alaskans or others who may be shareholders. Conflicts may arise, however, when the exploitation of land to maximize profits collides with the traditional lifestyles of village residents and shareholders. For instance, oil exploration activities might interfere with the ability of local villagers to fish and hunt for a living. Some of these conflicts may be settled at the local level. Unfortunately, many such disputes find their way to the courts, where they are often settled only at the cost of significant time and expense.

Congress had originally placed severe limitations on the transferability of village corporation stock, partly to prevent ownership of the corporation from passing into nonnative hands. Nevertheless, in the 1980s, Congress relaxed many of these restrictions by permitting these local entities to amend their governing documents, that is, their articles of incorporation, to determine to whom and when shares may be transferred. This has the potential to enable non–Native Alaskans to get control of the village corporation.

Although these village corporations may own land and occupy the same territory as an Alaska Native tribal government or local municipality, they are different organizations. Powers of self-government may be exercised to some degree by tribal governments organized under the Alaska Indian Reorganization Act of 1936 or by tribal groups that have been incorporated under state law as a municipality or city. Village corporations, as such, have no powers of self-government.

See also **Alaska Native Claims Settlement Act of 1971; Corporation; Regional Corporation**

W

Waiver of Sovereign Immunity Under the legal doctrine of waiver of sovereign immunity, a tribe may voluntarily—by tribal ordinance or some other procedure—give up its right to be immune from being sued in federal, state, or tribal courts. Generally, a tribe can clearly waive its immunity from suits against it in its own courts. Less certain is its right to waive immunity when it concerns other courts or where the subject of a lawsuit concerns trust, that is, restricted, property.

The issue of sovereign immunity has been a major concern of non-Indians doing business on a reservation. Such people often claim that they have no remedy against the tribe for wrongs they may suffer at its hands. This is one reason, whether justified or not, why non-Indians have been suspicious of tribal courts.

Of course, because Congress has plenary (that is, almost complete) authority over Indian affairs, it may enact legislation surrendering the sovereign immunity of tribal entities and allowing them to be sued in any court that Congress specifies. An example of this is found in the Indian Civil Rights Act of 1968, in which Congress allows tribes to be sued in federal court under a writ of habeas corpus against the tribe. However, under the Canons of Construction of Indian law (which hold that any ambiguities or unclarities in regulations, treaties, and so on must be interpreted in favor of Indians), such waivers cannot be implied. It must be shown that Congress clearly intended to waive such rights for the tribes.

Immunity from lawsuit generally extends only to a tribe itself and not to an individual, whether or not he or she is a member of the tribe claiming immunity or of another tribe or non-Indian. Under Indian law, sovereign immunity also does not extend to an individual tribal official. Some Indian tribes in the United States have renounced their immunity from lawsuits; others have not. A tribe may waive its immunity from certain types of lawsuits, such as for a debt owed by the tribe, and other tribal ordinances may allow suits against a tribe for wrongful acts, such as negligence by the tribe in performing its duties.

See also **Canons of Construction; Fee Simple; Sovereign Immunity; Trust Lands; Trust Responsibilities**

WARD A ward is a person whose important life decisions are made for him or her by a more responsible person. The usual relationship in which one person makes such decisions for another is that of parent and child. In most cases where there is no parent to make decisions for a child, a guardian-ward relationship is substituted. This is often the situation when an orphan is a minor (under the legal age) child who cannot make such decisions as deciding where to live or what medical advice to follow when sick and who cannot perform such legally binding actions as signing a contract. Those decisions are made by a responsible person or legal entity capable of exercising a sound and mature judgment as to those matters.

For instance, a minor child who inherits a fortune is often not capable of deciding how to maintain such wealth for his or her long-term benefit. A court would appoint a lawyer, some other person, or a bank or other financial institution to oversee the proper investment and use of that fortune for the child's benefit.

In Indian law, court decisions made during the earliest days of the United States used the term "guardian-ward relationship" to describe the relationship that the federal government had with Indian people, both individually and as tribes. Early non-Indian settlers believed that because Indian people and tribes did not work the land or live as the European settlers did, the Native Americans were incapable of managing their own affairs. Some Indian tribes in fact did farm. Others, which were nomadic, survived by hunting. Therefore, among the legal artifices used to justify taking Indian lands, first the European governments and later the U.S. government decided that the Indian people needed an experienced "partner" to help them manage their own internal affairs. This guardian-ward relationship was the early foundation for Indian-white relations, and it continues to this day. At the present time, in most cases, the Bureau of Indian Affairs acts as the "guardian" of many Indian assets, such as trust lands and other tribal property.

See also **Guardianship; Trust Lands; Trust Responsibilities**

***WARREN TRADING POST V. ARIZONA TAX COMMISSION* (1965)** *Warren Trading Post v. Arizona Tax Commission*, 380 U.S. 685 (1965), is a major U.S. Supreme Court case dealing with the authority of states to tax commercial activities in Indian country. The *Warren* decision involved a federally licensed trader on the Navajo

Indian Reservation. The State of Arizona levied a gross receipts tax on a non-Indian corporation (the Warren Trading Post Corporation) selling goods to Indians on a reservation. The Arizona Supreme Court upheld the tax, but the U.S. Supreme Court struck it down. In making its decision, the *Warren* Court shifted away from the infringement test of *Williams v. Lee*, 358 U.S. 217 (1959). Instead, it emphasized that the federal regulation of trade with Indian tribes is so extensive as to preclude state regulation in this matter; that is, it applied the preemption test.

This case is important in modern Indian law, for it signals a greater willingness by the judiciary to accommodate state concerns when states seek to extend their authority over activities on Indian lands. The courts have de-emphasized the importance of the infringement test when they are called upon to resolve tribal-state conflicts. The infringement test generally favors tribes, relying heavily on the notion that as political entities, they have inherent sovereignty. This means that tribes normally would have the same authority as states to govern people and activities within reservation borders, unless Congress has expressly taken away a particular authority. When courts used the infringement test, they asked first whether the proposed state action—that is, in this case, the taxing of reservation activities—interfered with the right of reservation tribal members to make and be ruled by their own laws. The U.S. Supreme Court continued to de-emphasize the importance of the infringement test in the subsequent case of *McClanahan v. Arizona State Tax Commission*, 411 U.S. 164 (1973). The *McClanahan* case is still widely followed today in settling tribal-state jurisdictional battles.

See also **Infringement Test**

WILLIAMS V. LEE (1959)

Williams v. Lee, 358 U.S. 217 (1959), is the U.S. Supreme Court's first modern statement on tribal-state relations. This case concerned a lawsuit brought in state court by a non-Indian trader to collect monies owed to him by Indians for goods sold to them on the Indian reservation. The state court held that since no federal law prohibited state jurisdiction over such lawsuits, it was proper for state courts to deal with the matter. On appeal, the U.S. Supreme Court held that the state courts have no authority to decide disputes in such cases if the tribe's legislative body has assumed that authority and given it to the tribal courts. In *Williams v. Lee* the Court decided that unless Congress has enacted a law on the subject in question, the test of whether the state or tribe shall assume jurisdiction over a particular activity is whether the "state action infringed on the rights of reservation Indians to make their own laws and be ruled by them." This is the infringement test used by courts to decide in a given case, absent federal law on the subject, whether a state has the authority to act in Indian country. With some exceptions, under this test, if an activity—such as a business, land use, and so on—conducted by non-Indians and carried out on a reservation has an impact on Indians or Indian property, that alone may give tribal courts the power to regulate or even forbid it.

The Court in this case followed its own earlier decisions, which held that tribes have some measure of inherent sovereignty, that is, the power to manage their own affairs and any activities that affect the tribe or tribal members on a reservation. Any government, in order to be sovereign, must have some authority to manage its own affairs. Else, it has no real authority and is really no government, or sovereign, at all. In recent years, however, some courts have adopted the preemption test (a legal doctrine that asks whether the national government, as permitted by the Constitution, has so regulated some activity that state or local governments are prevented from dealing with the same issues) rather than the infringement test to help resolve jurisdictional issues, that is, to decide whether a state or tribal court has authority over a particular dispute.

See also **Infringement Test; Preemption**

WINTERS DOCTRINE

The *Winters* Doctrine governs the water rights of Indian tribes and tribal members. The doctrine had its genesis in the U.S. Supreme Court case of *Winters v. United States*, 207 U.S. 564 (1908). The case arose when a non-Indian landowner wanted to dam a stream to use its water on his property. The dam prevented water in the stream from reaching the Indian reservation. *Winters* holds that whenever Congress creates an Indian reservation, it intends that there will be enough water available for the reservation's Indian residents to use the reservation for the purposes for which it was created. In most cases, that meant human survival, which might entail agricultural pursuits (such as raising livestock and crops) and in more recent times, industrial development and recreational uses. As one might imagine, water is critically important for economic development, as well as survival, and the *Winters* case is still influential today.

The *Winters* maxim is also known as the implied reservation of water rule in modern law. Congress rarely discussed water issues when it created an Indian reservation or otherwise set aside land for tribal use. Therefore, since Congress did not specifically mention water rights, the Supreme Court assumed that water rights attached to the lands that Congress set aside for Indian use. The logic of the *Winters* case was that Congress would not create Indian reservations without giving Indians the means to survive on such lands. There would be no reason to create a reservation for Indians if they were unable to live on such lands. Exactly how much water a tribe may use and for what purposes under the *Winters* doctrine are controversial issues, still being decided in the courts.

See also **Indian Water Rights**

WORCESTER V. GEORGIA (1832)

Worcester v. Georgia, 31 U.S. (6 Pet.) 515 (1832) is the third and final of the Trilogy Cases. It addressed, for the first time, the limit of state authority in Indian country. Samuel Worcester was a missionary living on the Cherokee Reservation in Georgia. He had the permission of the tribe to do so. At the time of this case, the people of Georgia, through their public officials, vigorously supported the national Indian removal policy of President Andrew Jackson. Jackson, in order to meet the demands of white settlers for land in the southeastern United States, embarked on a policy of encouraging the Indians, by treaty or by force, to move westward in order to open Cherokee land for settlement.

The Georgia legislature had passed laws forbidding whites to live or trade with the Cherokee. Worcester was arrested for violating this law. He was found guilty by the courts and sentenced to prison. He then appealed his conviction. The appeal ultimately came to the U.S. Supreme Court on the grounds that substantial federal and constitutional issues were involved.

Chief Justice John Marshall, writing for the Court, ruled that state laws had no effect on Indian reservations largely because the U.S. Constitution left to Congress the job of regulating trade with Indians and Indian affairs generally. Marshall also found that the European governments and the United States had a long history of dealing with Indian tribes on a government-to-government basis. The treaties that the United States signed with the Cherokee and other tribes also reflected this relationship. Under the treaties, the tribes were dealt with completely apart from the state governments. Thus, Worcester's conviction was reversed, as state law was found to have no effect on the reservation. Georgia's officials, however, refused to obey the Court's decision. A constitutional crisis was averted only when Jackson persuaded the governor of Georgia to pardon Worcester and another man also imprisoned for the same offense.

The Trilogy Cases—*Worcester; Johnson and Graham's Lessee v. William McIntosh,* 21 U.S. (8 Wheat.) 543 (1823); and *Cherokee Nation v. Georgia* 30 U.S. (5 Pet.) 1 (1831)—still form the basis for many of the present-day court rulings on Indian law cases. *Worcester* is still a rule of law, and state laws normally do not extend to Indian country unless Congress, exercising its constitutional power to regulate Indian affairs, chooses to allow the states such authority.

See also **Jurisdiction**

Z

ZONING In land use planning, a governmental body decides through zoning (marking off into sections) what any given piece of land may be used for. Typically, a local unit of government, such as a city or county, publishes a so-called master plan that specifies the allowable activities on any land within its jurisdiction. This means that a parcel of land may be restricted to certain broad areas of activity, such as agricultural, business, industrial, mining, or residential uses. Agricultural use would permit the raising of crops or livestock. A business classification would allow retail establishments, professional offices, and schools. Industrial uses would include factories, mills, warehouses, and the like. A mining classification would allow the extraction of natural resources from the earth. Finally, a residential use would allow dwelling units, ranging from multistoried apartments to single-family homes.

Such comprehensive plans are enacted to help ensure that property development in one area does not unduly impair the use of adjoining or near-by property. For instance, it would not make sense to allow a steel mill—with the noise, dust, and other pollution it generates—to be located next to a hospital or school. These master plans help ensure that activities that are unusually noisy, smelly, or dirty are not placed too near residential areas. Significant public input is usually taken before master plans or comprehensive zoning ordinances are adopted. Before the zoning classification of a particular area can be changed, any interested landowners as well as the general public must usually be given an opportunity to comment on the proposed changes.

In Indian law, under *Montana v. United States,* 450 U.S. 544 (1981), tribes may zone most land within their reservation boundaries, unless the land in question is predominantly of a non-Indian character and is privately owned by non-Indians, which must be determined on a case-by-case basis. As Indian tribes encourage economic development to boost their local economies, it becomes increasingly important for tribal governments to take an active role in regulating land use, especially where the operation of business enterprises may interfere with the traditional religious or cultural activities of tribal members.

See also ***Montana v. United States***

Table of Cases

Alaska v. Native Village of Venetie Tribal Government, 522 U.S. 520 (1998)
Arizona v. California, 373 U.S. 546 (1963)
Babbitt v. Youpee, 519 U.S. 234 (1997)
Brendale v. Confederated Tribes and Bands of Yakima, 492 U.S. 408 (1989)
Bryan v. Itasca County, 426 U.S. 373 (1976)
California v. Cabazon Band of Mission Indians, 480 U.S. 202 (1987)
Cherokee Nation v. Georgia, 30 U.S. (5 Pet.) 1 (1831)
DeCoteau v. District County Court, 420 U.S. 425 (1975)
Duro v. Reina, 495 U.S. 676 (1990)
Employment Division, Department of Human Resources of Oregon v. Smith, 494 U.S. 872 (1990)
Ex Parte Crow Dog, 109 U.S. 556 (1883)
Johnson and Graham's Lessee v. William McIntosh, 21 U.S. (8 Wheat.) 543 (1823)
Lincoln v. Vigil, 508 U.S. 182 (1993)
Lone Wolf v. Hitchcock, 187 U.S. 553 (1903)
Lyng v. Northwest Cemetery Protective Association, 485 U.S. 439 (1988)
Marbury v. Madison, 5 U.S. (1 Cranch) 137, 2 L.Ed. 60 (1803)
McClanahan v. Arizona State Tax Commission, 411 U.S. 164 (1973)
Menominee Tribe v. United States, 391 U.S. 404 (1968)
Montana v. United States, 450 U.S. 544 (1981)
Morton v. Mancari, 417 U.S. 535 (1974)
Morton v. Ruiz, 415 U.S. 199 (1974)
National Farmers Union Insurance Companies v. Crow Tribe of Indians, 471 U.S. 845 (1985)
New Mexico v. Mescalero Apache Tribe, 462 U.S. 324 (1983)
Oliphant v. Suquamish Indian Tribe, 435 U.S. 191 (1978)
Rice v. Cayetano, 98-818; 528 U.S. ___ (2000)
Santa Clara Pueblo v. Martinez, 436 U.S. 49 (1978)
Seminole Nation v. United States, 316 U.S. 286 (1942)
South Dakota v. Yankton Sioux Tribe, 522 U.S. 329 (1998)
Squire v. Capoeman, 356 U.S. 1 (1956)
Strate v. A-1 Contractors, 520 U.S. 438 (1997)
Talton v. Mayes, 163 U.S. 376 (1896)
Tee-Hit-Ton Indians v. United States, 348 U.S. 272 (1955)
Three Affiliated Tribes of the Fort Berthold Reservation v. Wold Engineering, PC, 476 U.S. 877 (1986)
Three Affiliated Tribes v. Wold Engineering, 467 U.S. 138 (1984)

United States ex. rel. Hualapai Indians v. Santa Fe Pacific Railroad, 314 U.S. 339 (1941)
United States v. Antelope, 430 U.S. 641 (1977)
United States v. Forty Three Gallons of Whiskey, 93 U.S. 188, 195 (1876)
United States v. Kagama, 118 U.S. 375 (1886)
United States v. McBratney, 104 U.S. 621 (1881)
United States v. Sioux Nation of Indians, 448 U.S. 371 (1980)
United States v. Washington, 384 F.Supp. 312 (W.D. Wash. 1974)
United States v. Wheeler, 435 U.S. 313 (1978)
United States v. Winans, 198 U.S. 371 (1905)
Warren Trading Post v. Arizona Tax Commission, 380 U.S. 685 (1965)
Washington v. Washington State Commercial Passenger Fishing Vessel Association, 443 U.S. 658 (1979)
Williams v Lee, 358 U.S. 217 (1959)
Williams v. United States, 327 U.S. 711 (1946)
Winans v. United States, 198 U.S. 371 (1905)
Winters v. United States, 207 U.S. 564 (1908)
Worcester v. Georgia, 31 U.S. (6 Pet.) 515 (1832)

Table of Statutes

2415 Claims Statute, 26 U.S.C. §§ 2415–2416

A Civil Rights Statute, 42 U.S.C. § 1983

Act Prohibiting the Use of Executive Order to Establish a Reservation, 43 U.S.C. § 150

Administrative Procedures Act of 1946, 5 U.S.C. § 551–559 and other places in the U.S. Code

Alaska Indian Reorganization Act of 1936, 25 U.S.C. § 473a

Alaska National Interest Lands Conservation Act of 1980, 16 U.S.C. § 3111 *et seq.*

Alaska Native Claims Settlement Act of 1971, 43 U.S.C. §§ 1601–1628

Alaska Statehood Act, 72 Stat. 339

American Indian Religious Freedom Act of 1978, 42 U.S.C. § 1996

American Indian Trust Fund Management Reform Act of 1994, 25 U.S.C. § 4001 *et seq.*

Assimilative Crimes Act of 1825, 18 U.S.C. § 13

Burke Act of 1906, 25 U.S.C. § 349

Buy Indian Act of 1908, 25 U.S.C. § 47

Citizenship Act of 1924, 8 U.S.C. § 1401(b) *et seq.*

Civil Service Act, 5 U.S.C. §§ 1101–1105 and other places in the U.S. Code

Dawes Act of 1887. *See* General Allotment Act

Federal Tort Claims Act of 1946, 28 U.S.C. § 1346(b) and other parts of the U.S. Code

Federally Impacted Areas Act of 1950, 20 U.S.C. § 238

General Allotment Act of 1887, 25 U.S.C. §§ 331–334 and other places in the U.S. Code

General Crimes Act. *See* **Indian Country Crimes Act of 1948**

General Severalty Act. *See* **General Allotment Act of 1887**

Hawaii Admission Act of 1959, Public Law 86-3, 73 Stat. 4

Hawaii Homes Commission Act of 1921, 42 Stat. 108, ch. 42

House Concurrent Resolution 108 (1953)

Indian Arts and Crafts Act, 18 U.S.C. §§ 1158–1159 and 25 U.S.C. § 350 *et seq.*

Indian Child Welfare Act of 1978, 25 U.S.C. § 1901 *et seq.*

Indian Civil Rights Act of 1968, 25 U.S.C. § 1301–1341

Indian Claims Commission Act of 1946, 25 U.S.C. § 70

Indian Country Crimes Act of 1948, 18 U.S.C. § 1151–1152, 25 U.S.C. § 1152

Indian Education Act, 20 U.S.C. §§ 241aa–241ff, as well as other parts of Title 20

Indian Financing Act of 1974, 25 U.S.C. §§ 1451–1453 and other places in the U.S. Code

Indian Gaming Regulatory Act of 1988, 25 U.S.C. §§ 2701–2721

Indian Health Care Improvement Act of 1976, 25 U.S.C. § 1601 *et seq.*

Indian Land Consolidation Act of 1982, 25 U.S.C. § 2201–2210

Indian Removal Act of 1830

Indian Reorganization Act of 1934, 25 U.S.C. §§ 461–479

Indian Self-Determination and Education Assistance Act of 1975, 25 U.S.C. § 450 *et seq.* and elsewhere in the U.S. code

Indian Tribal Governmental Tax Status Act of 1982, 26 U.S.C. § 7871

Johnson-O'Malley Act of 1934, 25 U.S.C. §§ 452–457

Kuleana Act of 1850, 2 Revised Laws of Hawaii § 2120 *et seq.* (1925 ed.)

Lacey Act, 16 U.S.C. §§ 3372(a)(1); 3373(d)(1)(B); and 3378(c)(2,3)

Major Crimes Act (MCA) of 1885, 18 U.S.C. § 1153

Museum Act. *See* National Museum of the American Indian Act of 1989

National Museum of the American Indian Act of 1989, 20 U.S.C. §§ 80q1–80q15

Native American Graves Protection and Repatriation Act of 1990, 25 U.S.C. §§ 3001–3013

Native American Housing Assistance and Self-Determination Act of 1996

Non-Intercourse Acts, 25 U.S.C. § 177

Oklahoma Indian Welfare Act of 1936, 25 U.S.C. §§ 501–509

Organic Act of Alaska, 56 Stat. 1016

Public Law 280, 18 U.S.C. § 1162; 25 U.S.C. §§ 1321–1326; 28 U.S.C. § 1360

Reindeer Industry Act of 1937, 25 U.S.C. § 500 et seq.

Rhode Island and Maine Claims Settlement Acts of 1980, 25 U.S.C. §§ 1701–1735

Snyder Act of 1921, 25 U.S.C. § 13

Taylor Grazing Act of 1934, 43 U.S.C. §§ 315–3160

Tort Claims Act of 1946, 28 U.S.C. § 1346 and other places in the U.S. Code

Trade and Intercourse Acts, 25 U.S.C. § 177 and other places in the U.S. Code

Tribally Controlled Schools Act of 1988, 25 U.S.C. §§ 2501 *et seq.*

Wheeler-Howard Act. *See* Indian Reorganization Act of 1934

Bibliography

BOOKS AND ARTICLES

Black, Henry Campbell. *Black's Law Dictionary.* 5th ed. Abridged. St. Paul, MN: West Publishing Co., 1982.

Bordewich, Fergus M. *Killing the White Man's Indian.* New York: Doubleday/Anchor Books, 1996.

Burton, Lloyd. *American Indian Water Rights and the Limit of Law.* Lawrence: University Press of Kansas, 1991.

Case, David S. *Alaska Natives and the Law.* Fairbanks: University of Alaska Press, 1984.

Cohen, Felix. *Handbook of Federal Indian Law.* 1982 ed. Charlottesville, VA: Michie Co., 1982.

Deloria, Vine Jr., and Clifford M. Lytle. *American Indians—American Justice.* Austin: University of Texas Press, 1983.

———. *The Nations Within.* New York: Pantheon Books, 1984.

Fixico, Donald L. *The Invasion of Indian Country in the Twentieth Century.* Niwot: University Press of Colorado, 1998.

Getches, David H., and Charles F. Wilkinson. *Federal Indian Law: Cases and Materials.* 2d ed. St. Paul, MN: West Publishing Co., 1986.

Getches, David H., et al. *Federal Indian Law: Cases and Materials.* 4th ed. St. Paul, MN: West Publishing Co., 1998.

Goldberg-Ambrose, Carole. *Planting Tail Feathers: Tribal Survival and Public Law 280.* Berkeley and Los Angeles: University of California Press, 1997.

Hawaii Revised Statutes, Annotated. 1995 ed. Charlottesville, VA: Michie Co., 1995.

Hoxie, Frederick E., ed. *Encyclopedia of North American Indians.* Boston: Houghton-Mifflin Co., 1996.

James, M. Annette, ed. *The State of Native America: Genocide, Colonization, and Resistance.* Boston: South End Press, 1992.

Jennings, Francis. *The Invasion of America.* New York: W. W. Norton, 1975.

Josephy, Alvin M., Joane Nagel, and Troy Johnson, eds. *Red Power: American Indians' Fight for Freedom.* 2d ed. Lincoln: University of Nebraska Press, 1999.

Levy, Neil M. "Native Hawaiian Land Rights." *California Law Review* 63 (1975): 848.

MacKenzie, Melody K., ed. *Native Hawaiian Rights Handbook.* Honolulu: University of Hawaii Press, 1991.

Maurer, Christine, and Tara E. Sheets, eds. *Encyclopedia of Associations.* 34th ed. Farmington Hills, MI: Gale Research, 1999.

McManamon, Francis P., and Larry V. Nordby. "Implementing the Native American Graves Protection and Repatriation Act." *Arizona State Law Journal* 24 (1992): 217–252.

Mitchell, Donald Craig. *Sold American: The Story of Alaska Natives and Their Land.* Hanover, NH: University Press of New England, 1997.

Nielsen, Marianne O., and Robert A. Silverman, eds. *Native Americans, Crime, and Justice.* Boulder, CO: Westview Press, 1996.

Nies, Judith. *Native American History: A Chronology.* New York: Ballantine Books, 1996.

Nowak, John E., Ronald D. Rotunda, and J. Nelson Young. *Constitutional Law.* 2d ed. St. Paul, MN: West Publishing Co., 1983.

O'Brien, Sharon. *American Indian Tribal Governments.* Norman: University of Oklahoma Press, 1989.

Pevar, Steven L. *The Rights of Indians and Tribes.* 2d ed. Carbondale: Southern Illinois University Press, 1992.

Philp, Kenneth R. *John Collier's Crusade for Indian Reform, 1920–1954.* Tucson: University of Arizona Press, 1977.

Prucha, Francis P. *American Indian Treaties: The History of a Political Anomaly.* Berkeley and Los Angeles: University of California Press, 1994.

———. *Documents on United States Indian Policy.* 2d ed. Lincoln: University of Nebraska Press, 1990.

Rawls, James J. *Indians of California: The Changing Image.* Norman: University of Oklahoma Press, 1984.

Reed, James B., and Judy A. Zelio, eds. *States and Tribes: Building New Traditions.* Washington, DC: National Conference of State Legislatures, 1995.

Shattuck, Petra T., and Jill Norgren. *Partial Justice: Federal Law in a Liberal Constitutional System.* Providence, RI: Berg Publishers, Inc., 1991.

Smith, Jane F., and Robert M. Kvasnicka, eds. *Indian-White Relations: A Persistent Paradox.* Washington, DC: Howard University Press, 1981.

Talbott, Steve. *Roots of Oppression: The American Indian Question.* New York: International Publishers, 1981.

Thornton, Russell. *American Indian Holocaust and Survival: A Population History since 1942.* Norman: University of Oklahoma Press, 1987.

Trope, Jack F., and Walter R. Echo-Hawk. "The Native American Graves Protection and Repatriation Act: Background and Legislative History." *Arizona State Law Journal* 24 (1992): 35–78.

United States Senate Committee on Indian Affairs. *Tribal Sovereign Immunity.* Hearing before the Committee on Indian Affairs. S. Hrg. 104–694. 104th Cong., 2d sess. (September 24, 1996). Washington, DC: Government Printing Office, 1996.

Utter, Jack. *American Indians: Answers to Today's Questions.* Lake Ann, MI: National Woodlands Publishing Co., 1993.

Washburn, Wilcomb E. *Red Man's Land—White Man's Law.* 2d ed. Norman: University of Oklahoma Press, 1995.

Weatherford, Jack. *Indian Givers.* New York: Crown Publishers, Inc., 1988.

Whitnah, Donald R., ed. *Government Agencies: Greenwood Encyclopedia of American Institutions.* Westport, CT: Greenwood Press, 1983.

Wilkins, David E. *American Indian Sovereignty and the U.S. Supreme Court.* Austin: University of Texas Press, 1997.

Wilkinson, Charles F. *American Indians, Time, and the Law.* New Haven, CT: Yale University Press, 1987.

INTERNET RESOURCES

Alaska Native Websites
http://www.codetalk.fed.us/Alaska_Native.html
Code Talk (federal government interagency web page dealing with Native American programs)
http://www.codetalk.fed.us/
National Congress of American Indians
http://www.ncai.org
Native American Law Constitution and Law Digitization Project (selected listing of tribal codes, constitutions, and other legal materials)
http://thorpe.ou.edu/
Native American Rights Fund
http://www.narf.org
Native Web (database of Native American cultural, legal, political, and spiritual issues)
http://www.nativeweb.org/resources/
Office of Hawaiian Affairs Homepage (the primary state agency that deals with Native Hawaiian issues)
http://www.oha.org/
Reifel, Benjamin. Papers. Manuscript Collections List. Brookings: South Dakota State University
www.sdstate.edu/li11/mss/scope/ma9.html
State of Hawaii Webpage (Native Hawaiian issues)
http://www.state.hi.us/index/nativeissues.htm
United States Bureau of Indian Affairs
http://www.doi.gov/bureau-indian-affairs.html
United States Commission on Civil Rights (commission information)
www.usccr.gov/cominfo.html
United States Department of Commerce, Economic Development Administration
www.doc.gov/eda
United States Department of Health and Human Services (fact sheet)
www.acf.dhhs.gov/programs/ana/anafs.htm
United States Fish and Wildlife Service, Federal Wildlife Laws Handbook
www.fws.gov/laws/federal/summaries/taylorgr.html
United States Indian Health Service
http://www.ihs.gov/
Useful Websites for Tribal Libraries
http://www.u.arizona.edu/~ecubbins/useful.html

Index

Gary A. Sokolow has practiced law in tribal courts on several reservations and has served as a judge on the Sisseton-Wahpeton Sioux Tribal Court in South Dakota. He also served in the South Dakota legislature. He is currently an instructor in the Administration of Justice Program at College of the Redwoods, Del Norte Campus, in Crescent City, California.